RELIGION IN AMERICA

OPPOSING VIEWPOINTS®

RELIGION IN AMERICA

OPPOSING VIEWPOINTS®

David L. Bender & Bruno Leone, *Series Editors*

Julie S. Bach & Thomas Modl, *Book Editors*
William Dudley, *Assistant Editor*

OPPOSING VIEWPOINTS SERIES ®

Greenhaven Press, Inc.   San Diego, CA

Library of Congress Cataloging-in-Publication Data

Religion in America.
  (Opposing viewpoints series)
  Bibliography: p.
  Includes index.
  1. United States—Religion. I. Bach, Julie S.,
1963-   . II. Modl, Thomas, 1963-   . III. Series.
BL2525.R465 1989   200'.973   88-24359
ISBN 0-89908-437-0
ISBN 0-89908-412-5 (pbk.)

"Congress shall make no law . . .
abridging the freedom of speech,
or of the press."

First Amendment to the US Constitution

The basic foundation of our democracy is the first amendment guarantee of freedom of expression. The *Opposing Viewpoints Series* is dedicated to the concept of this basic freedom and the idea that it is more important to practice it than to enshrine it.

Contents

Page

Why Consider Opposing Viewpoints?   9

Introduction   13

Chapter 1: Is America a Religious Society?

Chapter Preface   16

1. America Is a Religious Society   17
   Martin E. Marty

2. America Is Not a Religious Society   25
   Michael Harrington

3. Protestant Christianity Is America's Religion   33
   Terry Eastland

4. America's Cultural Heritage Is Its Religion   43
   Frederick Edwords

5. America's Identity Is Rooted in Religion   52
   William J. Bennett

6. America's Identity Is Secular   59
   John M. Swomley

A Critical Thinking Activity: 64
   Distinguishing Bias from Reason

Periodical Bibliography   66

Chapter 2: Should Religious Values Guide Public Policy?

Chapter Preface   68

1. Religious Values Preserve Democracy   69
   Russell Kirk

2. Religious Values Undermine Democracy   77
   Barbara Ehrenreich

3. Religious Leaders Should Challenge Public Policy   86
   James Gaffney

4. Religious Leaders Should Not Challenge Public Policy   94
   Dinesh D'Souza

5. Politicians Should Not Promote Their Religious Values   102
   Mario Cuomo

6. Politicians Should Promote Their Religious Values   109
   Christopher Wolfe

A Critical Thinking Activity: 115
Recognizing Deceptive Arguments
Periodical Bibliography   117

Chapter 3: Does Religious Discrimination Exist in America?

Chapter Preface   119
1. Banning School Prayer Is Religious Discrimination 120
    George Goldberg
2. Allowing School Prayer Is Religious Discrimination 127
    Robert L. Maddox
3. Government Should Override Personal Belief   133
    Arthur Caplan & Anthony Shaw
4. Government Should Not Interfere with Personal 139
   Belief
    Nathan Talbot
A Critical Thinking Activity: 146
Distinguishing Between Fact and Opinion
Periodical Bibliography   148

Chapter 4: Is Television Evangelism Positive?

Chapter Preface   150
1. Television Evangelism Is Legitimate   151
    Steve Wright & Dawn Weyrich
2. Television Evangelism Is Not Legitimate 158
    Henry Fairlie
3. Using Television Weakens Fundamentalists' 165
   Influence
    Harvey Cox
4. Using Television Strengthens Fundamentalists' 171
   Influence
    Jeffrey K. Hadden
5. The Church Should Use Television 176
    Jay Cormier
6. The Church Should Not Use Television 182
    Peter G. Horsfield
A Critical Thinking Activity: 189
Recognizing Statements That Are Provable
Periodical Bibliography 191

Chapter 5: What Is the Future of Religion in America?

Chapter Preface   193

1. Religious Faith Will Decline   194
   Burnham P. Beckwith
2. Religious Faith Will Not Decline   200
   Rodney Stark & William Sims Bainbridge
3. The New Age Movement Will Transform America   206
   Marilyn Ferguson
4. The New Age Movement Will Not Transform   214
   America
   Richard Blow

A Critical Thinking Activity: 222
   Understanding Words in Context

Periodical Bibliography   224

Organizations To Contact   225
Bibliography of Books   229
Index   231

Why Consider Opposing Viewpoints?

"It is better to debate a question without settling it than to settle a question without debating it."

Joseph Joubert (1754-1824)

The Importance of Examining Opposing Viewpoints

The purpose of the Opposing Viewpoints Series, and this book in particular, is to present balanced, and often difficult to find, opposing points of view on complex and sensitive issues.

Probably the best way to become informed is to analyze the positions of those who are regarded as experts and well studied on issues. It is important to consider every variety of opinion in an attempt to determine the truth. Opinions from the mainstream of society should be examined. But also important are opinions that are considered radical, reactionary, or minority as well as those stigmatized by some other uncomplimentary label. An important lesson of history is the eventual acceptance of many unpopular and even despised opinions. The ideas of Socrates, Jesus, and Galileo are good examples of this.

Readers will approach this book with their own opinions on the issues debated within it. However, to have a good grasp of one's own viewpoint, it is necessary to understand the arguments of those with whom one disagrees. It can be said that those who do not completely understand their adversary's point of view do not fully understand their own.

A persuasive case for considering opposing viewpoints has been presented by John Stuart Mill in his work *On Liberty*. When examining controversial issues it may be helpful to reflect on this suggestion:

> The only way in which a human being can make some approach to knowing the whole of a subject, is by hearing what can be said about it by persons of every variety of opinion, and studying all modes in which it can be looked at by every character of mind. No wise man ever acquired his wisdom in any mode but this.

Analyzing Sources of Information

The Opposing Viewpoints Series includes diverse materials taken from magazines, journals, books, and newspapers, as well as statements and position papers from a wide range of individuals, organizations and governments. This broad spectrum of sources helps to develop patterns of thinking which are open to the consideration of a variety of opinions.

Pitfalls To Avoid

A pitfall to avoid in considering opposing points of view is that of regarding one's own opinion as being common sense and the most rational stance and the point of view of others as being only opinion and naturally wrong. It may be that another's opinion is correct and one's own is in error.

Another pitfall to avoid is that of closing one's mind to the opinions of those with whom one disagrees. The best way to approach a dialogue is to make one's primary purpose that of understanding the mind and arguments of the other person and not that of enlightening him or her with one's own solutions. More can be learned by listening than speaking.

It is my hope that after reading this book the reader will have a deeper understanding of the issues debated and will appreciate the complexity of even seemingly simple issues on which good and honest people disagree. This awareness is particularly important in a democratic society such as ours where people enter into public debate to determine the common good. Those with whom one disagrees should not necessarily be regarded as enemies, but perhaps simply as people who suggest different paths to a common goal.

Developing Basic Reading and Thinking Skills

In this book, carefully edited opposing viewpoints are purposely placed back to back to create a running debate; each viewpoint is preceded by a short quotation that best expresses the author's main argument. This format instantly plunges the reader into the midst of a controversial issue and greatly aids that reader in mastering the basic skill of recognizing an author's point of view.

A number of basic skills for critical thinking are practiced in the activities that appear throughout the books in the series. Some of the skills are:

Evaluating Sources of Information The ability to choose from among alternative sources the most reliable and accurate source in relation to a given subject.

Separating Fact from Opinion The ability to make the basic distinction between factual statements (those that can be demonstrated or verified empirically) and statements of opinion (those that are beliefs or attitudes that cannot be proved).

Identifying Stereotypes The ability to identify oversimplified, exaggerated descriptions (favorable or unfavorable) about people and insulting statements about racial, religious or national groups, based upon misinformation or lack of information.

Recognizing Ethnocentrism The ability to recognize attitudes or opinions that express the view that one's own race, culture, or group is inherently superior, or those attitudes that judge another culture or group in terms of one's own.

It is important to consider opposing viewpoints and equally important to be able to critically analyze those viewpoints. The activities in this book are designed to help the reader master these thinking skills. Statements are taken from the book's viewpoints and the reader is asked to analyze them. This technique aids the reader in developing skills that not only can be applied to the viewpoints in this book, but also to situations where opinionated spokespersons comment on controversial issues. Although the activities are helpful to the solitary reader, they are most useful when the reader can benefit from the interaction of group discussion.

Using this book and others in the series should help readers develop basic reading and thinking skills. These skills should improve the reader's ability to understand what they read. Readers should be better able to separate fact from opinion, substance from rhetoric and become better consumers of information in our media-centered culture.

This volume of the Opposing Viewpoints Series does not advocate a particular point of view. Quite the contrary! The very nature of the book leaves it to the reader to formulate the opinions he or she finds most suitable. My purpose as publisher is to see that this is made possible by offering a wide range of viewpoints which are fairly presented.

David L. Bender
Publisher

Introduction

"God has marked the American people as His chosen nation to finally lead in the regeneration of the world."

Albert Jeremiah Beveridge

The pluralistic nature of religion in the United States finds little parallel in history. Yet despite this diversity, there is a unifying thread, a shared national faith, which has bound Americans throughout most of their past. Often referred to as America's "civil religion," this common faith is grounded in a conviction dating to colonial times that holds that God has graced America with a special mission in the world community of nations. As Indiana Senator Albert Jeremiah Beveridge said in a speech on the floor of the US Senate during the Spanish-American War, "This is the divine mission of America. . . . We are the trustees of the world's progress, guardians of its righteous peace."

Most historians agree that the belief in a "divine mission" originated with the Puritans in seventeenth-century New England and was perhaps Puritanism's most significant contribution to the social and political thought of America. The writings of such prominent Puritans as Samuel Willard, John Cotton, and John Winthrop overflow with claims of America being God's "new Israel" and Americans being the recipients of his "divine covenant." They believed that America was destined to bring spiritual and economic enlightenment to the world.

Throughout the colonial period, this lofty notion flourished. During the eighteenth century's national religious revival, the "Great Awakening," itinerant preachers journeyed throughout the thirteen colonies leaving not only a spiritual, but also a nationalistic fervor in their wake. Through the efforts of brilliant orators such as Jonathan Edwards and George Whitfield, a feeling of singularity enveloped the American people, fortified by the conviction that God had graced America with a divine purpose.

The subject of this book, religion in America, encompasses more than the intensely personal faith practiced in church, synagogue, or mosque. America's nationalistic religious heritage as expressed by the John Cottons, George Whitfields, and Albert Beveridges remains with us today. Yet the twentieth century—especially the latter half—has ushered in numerous issues which seriously call

13

into question the present value and future prospects of religion in America. The questions debated in this book reflect some of these issues. The chapters are Is America a Religious Society? Should Religious Values Guide Public Policy? Is Television Evangelism Positive? Does Religious Discrimination Exist in America? What Is the Future of Religion in America?

1 CHAPTER

Is America a Religious Society?

Chapter Preface

Is America a religious society? Surveys seem to show that it is. According to a 1985 Gallup poll, over 90 percent of Americans believe in God. Also, a large percentage of Americans belong to and attend a church, synagogue, or other place of worship. Do these facts reflect an American religious tradition that has continued since the founding of the United States?

Those who argue that America is and has been a religious society point to organized religion's continued strength. They maintain that although religious practice changes over time and religious movements rise and fall, religion's strength has been constant and will continue to be an important influence in American life.

Other people think that the influence of religion in American life is exaggerated. They believe that America's religious convictions are, in the words of Michael Harrington, "a mile wide and an inch deep." They contend that although surveys seem to indicate widespread religious belief, these same surveys often show that only a minority of Americans believe that religion plays a large role in their lives. Many of these skeptics conclude that secularism has replaced traditional religious belief.

The viewpoints in this chapter discuss these issues.

"[American] culture houses an impressive number of religious institutions that attract the loyalties of three out of five citizens . . . and are likely to continue to do so indefinitely."

America Is a Religious Society

Martin E. Marty

During the 1960s many members of the academic community were predicting that religious beliefs and practices would die out in American society. This point of view was symbolized by a famous 1966 *Time* magazine cover that asked "Is God Dead?" In the following viewpoint, Martin E. Marty takes issue with this view, and asserts that religion is a pervasive and constant presence in American life. Religion, Marty contends, is taking an increasing variety of forms but continues to be strong. Marty is a theology professor at the University of Chicago and the author of several books on the history of Christianity in the United States.

As you read, consider the following questions:

1. Why does Marty argue that many academics misread the strength and influence of religion in America?
2. What evidence has caused some sociologists to reexamine their belief that religion is dying out in America, according to the author?
3. What reason does Marty give for the increasing strength of fundamentalist Christianity in recent years?

From *Religion and Republic* by Martin E. Marty. Copyright © 1987 by Martin E. Marty. Reprinted by permission of Beacon Press.

For a great many years until mid-twentieth century, religion in the United States gave every indication of becoming increasingly secular, institutionalized, and less influential in American life. Yet the years since then have brought unanticipated changes in the relationship between religion and culture, and as a result, academic theorists have sought—and developed—fresh theories to account for these surprising cultural shifts.

First, contrary to expectations, religion is very much in evidence, which means that the secular paradigm and prophecy that had dominated Western academic thought have come to be questioned. Second, rather than being contained within formal institutions, religion has unmistakably and increasingly diffused throughout the culture, and has assumed highly particular forms in the private lives of citizens. Third, traditional religion has not fallen away, as expected, but has survived and staged an impressive comeback, establishing itself firmly and enduringly in large subcultures.

Academic Misperceptions

Before exploring these shifts, three important points must be made. The first is that continuity—especially with regard to religiosity and secularity, the social locations of religion, and the durability of traditional faiths in the face of change—has long been a fundamental feature of American religious culture. Though academic theorists have often overlooked it, it has not gone entirely unnoticed. The "consensus historians" of the 1950s, for example, took note of it, and by minimizing the stresses and strains of American life, accented the "givenness," the stable threads of American religion. Halfway through the period, historically informed sociologists, while impressed with the changes taking place, were able to keep their balance in the face of such change. In 1963 Seymour Martin Lipset, for example, in *The First New Nation* used the observations of both foreign visitors and American chroniclers to show that all-pervasive religion had characterized American culture through the years. While trying to do justice to the persistent secularity born of American pluralism—a secularity that manifests itself in the practical American temper—and the moral, as opposed to the transcendental, motif in much American faith, Lipset saw that voluntaryism was the source of religious strength. American citizens *chose* to be religious because they were free not to be; religious organizations survived because they had to compete for loyalty.

Second, academics trained in the sociology of knowledge—theorists in theology, religious studies, and humanistic or social scientific disciplines—were tuned in to certain of the more subtle shifts in American culture. They saw that most of those living *in* the culture have fewer options for their lives than is generally realized, fewer tools for analysis, and many motives for resisting

18

change. John Murray Cuddihy recognized that some core-culture analysts were theorists writing "from within the eye of the hurricane of modernization, where all [was] calm and intelligible." He knew that "for the underclass below, as for the ethnic outside, modernization [was] a trauma." In their humble dwellings, they had neither the peace nor the time to reflect on possible alternative courses: the wind was coming their way, and they had to put up the sandbags, move on, or be destroyed.

A High Commitment to Religion

Americans profess today a strikingly high commitment to religion. Over 70 percent of a national sample interviewed by Yankelovich, Skelly and White in December 1983 went so far as to state that they would not vote for a candidate for president who did not believe in God, "even if you really liked him and you shared his political views." About 58 percent of those interviewed by the National Opinion Research Center (NORC) in 1983 and 1984, as part of the General Social Surveys, said that they typically prayed at least once a day. The 1984 and 1985 NORC surveys found huge majorities professing traditional views of God and the Bible—for example, that the latter is either the literal or the inspired word of God, not an "ancient book of fables, legends, history, and moral precepts recorded by men.". . .

By all conventional measures, Americans are a pretty religious people when compared to their counterparts in other industrial countries, and they have been a religious people throughout their history.

Everett Carll Ladd, *Society*, March/April 1987.

Another way to put this is to caricature American society in terms borrowed from the comics and playpen; such an exercise leads to interesting results:

> Society can be diagrammed in a shape more or less like Al Capp's cartoon creation the Shmoo. The Shmoo's motion is largely in its head. A broad middle and a leaden bottom keep it earthbound. The child's roly-poly toy, all beaming and motion-filled in the face, is ungraspably broad in the middle, and burdened by weights so that it lands right side up when buffeted, and quickly comes to rest.

The academic specialist naturally notices exaggerated tilts of the head among elites; mass communicators consistently report on all signs of novelty and sensation. Thus, when late in the sixties, for example, the offspring of certain professors, mass media communicators, and middle-class suburbanites took up astrology and began to express a belief in omens, the media at once exploited this "occult explosion," while theologians and social thinkers felt called upon to come up with fresh theories about neo-religiosity or transcendence. In fact, the number of the new devotees did not significantly alter the proportion of the population that had always believed in such phenomena. The body of the societal shmoo—or the weighted portion of the cultural roly-poly—had barely moved. Both head and body merit observation; theories drawn from observing only one are inevitably vulnerable.

Religious Continuity

Proof of religious continuity in American life can be found in many ways, not least in the polling data. Thus, for example, in a poll taken in 1952 as compared with one in 1965, the data seemed to show a widespread, if shallow, *revival* of religion, followed immediately by a sort of *revolution* in religion. There were [according to Martin Marty, Stuart Rosenberg and Andrew Greeley] "startling indications of change and . . . more puzzling indications of nonchange."

> Some . . . recalling the drama of the last dozen years, may look for more in these polls than they will deliver. Often . . . readers may have "felt in their bones" that epochal change in the world of science and the mass media or education will have induced epochal change in one or another of the sectors of the churches' lives. They will consult the statistics of those sectors and find a relatively undramatic change in percentages from 1952 to 1965.

Polls today show that continuity persisting. This is not to say that there have not also been certain quite sudden documentable and dramatic changes. Attendance at mass and other religious obser-vances, for example, fell off significantly after Vatican II, when true voluntaryism hit Roman Catholicism. Mainline Protestant and Jewish organizations have shown a continuing decline in their relative place among denominations, though it must be noted that this follows a trend as old as the one that began with the Methodist and Baptist revivals around 1800, when Episcopalians, Congrega-tionalists, and Presbyterians began to lose primacy. The fundamen-talist, Pentecostal, and evangelical churches have clearly gained in visibility, morale, and strength; their code words have become a part of American culture. Recent Gallup polls, for example, have found Americans more ready than ever to identify themselves as "born again." Yet such shifts tend to occur within the borders of an "all-pervasive religiousness" and a concurrent and "persistent secularity."

It is essential to think of these issues in a context that takes ac-count also of generations—our third point. Two or more must always coexist. If there are two generations of Americans with different religious experiences, there are as well two generations of academic theorists with quite different outlooks. A generational shift appears to separate the period from roughly the end of World War II (or the beginning of the Eisenhower era) through the mid-sixties, from the late sixties into the 1980s. . . .

In the years following mid-century, as theorists not only found more evidence of religion than they had foreseen, but had to account for it as well, they began to waver in their support for the secular paradigm. They were committed by their academic "upbringing" to the view that, over the long haul, industrial societies like America could not do otherwise than become increasingly secular, yet plausible explanations were needed to account for the postwar revival of religion. Why, going against all trends, was so much favor shown to religious institutions in the 1950s? Theorists like Lipset believed that the revival was no more than a continuation of the all-pervasive religiousness of American life. Charles Y. Glock believed that there was more *talk* about revival than revival itself. And as Michael Argyle looked at America from England, he tried to make sense of the signs of revived religiousness in America, noting their absence in Europe. He cited Thomas Luckmann, who argued that, while "traditional church religion in Europe kept its religious functions and was pushed to the periphery of modern life, . . . in the USA, church religion has undergone a process of internal secularization, which has kept it 'modern' and visible." Religiosity was merely a veneer covering a deeper secularity. Argyle found a psychosocial explanation for religiosity in work done by Marcus Lee Hansen and Will Herberg in 1952 and 1955: they saw American religiousness as a secular search for identity, a "third generation return." Americans, they said, feel "alienated and unidentified unless they belong to one of the major religious divisions." Argyle also cited earlier conventional explanations that tied religiosity to immigration, ethnicity, and urbanization, and found it plausible to assume that "religion in America . . . is mostly secularized."

An Actively Religious Nation

It is not my business to judge the depth of our national spiritual commitments—a judgment best left to God—but I can say that America is the most actively religious nation in the Western World, with the possible exception of Ireland. In any given week 30 to 40 percent of the American adult population attend some form of religious worship. The American religious enterprise, in its multiple expressions, gives evidence of vigor. A broad, important, if doctrinally imprecise religious tradition pervades American society.

Robert L. Maddox, *Separation of Church and State,* 1987.

Scholars who looked at the problem in these terms tended to see religious people as being, in Cuddihy's terms, "underclass" or "ethnic" and marginal. Yet in the core-culture, the majority were entering the mainstream of Western industrial, technological, and hence, secular culture. Avant-garde theologians, reared in the same "disciplinary matrix" as humanists and social scientists, began to use the paradigm—and even exaggerated it—in what came to be called "secular theology," a school that emerged precisely at the end of the first of the two generations. By now it is no longer rude, it is merely boring, to keep showing how wide of the mark their theories and extrapolations were. . . .

Pervasive Religion

Humanists, social scientists, and theologians, it appears, are as susceptible to fads as other mortals. In the second of these generations, they saw religiousness everywhere, for by 1970, religion was "in." Scholars who at one time could account for its signs merely by saying that religiousness was an underclass phenomenon, or that it belonged on the ethnic margins of society, could no longer do so. Too many of their own children were caught up in cults and the occult. The Beautiful People were "into" an alphabet of phenomena, from astrology to Zen. Middle-class Catholics and Episcopalians were "speaking in tongues" in pentecostal enclaves. Certainly, the fervent evangelical culture could not be classified as "marginal" when successive presidents—Ford, Carter, and Reagan—openly claimed membership in it. All this occurred, paradoxically, while a moderate, but still marked, decline in support of mainline religious institutions was so clearly taking place.

The cultural turn that was evident among elites, and the durable, but newly visible, "pervasive religiousness" in the broad culture, found theorists with explanations in hand. Some employed a neo-Marxist view that saw religion as the "opiate" for the failed "revolution" of the late sixties. Freudian observations about the need for new illusions, Sartrean suggestions of bad faith as evasions of reality, or Weberian notions about how authentic and deeply held religious views could alter the social and cultural environment were used by others. None need concern us here. Instead, our focus will be the fundamental shift in paradigms; here "modernity," which could include diffused religions, replaced—or at least challenged—"secularity," which had to explain religion away. This occurred, first, when scholars redefined religion and saw it diffused in culture; and second, when they amplified the model of what it is to be human in culture. For the redefinition of religion, the notion of modernity as differentiation was rescued from Talcott Parsons's macrotheory. Cuddihy summarized well the "differentiated modernity" motif:

> Differentiation is the cutting edge of the modernization process, sundering cruelly what tradition had joined. It . . . separates church from state (the Catholic trauma), ethnicity from religion (the Jewish trauma). . . . Differentiation slices through ancient primordial ties and identities, leaving crisis and "wholeness-hunger" in its wake. . . .

The shift from the secular paradigm to religion as all-pervasive forced theorists, perhaps *enabled* them, to look for dimensions they had at another time ignored. Certain social scientists were able to confirm trends in their earlier work. Daniel Bell began to speak up for the values of the sacred and the transcendent. Philip Rieff awaited the recovery of the sacred after the triumph of the therapeutic. Scholarly definitions of *the sacred* were perhaps not what ministers, priests, and rabbis had in mind when they spoke of God. Humanistic thinkers, however, have often been in advance of theological thinkers; in this case, certainly, for avant-garde theologians who had accepted the secular paradigm now had to account for the survival of the sacred. The counterculture, the Age of Aquarius, the Jesus People, all had come and gone, leaving as their marks new evidence that humans seemed to be durably religious. . . .

A Religious People

Americans remain, despite recent incursions by civil humanism among cultural elites and relentless promotion of egoism by advertising and entertainment media, overwhelmingly, in Justice William Douglas's words, "a religious people." By all the indices of public opinion surveys, most Americans regard religion as either "very important" (56 percent in 1984 according to Gallup) or "fairly important" (30 percent) in their personal lives. More than 90 percent of Americans indicate some kind of religious attachment, all but about 2 percent within the Judeo-Christian tradition. How much deep religious experience these figures represent is open to question—probably more than many academic commentators assume.

A. James Reichley, *Religion in American Public Life*, 1985.

Through the two generations when secularism reigned, one large subculture resisted its sway. It included Hassidic and other mystical or orthodox movements in Judaism; numbers of American-born "sects" like the Latter-Day Saints, Jehovah's Witnesses, and Adventists; Pentecostal and charismatic movements in conventional Christianity; traditionalist Catholicism, to a lesser extent; and to a greater one, evangelical and fundamentalist Protestantism. That subculture is now resurgent. In 1980 it could claim the loyalty of all three major presidential candidates, along with entertainers and entrepreneurs, athletes and beauty queens. Obviously, such a subculture can hardly be described as marginal.

Its recent gains come in substantial measure from the selective use of secular techniques and modern technology; it is characterized by certain signs of secular "worldliness" and modern "diffusion." Yet these appear to be inadequate to account for the survival and strength of this steadfastly antimodern force. If religion elsewhere in the culture is so diffuse, why is it here so organized? If most religious institutions have become "refined" and civil, why are these so belligerent and aggressive? If a good deal of religiosity dissolves into the culture, why does this variety remain lumpish, unwilling to be filtered? . . .

This "old-time" religion never really disappeared; packaged in modern forms and transmitted through sophisticated media, it came back with a vengeance during the second of the two generations. In its Catholic form, it survived in various traditionalist movements or in its selective support for certain of the more conservative policies of Pope John Paul II. Among Jews, it became a charismatic movement, attracting those who had a predilection for Hassidic or mystical forms of Judaism, as well as those whose faith encompassed biblical claims to the land of Israel. Among the elites in mainline Protestant denominations, it took form in movements of "lay concern" against liberal theology, and in opposition to liturgical revision. . . .

Don't Overlook Religion

We are left now with a many-layered culture. Legally, at base, and in many parts of the ethos, America is a secular, nonreligious culture; in practice, a pluralistic one. But that culture houses an impressive number of religious institutions that attract the loyalties of three out of five citizens, and the weekly participation of two out of five—and are likely to continue to do so indefinitely. Over these is a layer of particled religion, whose institutions count for less and which many take the form of private support. Some would put the whole complex in a container called "civil" or "public" religion, the consensus that presumably holds America together. Meanwhile, as we await a *new* consensus, traditionalist religion thrives. Through it all, a paradigm that seems ambivalent and equivocal, combining as it does both religious and secular elements, does justice to the viscous aspects of American cultural life.

The rediscovery of American religion implies a long tradition. . . . For the present, at the very least, informed Americans are learning that their university, communication, literary, governmental, and intellectual elites overlook the dynamism of religion at their peril. In the emerging generation, during what appears to be a major cultural restructuring that goes from the nation's capital to its most remote precincts, to misperceive the role of religion, in what Jose Ortega y Gasset called the effort "to meet the problems and necessities of life, as well as those which belong to the material order as the so-called spiritual ones," will be more foolish than ever before.

"Religion in this country has generally been a mile wide and an inch deep, pervasive but not too important as a belief."

America Is Not a Religious Society

Michael Harrington

In the following viewpoint, Michael Harrington contends that America is not now and never has been a religious society. He argues that surveys showing levels of religious belief and practice in America indicate that as people become more educated and more a part of modern industrial society, they will become even less religious. Religion, though still in existence in American society, was never very powerful and is getting weaker. Harrington is a political science professor at Queens College in New York, and the author of numerous books, including *The Other America*.

As you read, consider the following questions:

1. How does Harrington explain the fact that there is more religious observance in the United States than in other industrialized nations?
2. Why does the author believe that Americans' practice of religion is not a sign of deep religious conviction?
3. What conclusions does Harrington draw from the results of the Connecticut Mutual Life survey on religious belief?

From THE POLITICS AT GOD'S FUNERAL: THE SPIRITUAL CRISIS OF WESTERN CIVILIZATION by Michael Harrington. Copyright © 1983 by Michael Harrington. Reprinted by permission of Henry Holt and Company, Inc.

America, Edmund Burke shrewdly said, "is the dissidence of dissent, and the Protestantism of the Protestant religion." The frontier turned European churches into sects—and then the establishment of an ordered society transformed sects into churches. As [Samuel] Huntington puts it, "America is unique in the world in the number of religious bodies to which it has given birth since the early seventeenth century" even though it "produced no significant theologian between Jonathan Edwards and Reinhold Niebuhr. . . ." This exuberant pluralism led to the "Americanization" of religion, since the national creed was the only one accepted by all the churches and sects. But it also promoted Biblical literalism—and the only fundamentalist movement in the West— because there was no established church to interpret the Holy Scriptures authoritatively.

Were it not for the United States and Canada, Walter Dean Burnham documents, there would be a one-to-one relationship between economic development and secularization (measured crudely by church attendance, which declines as the GNP [Gross National Product] rises) in the world. . . .

Most paradoxical of all, America has always been as secular as it is religious; or, rather, it has always been simultaneously very secular and very religious. Religion in this country has generally been a mile wide and an inch deep, pervasive but not too important as a belief. [Alexis de] Tocqueville was one of the first to see that.

A Mile Wide and an Inch Deep

The nation began with a theocratic dream of a "city on the hill" in the Massachusetts Bay Colony but quickly moved toward tolerance. Even in Virginia, where there was an established church, the fight against the Crown began as a struggle for religious freedom led by, among others, the young Patrick Henry. And even though the Revolution had roots in the eighteenth-century "awakening," it was led by *philosophes*, occurred at a time when religion was at a low ebb and drove the Tory Anglicans out of the country. But then there was a new, typically American surge of religious fervor, the Second Great Awakening in the New England of the turn of the century. After that, in the first decades of the nineteenth century, evangelism—primarily Baptist and Methodist—swept across Kentucky, Tennessee and southern Ohio. These typically American churches were frontier institutions, democratic, uncontrolled by hierarchies.

Tocqueville came to America during that religious surge in the early nineteenth century. And yet, as he himself intuited, secularism was powerful even then. In the early days of the Republic there was resistance to any notion that this country was "Christian." In 1810, Congress passed a law which provided that the mail should be delivered seven days a week in order to emphasize that the government did not keep the Sabbath holy, whatever the churches might do. That commitment to public services on Sunday was confirmed in 1825, and in 1829 a Senate committee declared that irreligion had the same rights as religion. To proclaim Sunday a day of rest, the committee said, would be unjust to both non-Christians and the irreligious.

Religiousness Without Religion

Yet it is only too evident that the religiousness characteristic of America today is very often a religiousness without religion, a religiousness with almost any kind of content or none, a way of sociability or "belonging" rather than a way or reorienting life to God. It is thus frequently a religiousness without serious commitment, without real inner conviction, without genuine existential decision. What should reach down to the core of existence, shattering and renewing, merely skims the surface of life, and yet succeeds in generating the sincere feeling of being religious. Religion thus becomes a kind of protection the self throws up against the radical demand of faith.

Will Herberg, *Protestant-Catholic-Jew*, 1955.

Religion itself, for all of its ubiquity, had strangely secular qualities. Tocqueville noticed the indifference of the American faithful to religious doctrine. This quality, he said, did not diminish "the fervour of each for the cult he had chosen"—but it did make each remarkably tolerant of the other churches (Roman Catholicism was often an exception to this rule because it was suspected of being systemically and structurally intolerant, hostile to democracy). The sermons, Tocqueville wrote, concerned morality, not dogma. Later on, when Max Weber visited America, he came to much the same conclusion. Church membership, he commented in *The Protestant Sects and the Spirit of Capitalism*, was something required of a good businessman who wanted to establish his credit-worthiness. You can believe anything you want, a salesman told him—as long as you believe something.

Everywhere and Nowhere

Historically, then, religion played a particularly diffuse role in America; it was everywhere and nowhere. That trend, [Seymour Martin] Lipsett writes, was then further accentuated by urbanization and industrialization, which broke up the old, homogeneous communities. Gerhard Lenski, one of the sociological defenders of religion, made the same discovery in his empirical study of contemporary urban churches: the cities, bringing together so many diverse kinds of people, require that they tolerate one another's faiths. But perhaps the shrewdest recent application of this paradigm is found in the book that summarized the great "religious revival" of the 1950s, Will Herberg's *Protestant, Catholic, Jew.*

That decade was the period of the highest level of church attendance in American history (49 percent average weekly attendance). Yet Herberg understood the paradox which was later traced by Lipsett back to nineteenth-century American history. "America," Herberg wrote, "seems to be at once the most religious and the most secular of nations." There were, he argued, secular reasons for religious observance: "With the religious community as the primary context of self-identification and social location, and with Protestantism, Catholicism and Judaism as the three culturally diverse representatives of the same 'spiritual values,' it becomes virtually mandatory for the American to place himself in one or another of these groups."

That trend, Herberg continued, was also influenced by one of the great social facts of the fifties: the baby boom. Parents with younger children often join a church, not so much out of great religious commitment, but because they believe that the young should have some form of religious (moral) education. There was, Herberg said, a "faith in faith" which was also part of the American "civil religion." These perceptions were, I think, telling and complex, but they dealt with a volatile subject matter. The seemingly pious fifties were followed by the turbulent sixties. The Roman Catholic Church, a rather orthodox, mainstream faith, lost 25 percent of its college graduates in the period immediately following Paul VI's 1967 reaffirmation of the traditional teaching with regard to birth control; between the mid-sixties and the mid-seventies, the number of Catholics attending mass declined from 71 percent to 50 percent. . . .

An Advancing Trend

So what are the "American" qualifications which our particular history requires when we are generalizing from the experience in this country to that of the West as a whole? On the one hand, it can be fairly said that a drop in the more obvious forms of religious observance in the United States—church attendance, for instance—would suggest that these trends are probably *more* advanced in the other late capitalist societies of European origin. Since the American numbers describe the most religious Western nation in terms of conventional church faith, they make a particularly strong case. In this country, one survey showed, 85 percent of the people believe in heaven—as against 50 percent for the Swiss and 39 percent for the French—and 56 percent say they think religion is "very important," compared with 17 percent in West Germany and Scandinavia (and 12 percent in Japan).

At the same time, . . . such facts must be taken with a grain of salt. God and heaven, we have seen, have always been treated more casually in the United States than in most other Western nations. It is important, then, to distinguish between religious rhetoric and religious belief. That is one reason that I will focus on one survey—*The Impact of Belief*, a report commissioned by the Connecticut Mutual Life Insurance Company and published in 1981. By dealing with a single, comprehensive source, I hope to avoid many of the definitional problems which arise when one picks and chooses among the endless data. Moreover, *The Impact of Belief* is enthusiastic about its findings and interprets them as proving that "the impact of religious belief reaches far beyond the realm of politics and has penetrated virtually every dimension of American experience. This force is rapidly becoming a more powerful factor in American life than whether someone is liberal or conservative, male or female, young or old, or a blue collar or a white collar worker." Since this conclusion is diametrically opposed to my own, if I can make my case from its numbers that certainly guarantees that I have not used statistics biased in my favor. . . .

Secular from the Beginning

In the early days of the Republic there was resistance to any notion that this country was "Christian."

Connecticut Mutual asked eight questions of a weighted sample of the population. There were approximately sixteen hundred respondents. It also mailed a questionnaire to 4,383 leaders and received 1,762 answers. The latter were treated separately from the poll data on general public attitudes. The eight questions put to the general public asked whether the respondent (1) feels that God loves him or her; (2) engages in prayer; (3) attends religious service; (4) reads the Bible; (5) has had a "religious experience"; (6) participates in a church social activity; (7) encourages others to turn to religion; (8) listens to a religious broadcast. Those who said they "frequently" did seven or eight of these activities were in the "highest" category of religious commitment; positive answers to five or six items put an individual in the "high" category; three or four described a "moderate"; one or two was categorized as "low" and zero was the "lowest" on the scale of religious commitment.

Given this measure, 10 percent of the sample were in the highest, 16 percent high, 24 percent moderate, 32 percent low and 18 percent lowest. For Connecticut Mutual, the fact that 26 percent of the American people were in the top two categories "identifies a cohesive and powerful group of Americans approximately

45 million strong [as a percentage of the 174 million Americans over 14 years of age] as 'intensely religious.' . . .'' There is another way of looking at the same figures. The number of Americans with zero positive responses to the eight questions was almost twice as high as those at the highest level of commitment (18 percent as against 10 percent). Fully one-half of the population were found with no more than two positive responses (18 percent with zero, 32 percent with one or two "religious" answers). And three-quarters of the people were positive about half or fewer of the questions (adding the 24 percent of moderates to the 32 of low and the 18 percent of lowest). Since the Gallup Poll found 59 percent of the American people to be church members, belonging to a church must be compatible with moderate, low—or perhaps even zero—religious commitment.

Clearly, however, it would be difficult to settle the argument between my interpretation of the statistics and that of *The Impact of Belief* since there is no objective criterion for determining whether the glass is half full (their reading) or half empty (my thesis). However, this report provides other figures which do, I think, offer the possibility of an even more persuasive rejection of the conclusions it draws from them.

Fewer Religious People

The analysis which resolves the impasse is dynamic: that is, it deals with characteristics of religious people, and our knowledge about whether those characteristics are, in general, increasing or waning. It discovers that the most religious people belong to groups which have been least affected by the cultural revolution of modernity. Since that revolution continues to proceed apace, the religious attitudes found in those groups are not simply held by a declining percentage of the population but have less and less social and political weight.

Who are the most committed religious people according to *The Impact of Belief?* They are disproportionately older, Southern, black, female and low-income, with low levels of education and from small cities and rural areas. The Connecticut Mutual study attempts to deal with the age-distribution statistics by arguing that they represent, not a progressive decline in religion over the generations, but a life-cycle pattern within each generation. This was demonstrated, the report says, because 75 percent of the people in *every* age group said that religion would become more important to them if they knew they had only six months to live. That strikes me as an extremely casual way to settle a major question. However, without elaborate argument, I will simply assume that the age distribution of religious belief is a function of both a life-cycle pattern *and* the fact that recent generations have been born into a more secular society. The basis for this assumption is to be found in the evidence all the other data about the characteristics of the highly committed religious people provide as to the importance of cultural effects which have been intensifying over time. And this suggests intra- as well as intergenerational differences.

The South is over-represented at the highest level of religious commitment (35 percent, against 28 percent in the Midwest, 22 percent in the West and 17 percent in the Northeast) because it is more black, poorer and less educated than the other regions. Those sociological determinants, I would suggest, are the most important discovered by the Connecticut Mutual research. Why is it that the blacks (and, in the *New York Times* Christmas 1981 survey, the Hispanics in New York City) are so much more religious than the whites? As a result of discrimination, black people (and Hispanics) have been disproportionately excluded from the most "modern"—scientific, technological—sectors of the society. Indeed, while a participant-observer in the civil-rights movement of the fifties and sixties, I argued that "soul" was less an innate quality of black people than a characteristic of all groups who had not been through the capitalist cultural revolution. . . .

A Casual Attitude

God and heaven . . . have always been treated more casually in the United States than in most other Western nations.

The education and income figures—which are obviously related to one another—refract the same cultural-social trends. The more money and the more education one has, the more likely it is that one has been exposed to secular cultural influences—for instance, that one has been to a college where the Bible is studied, even if under the direction of a deeply religious professor, as history, sociology or literature and not simply as the revealed Word of God. So it was that *The Impact of Belief* also found out that "leaders" in the United States were less likely to consider themselves religious than the people as a whole: 74 percent for the public, 66 percent for the leaders. And that last figure is obviously affected by the fact that one of the leadership groups surveyed was religious leaders, 100 percent of whom considered themselves to be religious. Indeed, the spectrum of opinion among leaders corroborates the general thesis being urged here: 100 percent of the religious leaders define themselves as religious, 80 percent of the business leaders, 67 percent in the military, 64 percent in voluntary associations, 64 percent in news media, 63 percent in education, 57 percent in government (*sic!*), 53 percent in law and justice and 50 percent in science. The sciences and humanities—the areas most effected by the cultural revolution of the past several centuries—are thus the least religious areas. . . .

What do all these figures have to do with statistical debate over secularization? They indicate that the internal social and cultural processes in the United States—when prescinded from immigrants with different kinds of societal backgrounds, that is—are eroding the social sources of faith in the most religious groups (black, poor, Southern, women). . . .

The major social determinants affecting the future of religion in America are, I believe, the ones unwittingly defined in the Connecticut Mutual study. And they predict further secularization.

"Protestant Christianity has been our established religion in almost every sense of that phrase."

Protestant Christianity Is America's Religion

Terry Eastland

In the following viewpoint, Terry Eastland maintains that Protestant Christian values are the basis of American society. He further argues that the trend toward the secularization of government and society is weakening both. Eastland is an author and journalist and the former special assistant to Attorney General Edwin Meese in the Reagan administration.

As you read, consider the following questions:

1. What examples does Eastland give to show that, from the beginning, the United States considered itself a Christian nation?
2. According to the author, how has Protestant Christianity influenced American culture?
3. What have been the consequences of the decline of the influence of Protestant Christianity on American society, according to Eastland?

"In Defense of Religious America" by Terry Eastland, from *Commentary*, June 1981, reprinted in *America: Christian or Secular?* edited by Jerry S. Herbert and published by Multnomah Press, Portland, OR. Copyright © 1984 by Christian College Coalition, Inc., 329 Eighth Street, NE, Washington, DC 20002. Used by permission.

It is only from history, not from clichés about history, that we can understand what we once were as a nation in regard to religion, and what we have since become. Let me therefore start with these propositions: that there was a principal religion in American life from 1620 until roughly 1920; that this religion was Protestant Christianity; and that Protestant Christianity has been our established religion in almost every sense of that phrase.

The one sense in which Protestant Christianity was *not* established, of course, was as our national religion. There never has been a Church of the United States, complete with a bishop and supported by tax revenues, as in England. Nor can there be one: the First Amendment to the Constitution did make sure of that. But nothing more than that.

The intention of the framers of the First Amendment was not to effect an absolute neutrality on the part of government toward religion on the one hand and irreligion on the other. The neutrality the framers sought was rather among the sects, the various denominations. Accordingly, as Michael J. Malbin has shown, although there could be no national establishment of a sect, there could be state aid to religious groups so long as the assistance furthered a public purpose and so long as it did not discriminate in favor of some or against others; all sects, in other words, would have to be benefited. . . .

The Anglican establishments in Maryland, South Carolina, North Carolina, and Georgia were wiped out before 1776, and Virginia's died finally in 1802. Congregationalism held on long past 1791 in Massachusetts, Connecticut, and New Hampshire, but by 1833 had lost its privileged status in all of these states. . . .

Government Support of Christianity

The particular sects, then, had been disestablished at the state level by 1833. But Christianity had not been, and would not be, until much later. In the early part of the nineteenth century, states set up both constitution and statute provisions declaring it the duty of all men "to worship the Supreme Being." States also regulated membership in Christian denominations, imposed fines for failure to fix the worship hour on Sundays, and even mandated that elected officials believe in "the Christian religion."

State courts did their part to support the Protestant faith. In 1811 the New York state court upheld an indictment for blasphemous utterances against Christ, and in its ruling, given by Chief Justice Kent, the court said, "We are Christian people, and the morality of the country is deeply engrafted upon Christianity." Fifty years later this same court said that "Christianity may be conceded to be the established religion."

The Pennsylvania state court also affirmed the conviction of a man on charges of blasphemy, here against the Holy Scriptures.

The Court said: "Christianity, general Christianity is, and always has been, a part of the common law of Pennsylvania . . . not Christianity founded on any particular religious tenets; nor Christianity with an established church and tithes and spiritual courts; but Christianity with liberty of conscience to all men."

States also required the teaching of the Christian religion in state colleges and universities, and in prisons, reformatories, asylums, orphanages, and homes for soldiers. Furthermore, public aid was given to church-run hospitals and orphanages. Last, but certainly not least, many states required Bible reading and prayers in the elementary and secondary public schools. . . .

As with the public schools, so with almost every area of American life. The establishment of Protestant Christianity was one not only of law but also, and far more important, of culture. Protestant Christianity supplied the nation with its "system of

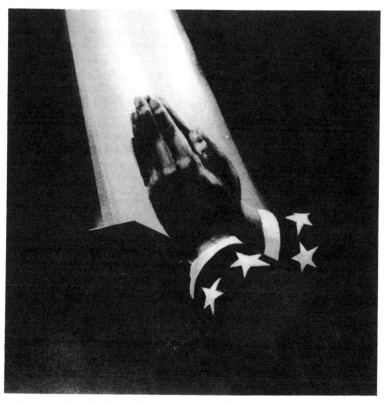

Illustration by Don Eckelkamp. First appeared in the June 20, 1988 issue of *The New American* and is reprinted by permission of the publisher. All rights reserved.

values"—to use the modern phrase—and would do so until the 1920s when the cake of Protestant custom seemed most noticeably to begin crumbling. But before coming to that moment we should reflect on the content of the particular religion that held sway in American life for the better part of 300 years, and remark more precisely on the significance of its "cultural" establishment.

As a general metaphysic, Protestant Christianity was understood in ways Catholics and Jews and deists could accept. Not only Protestant Christians but most people agreed that our law was rooted, as John Adams had said, in a common moral and religious tradition, one that stretched back to the time Moses went up on Mount Sinai. Similarly, almost everyone agreed that our liberties were God-given and should be exercised responsibly. There was a distinction between liberty and license.

Puritan in Outlook

Beyond this it is possible to be much more specific. Protestant Christianity was Reformed in theology, Puritan in outlook, experiential in faith. It was also evangelical in its orientation toward the world. These propositions held true of not only the denominations of Puritan origin (such as the Congregational, Presbyterian, and Baptist churches) but also those with more highly qualified views on the issue of predestination (such as the Methodist church) and those we might today consider "High Church" (such as the Episcopal church). Almost everyone drank from the same Reformation well, which happened to be the Westminster Confession of 1643. Reformation theology placed emphasis on the sovereignty of God and the depravity of man. It was a religion of the book—the Bible—that demanded the individual conversion of man and, in consequence, the living of a changed life.

This point had enormous social and political consequences. It is unlikely that a predominantly Catholic or Jewish America would have given birth to the type of society that eventually evolved by the late eighteenth century. The reason is that neither would have emphasized to the degree the American Puritans did the importance of personal development in the moral (and for them spiritual) sense of character formation. The Westminster Confession describes the preaching of the word as "an effectual means of driving them [sinners] out of themselves" and "of strengthening them against temptation and corruption, and of building them up in grace.". . .

The American Protestant characteristically was driven out of himself, not only into Christ but also into the world. Hence the description—"this-worldly ascetic"—so often applied to individuals in Reformed communities. The change in the history of Christianity that this phrase suggests is seismic. After Martin Luther it was no longer necessary to withdraw from the world

36

(and into a monastery) to serve God. A man could serve God in the secular world. ("What is the chief and highest end of man?" asks the first question of the Larger Catechism of the Westminster Confession. "Man's chief and highest end is to glorify God and fully to enjoy Him forever.") Every job had a purpose, every man a calling, a vocation, no matter how lowly or how exalted. Working in *this* world, furthermore, men could transform the society about them, as the New England Puritans tried to do in their Bible Commonwealths. Though these societies failed according to their own ideals, the impulse to change society remained and would manifest itself in numerous ways, including the voluntarism of the nineteenth century, which became such a mainstay of American life.

Christianity Shaped Society

Protestant Christianity tutored the first generations of Americans. It provided what we today would call the value system of the society. It is, of course, true that many early Americans did not go regularly to church; many were nominal Christians. But even these Americans tended to be well acquainted with the Bible and the fundamentals of Christian faith. Most Americans had a common frame of reference, and, whatever the degree of belief on the part of each individual, this frame of reference was deeply influenced by Christianity. . . .

This, then, was America at its birth—a product not only of the Enlightenment but also Protestant Christianity. If America was an impossibility before the Enlightenment, it was equally an impossibility before the Protestant Revolution. This peculiar nation was not explicitly Christian—in the sense of a Constitution that declares fidelity to Christian faith. But it was in its guts Christian, for Christianity shaped the society and the individuals who lived in it.

Terry Eastland, in *Whose Values?*, 1985.

American Protestantism not only taught spiritual values but also the less heroic ones of sobriety, honesty, prudence, temperance, and diligence. In the context of these virtues, as Irving Kristol has often pointed out, capitalism made ethical sense. Protestantism was understood to tame and direct a man's interests, including his economic ones, toward worthy ends. Man was understood to be a steward upon earth, and he was to use his liberty and his talents responsibly (and diligently; there was to be no idleness, no sloth). There may be no more interesting text on this than Question 141 of the Larger Catechism of the Westminster Confession, which even as late as 1844 was described by Philip Schaff, a German writing on America's religious life, as "the reigning theology of the country." The question refers to the Eighth Commandment ("Thou shalt not steal") and asks what duties it requires:

> The duties required . . . are: truth, faithfulness, and justice in contracts and commerce between man and man; rendering to everyone his due; restitution of goods unlawfully detained from the right owners thereof, giving and lending freely, according to our abilities, and the necessities of others; moderation of our judgments, wills, and affections; concerning worldly goods; a provident care and study to get, keep, use, and dispose of those things which are necessary and convenient for the sustentation of our nature, and suitable to our condition; a lawful calling, and diligence in it; frugality; avoiding unnecessary lawsuits, and suretyship, or other like arrangements; and an endeavor by all just and lawful means to procure, preserve, and further the wealth and outward estate of others, as well as our own.

This answer offers much to reflect on; there is, for instance, the implicit approval of both commerce and the creation of wealth, even of one's own wealth. But the principal concern is man's duty, which is to have moderating effects upon his commercial activities. Alexis de Tocqueville observed that the law allowed the American people to do everything, but that there are things which their religion prevented them from imagining and forbade them to dare. Religion—the Protestant religion here described—was thus a major source of the virtues a nation conceived in liberty always would need. It shaped the society and the individuals within it. Protestant Christianity helped answer the oldest of political questions: What kind of people, having what kind of character, does a society produce?

Tocqueville therefore was right to say that religion was America's "foremost political institution." It was the branch of government that the Constitution, based on self-interest and envisioning a commercial Republic, obviously could not create. Yet it was the branch essential to the maintenance of the Republic. It provided a check on the liberty guaranteed by our conventional political institutions. It was responsible for the character of the people. And as this "informal" branch of government, as our "foremost political institution," Protestant Christianity enjoyed its most significant form of "establishment."

The Decline of Protestantism

In the past sixty years, we have witnessed the disestablishment of this religion. One could argue that it was bound to happen. Good American theory—as given by James Madison—holds that the more factions the better for the Republic's chances of survival. This theory applies not only to economic interests but also to religious ones. Despite the fact that the nation had been settled by Protestants, other religious peoples could settle here, too, and eventually they did. The great immigrations from Southern and

38

Eastern Europe after the Civil War brought millions of Catholics to the United States, and by the end of the nineteenth century a sizeable number of Jewish and Eastern Orthodox communities were also flourishing.

Meanwhile, something was happening to the old Protestantism itself. Evangelical Protestant Christianity (revitalized by the Second Awakening in the early years of the Republic) had held on strongly throughout the first half of the nineteenth century, but after the Civil War the tendencies toward Arminianism—i.e., the belief in divine sovereignty *and* human freedom—that had been present even in the eighteenth century became far more pronounced.

A Christian Nation

The Constitution was written by men who were either Christians themselves or were influenced by Biblical teachings on law and government. This Christian bias is evident in the precepts of the Constitution. Professor John Eidsmoe has identified over a dozen examples of Biblical teachings incorporated into the Constitution, including: the equality of man, God-given rights, government by the consent of the governed, the fallen nature of man, the rights of criminal defendants, property rights, and the sanctity of contracts. . . .

America was founded as a Christian nation; from the planting of the colonies in the 1660s, through the revolutionary struggle of the 1770s and 1780s, to the establishment of the Constitutional Republic in 1787-89, the teachings of the Bible and the Christian religion have been pivotal in the formation of the United States of America.

Kirk Kidwell, *The New American,* June 20, 1988.

On the one hand, a liberal variety of Protestantism developed. Liberal theology had little interest in Original Sin; indeed sin to it was nothing more than mere error. Liberal Protestantism emphasized instead man's freedom and his natural goodness. Dogma and the sacraments were slighted, and there was immense optimism about the human race. Influenced by Immanuel Kant, liberal Protestants reduced Christianity to morality; they had no prophetic voice to speak of (or with). Liberal Protestantism was an accommodation to culture. H. Richard Niebuhr perhaps best described its God as One "without wrath" Who "brought men without sin into a kingdom without judgment through the ministrations of a Christ without a cross."

Liberal Protestantism was not the only accommodation to culture. More conservative Protestants—the keepers of the old religious flame—proved to be poor stewards of it. The old Protestantism descended into revivalistic orgies, as brought to us most sensationally by Billy Sunday. Christianity was presented as something dulcet and sentimental, and as often as not it was allied to the pursuit of profit. Frequently the old Protestantism was served up as a civil religion—a heresy, as Jonathan Edwards, but not Billy Sunday, would have recognized. Here too, and not surprisingly, dogma was neglected. A remark by Dwight Moody perhaps best captures this. "My theology!" he exclaimed, when asked about it. "I didn't know I had any."

In the 1920s H.L. Mencken would acidly but correctly assert that "Protestantism is down with a wasting disease." One of the deepest reasons for its condition was that the Enlightenment had finally made its way to America. By the end of the nineteenth century the higher biblical criticism had disturbed the Protestant theologians' confidence in their ultimate authority, the Bible. So had the modern sciences, not only the physical sciences (especially biology in the form of Darwinism) but also the newer social sciences. Truth no longer seemed absolute but relative to time and place, and the insights into personality and society provided by psychology and sociology seemed at least as plausible as those found in the Bible.

The half-decade following the Civil War had been the great age of urbanization. The rise of the city had also seen for the first time in American history the development of an intellectual class, and it was not kind to the old Protestant faith. By the 1920s it had become intellectual fashion not to believe in God and, if one were a writer, to attack "Puritanism."

The Disestablishment of Protestantism

With the great immigrations, the decline of the old Protestant religion, and the rise of an intellectual class not merely indifferent but hostile to religion, the stage had been set by the 1920s for the cultural disestablishment of the old faith. Indeed, it had begun earlier. The end of World War I in 1918 had inaugurated a period of laxity in morals and manners. This is typically what happens after wars, but the decade of the 20s eventually would prove to be a dramatic break from the past. For it was not followed by a recovery of the old morals and manners, as also typically happens after social upheavals; the Victorian era stayed firmly in the past. Church attendance declined throughout the 20s. People lost their fear of Hell and had less interest in Heaven. They made more demands for material fulfillment.

Such demands, of course, are as American as the Declaration of Independence, which after all sanctified the idea of the pursuit of happiness. That idea owed more to the Enlightenment than to the Bible; certainly it did not sail to America aboard the Mayflower. Since the Declaration of Independence America had held its commitments to liberty and to virtue in tension. By the

20s it was clear the tension had begun to resolve itself in favor of liberty. Americans now insisted, as William Leuchtenburg has noted, not only on the right to pursue happiness but also on the right to possess it. The 20s saw the beginnings of the installment-buying plan; it is impossible to imagine such a purchasing scheme in the American culture of 200 or even 100 years earlier.

Since the 20s the disestablishment of the old Protestant religion has taken place most obviously in the intellectual, governing, bureaucratic, and cultural classes, and to a lesser but no less real and increasing degree in the rest of society. Today the disestablishment is perhaps more easily detected on the college campus. Logical positivism may have long ago fallen out of favor among philosophers, but as a cultural attitude among intellectuals and academics it is still going strong. God-talk (the literal meaning of theology) is not fashionable, not even, it sometimes seems, in a college chapel. . . .

Founded on Biblical Principles

America must not turn away from the God who established her and who blessed her. It is time for Americans to come back to the faith of our fathers, to the Bible of our fathers, and to the biblical principles that our fathers used as a premise for this nation's establishment.

Jerry Falwell, *Listen, America!*, 1980.

Other evidences of disestablishment abound. Today the old idea that law has its roots in the Judeo-Christian ethic, as was believed at the Founding and throughout most of American history, is no longer much discussed, let alone believed in by many American legal philosophers and judges. The public philosophy of America, as Harold Berman has pointed out, has in the past two generations "shifted radically." Law is in theory no longer religious but secular; no longer moral but political and instrumental; no longer communitarian but individualistic. (People increasingly engage in "unnecessary lawsuits.") It is no wonder that Aleksandr Solzhenitsyn, at Harvard for the commencement address [in 1981], left his audience stunned when he spoke of law in a religious context. . . .

A Voice of Constraint and Responsibility

We have all witnessed the proliferation of rights with no concomitant responsibilities that has been the result. With traditional religion now pushed to the margin of our public life, not only thanks to the Court's doctrines of neutrality and secularism but also, and more important, thanks to the pedagogy of school and college teachers alike, religion is less able to exercise its historic role as a political counterweight, as the voice of constraint and responsibility.

The shift in ethical thinking away from character formation toward personality adjustment and values clarification on the one hand, and social problems on the other, is perhaps the most disturbing change of all. The emphasis on virtues that the old Protestant culture provided was precisely what the Founding Fathers acknowledged their new Constitution could not provide. And yet the Founders also knew that just these virtues were what the best thinkers in antiquity had thought necessary to the maintenance of a republican order. If the old evangelical Protestantism had a special fire in it that burned the ancient virtues into the souls of men, the virtues themselves were not special to that faith. For these were virtues agreeable to Catholic and rabbinical tradition, to the Deists of the Founding period, to the Greeks and Romans. The old Protestant religion understood, as ancient philosophy did, that politics is ultimately about the cultivation of character. It is unclear today that our modern culture even understands this point, let alone wants to deal with it.

Even so, it is answered, by default if not by design. Protestant Christianity is no longer America's "foremost political institution," but this fact does not obviate the need for a system of values in which Americans can move and live and have their commercial (and now leisure) being. If our morality is not engrafted upon Protestant Christianity, it will be engrafted on something else—God only knows what. The brilliance of the Founding Fathers did not anticipate this situation, but surely they did not believe that any institution could ever be "value-free." We are all the time engrafting our way of life upon *some* set of values. . . .

A New Religion

The trends go against even the minimal kind of free exercise of religion. It has been argued by serious public philosophers that only a rational, utilitarian morality should ever be enforced by law, and that this morality by definition would exclude any influenced by or grounded in religious considerations. Today this argument, spoken by non-philosophers, is used against the Moral Majority and their kind. You cannot legislate morality, it is said, meaning you cannot legislate a particular kind of morality—the kind having to do with religion as traditionally conceived. . . .

If someday people with traditional religious views should be effectively banned from public debate, not only will the free exercise of religion have been denied but a new religion will have been culturally established as our "foremost political institution." It would no doubt look very much like what the Supreme Court alluded to in its *Torcaso* ruling—the religion of "secular humanism." God save us from that.

"The United States is indeed a religious nation, but its unifying religion is not Christianity. . . . It is instead a unique national belief system best called Americanism.*"*

America's Cultural Heritage Is Its Religion

Frederick Edwords

Some sociologists have identified what they call a "civil religion," drawn from the history of the United States, with its own sacred writings, saints, and martyrs. In the following viewpoint, Frederick Edwords, executive director of the American Humanist Association, argues that this collection of national myths constitutes a creed which he calls Americanism, and that this Americanism, not any form of Christianity, is America's religion.

As you read, consider the following questions:

1. According to Edwords, why did this national religion come into being?
2. According to the author, why do some religious groups make great efforts to associate their religious traditions with American patriotism?
3. Why does Edwords believe that Americanism is necessary and good for the United States?

Frederick Edwords, "The Religious Character of American Patriotism." This articles first appeared in *The Humanist* issue of November/December 1987 and is reprinted with permission.

As Americans we do not belong to a single racial group, do not share the same religion, and are mostly relative newcomers to the national soil we inhabit (so new, in fact, that many British still refer to the United States as "the colonies"). Lacking, then, a single racial, religious, or longstanding geographical identity, our cultural unity and patriotic zeal seem hard to explain.

What is it, then, that binds us? The answer can be found in a set of ideals and myths pervading our national consciousness that has been growing for two centuries. Whether we admit it or not, and even if we claim we are not religious, we frequently tend to operate according to the prophetic vision, dogma, and rituals of a generally unacknowledged religious tradition. Our behavior belies this as we take pilgrimages to this tradition's shrines, view its relics, sing its songs, celebrate its holy days, show respect to its saints and martyrs, and respond to its symbols. The United States is indeed a religious nation, but its unifying religion is not Christianity or any other world faith—not even "the religion of secular humanism," as has been claimed of late. It is instead a unique national belief system best called *Americanism*.

Consolidation of Tribes

New nations are frequently formed when an already existing ethnic or religious group re-identifies itself and breaks away from a larger body. In the ancient past, new nations formed from the consolidation of similar tribes. In both cases, however, a long prior tradition existed, a tradition that cemented the union. But in 1776, a group of people from diverse linguistic, national, ethnic, and religious traditions, isolated on the coast of a continent they had only recently inhabited, suddenly decided to set themselves apart from the rest of the world. This must have seemed a preposterous undertaking to many.

Could a nation last without a common bond in some time-worn ground for unity? This was a bold experiment—a government invented out of the whole cloth. If the project was to work, a unifying tradition would have to be invented to go along with it.

In his Centennial Oration of July 4, 1876, the great American agnostic Robert Ingersoll gave his view of how this came about:

> There were the Puritans who hated the Episcopalians, and Episcopalians who hated the Catholics, and the Catholics who hated both, while the Quakers held them all in contempt. There they were, of every sort, and color and kind, and how was it that they came together? They had a common aspiration. They wanted to form a new nation. More than that, most of them cordially hated Great Britain; and they pledged each other to forget these religious prejudices, for a time at least, and agreed that there should be only one religion until they got through, and that was the religion of patriotism.

44

But the religion was more than just patriotism. As early as 1749, Benjamin Franklin pointed to "the Necessity of a Publick Religion" that would promote good citizenship and ethical standards. Later, in his *Autobiography*, he laid out "the essentials of every religion," limiting them to the following few items:

The existence of the Deity; that he made the world and govern'd it by his Providence; that the most acceptable service of God was the doing good to men; that our souls are immortal; and that all crime will be punished, and virtue rewarded, either here or hereafter.

He then proceeded to accord "different degrees of respect" to existing religions depending upon how far they departed from this outline and to what degree they added other doctrines that were divisive or unhelpful to public morality. His ideas were shared by many of the founders.

For example, in his first inaugural address, Thomas Jefferson asked his listeners to pursue good government, which he defined as being:

enlightened by a benign religion, professed, indeed, and practiced in various forms, yet all of them inculcating honesty, truth, temperance, gratitude, and the love of man; acknowledging and adoring an overruling Providence, which by all its dispensations proves that it delights in the happiness of man here and his greater happiness hereafter.

Other elements of this public religion were set forth in the Declaration of Independence. However, they were presented not as the absolute or God-given truths of prior religions but as "self-evident" truths discoverable by human beings. Furthermore, these truths were not a decalogue of divine commands but an assertion of "unalienable rights," a notion no less religious for not being traditional. Noticing this, British journalist Gilbert K. Chesterton wrote in 1922 that America is "the only nation in the world that is founded on a creed. That creed is set forth with dogmatic and even theological lucidity in the Declaration of Independence."

God Involved in History

Conspicuously absent from the writings of many of the nation's founders and first presidents are indications of belief in Christ, hell, and Original Sin. But they all mentioned God—and not merely the clockwork God of deism but a God actively involved in history. Their "public religion" clearly was not Christianity, though it could include Christians and others within its embrace. In some ways it harked back to the Old Testament with its view of America as "the promised land." This was prevalent in many writings of the time. Jefferson concluded his second inaugural address in this vein:

I shall need, too, the favor of that Being in whose hands we are, who led our fathers, as Israel of old, from their native land and planted them in a country flowing with all the necessaries and comforts of life; who has covered our infancy with His providence and our riper years with His wisdom and power. . . .

No religion is complete, however, if it only has a unifying doctrine. It also needs a unique history, complete with saints and martyrs. Thus, it was not long before the principal figures in the saga of the United States' founding began to take on a heroic character.

In the growing mythology, George Washington, "the father of his country," came to be immortalized as a type of latter-day Moses who led his people out of British bondage and to a "sweet land of liberty." Benjamin Franklin was immortalized, too, as the intellect behind the "holy" cause. These two became the most prominent among the stock characters of nineteenth-century children's U.S. history textbooks. . . .

Not a Christian Nation

We must dispel the faulty notion that America ever *was* a Christian nation. Certainly the Pilgrims came here to be "a city set upon a hill" that would shine the light of Christ's kingdom. But it is no secret that many of our famous Founding Fathers were deists (at best), not Christians. Their ideal was a land of religious freedom—not a Christian land. They gave us a Constitution that specifically guarantees the freedom to follow any faith—or none at all. And the church flourished here in large part because of its divorce from the civil domain.

Rick McKinniss, *Christianity Today,* February 5, 1988.

But the Old Testament analogy does not end here. Like the Hebrews who followed Moses, the brave patriots who followed Washington soon strayed from the truth and fell from grace. Robert Ingersoll, in his Decoration Day oration of 1888, summed it up in a manner common to the oratory of his time:

> When their independence was secured they adopted a Constitution that legalized slavery, and they passed laws making it the duty of free men to prevent others from becoming free. They followed the example of kings and nobles. . . . They forgot all the splendid things they had said—the great principles they had so proudly and eloquently announced. The sublime truths faded from their hearts. The spirit of trade, the greed for office, took possession of their souls.

And so a war was required to redeem the nation, Ingersoll maintained:

> The conflict came. The South unsheathed the sword. Then rose the embattled North, and these men who sleep tonight beneath the flowers of half the world, gave all for us.
>
> They gave us a Nation—a republic without a slave—a republic that is sovereign, and to whose will every citizen and every State must bow.

Added to the liberation imagery of the American Revolution were the new elements of a fall, repentance, sacrifice, death, and rebirth. Abraham Lincoln was especially adept at getting this

47

message across. In his Gettysburg Address, he spoke of "those who here gave their lives that that nation might live," the honored dead who "gave the last full measure of devotion" so that "this nation, under God, shall have a new birth of freedom; and that government of the people, by the people, and for the people, shall not perish from the earth." One almost feels need for the concluding phrase: "but shall have everlasting life." It's hardly surprising that generations of American school children were once required to memorize and recite the Gettysburg Address. The address was a ritual and a sacrament of the national religion, much as the Pledge of Allegiance is today.

A Martyr

The Gettysburg Address took on an even greater meaning after Lincoln was shot. For then it was Lincoln who had become the blood sacrifice so that the nation might be reborn. The imagery of Lincoln as savior, as an American Christ, arose immediately in the sermons that resonated from the pulpits of a grieving nation. The Reverend John McClintock in New York said it most explicitly:

> We had no fear about Abraham Lincoln, except the fear that he would be too forgiving. Oh! what an epitaph—that the only fear men had was that he would be too tender, that he had too much love; in a word, that he was too Christ-like! And how Christ-like was he in dying! His last official words in substance were, "Father, forgive them, they know not what they do." And on Good Friday, he fell a martyr to the cause of humanity. . . .

To this day, whenever an American hears the "Battle Hymn of the Republic," he or she thinks of Lincoln and his death. What is the song about? Think of the words. It is about "the glory of the coming of the Lord" in the last days when "his terrible swift sword" shall destroy the wicked. Yet, our mental associations turn to Lincoln who died for the sins of a nation and whose "truth is marching on."

A Vision of Paradise

The song is appropriate in a way, however, for in the religion of Americanism there is also a vision of the millennium, a paradise on Earth to come. Ingersoll offered his version of this at the conclusion of his Decoration Day oration of 1888:

> A vision of the future rises:
> I see our country filled with happy homes, with firesides of content,—the foremost land of all the earth.
> I see a world where thrones have crumbled and where kings are dust. The aristocracy of idleness has perished from the earth.
> I see a world without a slave. Man at last is free. Nature's forces have by Science been enslaved. Lightning and light, wind and wave, frost and flame, and all the secret, subtle powers of earth and air are the tireless toilers for the human race.
> I see a world at peace, adorned with every form of art, with

music's myriad voices thrilled, while lips are rich with words of love and truth; a world in which no exile sighs, no prisoner mourns; a world on which the gibbet's shadow does not fall; a world where labor reaps its full reward, where work and worth go hand in hand . . . —and, as I look, life lengthens, joy deepens, love canopies the earth; and over all, in the great dome, shines the eternal star of human hope.

Of this speech, the *New York Times* of May 31, 1888, reported:

Enthusiastic cheers greeted all his points, and his audience simply went wild at the end. . . . Nor did the enthusiasm which Col. Ingersoll created end until the very last when the whole assemblage arose and sang "America" in a way which will never be forgotten by anyone present.

Ingersoll was popular, even with many who opposed his agnosticism, because he advanced a common doctrine using inspiring and emotional language that spoke to the heart. One could either espouse traditonal religion or advocate free thought and still be inspired by a religious display of Americanism.

A Vehicle of Self-Understanding

What we have from the earliest years of the republic is a collection of beliefs, symbols, and rituals with respect to sacred things and institutionalized in a collectivity. This religion—there seems no other word for it—while not antithetical to and indeed sharing much in common with Christianity, was neither sectarian nor in any specific sense Christian. At a time when the society was overwhelmingly Christian, it seems unlikely that this lack of Christian reference was meant to spare the feelings of the tiny non-Christian minority. Rather, the civil religion expressed what those who set the precedents felt was appropriate under the circumstances. It reflected their private as well as public views. Nor was the civil religion simply "religion in general." While generality was undoubtedly seen as a virtue by some . . . the civil religion was specific enough when it came to the topic of America. Precisely because of this specificity, the civil religion was saved from empty formalism and served as a genuine vehicle of national religious self-understanding.

Robert Bellah, *Beyond Belief,* 1970.

Because of the power this common religion has held over the imagination of Americans, different groups have continually tried to claim it as wholly their own. For example, in 1912 *An American Bible* by Elbert Hubbard was published. This was a collection of selected sayings from eight American "prophets"—Benjamin Franklin, Thomas Jefferson, Thomas Paine, Robert Ingersoll, Walt Whitman, Abraham Lincoln, Ralph Waldo Emerson, and Hubbard himself (who devoted nearly half of the book to his own writings). The selections had a decidedly free thought slant, and the book was a bestseller in its time and remained popular into the 1940s.

When I attended the annual Hill Cumorah Pageant put on by the Mormons in Palmyra, New York, I noted how cleverly they used Americanism to make their bizarre religious ideas more palatable to non-Mormons. American flags flew on flagpoles throughout the pageant area, the program opened with the national anthem, and a giant flag on a hillside was waved by over a hundred Mormon youth. Then there were fifteen minutes of bicentennial hoopla involving claims that America's founders were guided by God in all their actions. Only after this common emotional ground was established did the uniquely Mormon part of the program get under way. And even in this latter part, the mythical pre-Columbian followers of Christ in the Americas were depicted as advocates of liberty and democracy—an indication of the influence Americanism had on Joseph Smith when he published *The Book of Mormon* in 1830.

And Christian fundamentalists constantly try to tell us, in spite of well-established evidence to the contrary, that our forefathers were practically all devout Christians. . . .

Religion and Patriotism

That America is most religious when it is most patriotic cannot, I think, be denied. A common religiosity seems to run through our national life. The evidence of it is everywhere. One event sticks in my mind. When I was a teenager, I attended a summer camp for boys, established by the U.S. Marine Corps. We all had drill instructors who, to us, seemed pretty rough. Because of this, one teenager wanted to go home. But when our sergeant told us that this teenager had said he would "walk across the American flag" to get out of there, the people in my group went crazy with rage and wanted to kill him. He had to be moved to a different group for his own protection.

This is one of the dangers of Americanism. It leads to fanaticism and bigotry. And because it calls upon ideals that are sometimes seen as higher than the law, it makes possible an Oliver North and, worse, a public admiration of an Oliver North.

We are inculcated with this Americanism in our youth and we reflexively respond to key words, strains of music, symbols, and imagery. It is no wonder that religious, political, and social organizations deliberately seek to usurp patriotic responses.

But, in spite of the fact that blind patriotic belief, like any such belief, is dangerous, there is a positive side to it as well. By its very nature, it is the glue that holds this diverse nation together. As such, it is the best reply to the charge that America will collapse in a post-Christian era, floundering without roots or religious moorings. It will not, for America does have roots and religious moorings, even without Christianity. The Christian Reconstructionists sense this and are none too happy about it. . . .

Americanism, for all its shortcomings, dangers, and new problems, has successfully served for two centuries as the religious unifying factor thought so necessary for successful governments by Roman statesman Cicero, by America's founders, and even by humanist historians Will and Ariel Durant. Whether it will continue, and whether it should, are questions to ponder as we celebrate our various national anniversaries.

"Religious beliefs do deserve . . . common acknowledgment, mutual respect, and public encouragement."

America's Identity Is Rooted in Religion

William J. Bennett

The vast majority of Americans claim to believe in God. In the following viewpoint, William J. Bennett argues that public officials should encourage religious belief while not favoring any particular sect and while showing respect for non-believers. Bennett contends that religion encourages responsibility, tolerance, and morality, thus contributing to a healthy society. The author is a former secretary of education in the Reagan administration.

As you read, consider the following questions:

1. Why does Bennett believe that a religious society is more likely to provide religious freedom?
2. What two extreme views does the government encourage by being neutral toward religion, according to the author? What dangers does he see in each?
3. According to Bennett, what role does the Judeo-Christian tradition have in our government?

William J. Bennett, "Religious Belief and the Constitutional Order," speech given at the University of Missouri, September 17, 1986.

From Sam Adams to Patrick Henry to Benjamin Franklin to Alexander Hamilton, all of the Founders intended religion to provide a moral anchor for our liberty in democracy. Yet all would be puzzled were they to return to America today. For they would find, among certain elite circles in the academy and in the media, a fastidious disdain for the public expression of religious values—a disdain that clashes directly with the Founders' vision of religion as a friend of civic life. That is why, on the bicentennial of the Constitution, it is not enough merely to identify the intent of the Founders. It is also necessary actively to *defend* the intent of the Founders.

The first question we should ask ourselves is: Why did the Founders see a connection between religious values and political liberty? [Alexis de] Tocqueville, as always, points to an answer. "Liberty regards religion . . . as the safeguard of morality, and morality as the best security of law and the surest pledge of the duration of freedom. Religion promotes self-restraint, in the rulers and the ruled, and mitigates the individualist tendencies that atomize society." In short, Tocqueville concluded, "religion is much more needed in democratic republics than in any others."

But it is not necessary to go back to Tocqueville to see the connections between religion and liberty in democracy. It's simply common sense: Our commitment to liberty of conscience—including the freedom to believe or not to believe—follows, in good part, from the respect for religion felt by the majority of Americans. It is ironic that anyone who appeals today to religious values runs the risk of being called "divisive," or attacked as an enemy of pluralism. For the readiness of most Americans to defend tolerance and equality does not derive only from an abstract allegiance to Enlightenment ideals. It comes also from a concrete allegiance to the Judeo-Christian ethic.

Religion Promotes Tolerance

The connection between religion and liberty is one reason that the Founders considered religion to be indispensable to democracy. I'd like to propose two more reasons. One: At its best, *religion deepens politics*. It is a wellspring of the civic virtues that democracy requires to flourish. It promotes hard work and individual responsibility. It lifts each citizen outside himself and inspires concern for community and country. At the same time, it offers a sense of purpose and a frame of reference for the claims that transcend everyday politics—claims like our collective responsibility to foster liberty around the globe, and to be kind and good and decent and forgiving in our homes, our schools, and our communities.

Two: *Religion promotes tolerance*. This sounds like a paradox. Religion, after all, is about absolute truth, and does not the search for absolute truth lead to absolutism and to *intolerance*? Not necessarily—and, in America, thankfully, not very often. At its most sectarian, religion can indeed be used in the service of intolerance. When religion is "kindled into enthusiasm," as Madison said, it may "itself become a motive to persecution and oppression." But more often in America, religion has had the opposite effect. I am always struck by the way different schools receive me when I speak. I remember starting off a recent speech at a Baptist college—known for its enthusiasm—by stipulating that I spoke as a Catholic. The audience was at first surprised by my frankness, but quickly settled down and courteously listened to what I had to say. Many even liked it. On the other hand, some in the so-called "enlightened" universities—aggressively secular, perhaps even intolerantly so—are more likely to greet me as an ayatollah or to shout down speakers with whom they disagree. In this instance, strongly held religious convictions seem to go hand in hand with respect for the convictions of others. . . .

State Should Mandate Religious Education

While it is not and should not be the function of the state to teach religion, it is in the interest of the society which the state governs that religion should be taught. We need consequently to rethink the proposition that religious freedom consists primarily or exclusively in a separation of church and state made as absolute as possible. Political society and the state depend on social forces which they cannot create but can destroy, and among these religion is one of the principal ones. Some relationship between the state and religion more nuanced than neutrality between religion and irreligion is needed, in the interest of society and the state.

Francis Canavan, in *Whose Values?*, 1985.

The question of tolerance, moreover, points to a protection at the very heart of the Constitution: equal justice under law, for non-believers as well as for believers. When Patrick Henry proposed a tax for the "annual support of the Christian religion," Madison successfully opposed it on these grounds: "Whilst we assert for ourselves a freedom to . . . observe the religion which we believe to be of divine origin, we cannot deny an equal freedom to those whose minds have not yet yielded to the evidence which has convinced us." And Jefferson agreed, in his Virginia statute for religious freedom: "No man," he said, "shall be compelled to frequent or support any religious worship place, or ministry whatsoever."

This is an important point, and I will stress it. Absolute freedom of conscience is the first of our freedoms. The American people and this Administration are irrevocably committed to equal rights for all. No one can or should ever be forced in America to assent to any particular religious belief, or even to the general religious beliefs derived from the Judeo-Christian tradition and embedded in our common culture. At the same time, however, religious beliefs do deserve, in our time, common acknowledgment, mutual respect, and public encouragement. And we tend to forget that the Founders saw no conflict between our individual rights and our common values. In their minds, *complete neutrality between particular religious beliefs can and should coexist with public acknowledgment of general religious values.*

This is not merely a question of constitutional principle, though it is that. It is also a question of civic health. My point is not simply that children who go to church are less likely to take drugs, or that empirical studies show an inverse relation between religious belief and teen age pregnancy, although both are true. My point is that we are coming to recognize the extent to which many of our social problems require for their solution the nurture and improvement of character. And for many of us, for most of us, religion is an important part of the development of character. That is not to say that religious faith is necessary for sound character. But that it can help, and that it has helped many—who can doubt? And so, as we move toward a national consensus that, in dealing with social problems, we must improve the character of our citizenry—of ourselves—we should not, out of a misplaced fastidiousness, spurn the vast resources of ethical precept and practice that are inspired, and reinforced, by religious belief. . . .

Excluding Religion

In America today, we face misunderstandings from both ends of the spectrum—from the secularists on one side and from the sectarians on the other. First there is the secularist orthodoxy, which seeks to eradicate all signs of religion from public life. With a reckless disregard for both American history and the American people, some secularists are not content to pursue government neutrality among beliefs, or even government protection of non-belief. Instead they seek to vanquish religion altogether. For as former Supreme Court Justice Potter Stewart has pointed out, the banishment of religion does not represent neutrality between religion and secularism; the conduct of public institutions without any acknowledgment of religion is secularism. . . .

In recent years, we have shown a reluctance to tell the whole truth. We have excluded religious history from our textbooks. We have excluded religious values from our public life. And we have paid a double price. First, our efforts to deny religious values in the name of religious liberty threaten the very toleration that it affirms. As John Locke reminds us: "Those that by their atheism undermine and destroy all religion, can have no pretence of religion whereupon to challenge the privilege of toleration." Second, we have created, in the words of Richard John Neuhaus, something like a "naked public square." We seem to be unable to celebrate in public the common values that most of us still affirm in private. And so our politics, deprived of religion, has threatened to become short-sighted and self-interested. And so, as we might expect, religion, excluded from politics, has threatened to become resentful, extremist, and sectarian.

Sectarian Distortions

Ironically, those who seek to exclude religion from politics may end by inciting the dangers they fear. For there are some whose vision of America yields nothing in dogmatic certainty to the opposing vision of the secularists, and who, no less than the secularists, misunderstand the character of our constitutional order. There are those in America today who believe, like Samuel Adams, that America should be a "Christian Sparta." They properly deserve the name "sectarian" rather than "religious." For though they sometimes speak in the name of religion in general, they would promote their own particular brand of religion into a favored position in public life. Not content to bring religious values into the public square, they would deny the government's constitutional obligation to be neutral among particular religious communities.

Neutrality Not Necessary

The First Amendment does not require the government to be neutral on the subject of religion. It requires it to be neutral only on any one particular form of religion.

The purpose of the First Amendment was to encourage religion, not to be neutral. Does anyone suppose the very same amendment requires the government to be neutral on the subject of free speech, a free press, the right of peaceable assembly and petition? Of course not. On these subjects even the church-haters loudly proclaim that the purpose is to encourage the exercise of these rights.

Neutrality my foot.

Charley Reese, *Manchester Union Leader,* September 5, 1987.

Like their secular antagonists, these zealots suffer from a misreading of history. If the secularists assert, wrongly, that the Founders meant to exclude all public support of religion, then the sectarians assert, wrongly, that the Constitution was designed, first and foremost "to perpetuate a Christian order." One scholar argues that Christianity was the primary cause of the American revolution. He calls for a "Christian historiography and a Christian revisionism" to foster a "return to the Protestant restoration of feudalism." A newspaper columnist insists that the Founders intended that all schoolchildren should be taught to acknowledge the divinity of Christ. . . .

A public figure recently said that Christians feel more strongly about love of country, love of God and support for the traditional family than do non-Christians. This sort of invidious sectarianism must be denounced in the strongest terms. The vibrant families and warm patriotism of millions upon millions of non-Christian and non-religious Americans give it the lie. Its narrowness would have disappointed the Founders. And its intolerance clashes with the best traditions of our democracy.

The same public figure was on much firmer ground when he later observed: "I don't think we should invest any candidate with the mantle of God." This point is crucial. On the one hand, religion should never be excluded from public debate. But on the other, it should never be used as a kind of divine trump card to foreclose further debate. Those who claim that their religious faith gives them a monopoly on political truth make democratic discourse difficult. Disagree with me and you're damned, they seem to suggest. In doing so, they insult the common sense and the tolerant spirit of the American people. . . .

America Not a Christian Nation

So to those today who make others afraid by calling America a "Christian nation," this is my reply: You are wrong. Sam Adams was wrong. We are not a "Christian Sparta." But Justice William Douglas was right when he said, "We are a religious people." We are indeed—the most religious free people on earth. A recent survey showed that while 76 percent of the British, 62 percent of the French, and 79 percent of the Japanese said they believed in God, fully 95 percent of Americans said they did. It is noteworthy that in each case, a similar percentage said they were willing to die for their countries. For the virtues that inspire patriotism— hard work, self-discipline, perseverance, industry, respect for family, for learning, and for country—are intimately linked with and strengthened by religious values. In short, the democratic ethic and the work ethic flourish in the context of the Judeo-Christian ethic from which they take their original shape and their continued vitality.

Let me be clear. The virtues of self-discipline, love of learning, and respect for family are by no means limited to the Judeo-Christian tradition alone, or to any religious tradition. My point is that in America, our civic virtues are inseparable from our common values. And values such as courage, kindness, honesty, and discipline are, to a large degree, common to almost *all* religious traditions. But it is the Judeo-Christian tradition that has given birth to our free political institutions; and it is the Judeo-Christian tradition that has shaped our national ideals. Although we should never forget the contributions of a host of people from other religions and cultures who have come to our shores in search of freedom and opportunity, we should also acknowledge that freedom and opportunity have flourished here in a political and social context shaped by the Judeo-Christian tradition. . . .

Don't Separate Government and God

The First Amendment to our Constitution states, "Congress shall make no law respecting an establishment of religion, or forbidding the free exercise thereof. . . ." This was included in the Bill of Rights because in England the state church had been determined by the religion of the monarchy; the intention of our Founding Fathers was to protect the American people from an established government church, a church that would be controlled by the government and paid for by the taxpayers. Our Founding Fathers sought to avoid this favoritism by separating church and state in function. This does not mean they intended a government devoid of God or of the guidance found in Scripture. . . .

To separate personal religious preference from a forced establishment of religion is far different from separating godliness from government. The establishment of a state religion such as that which was established in England, the Church of England, and severing the relationship between God and government are two entirely different matters. Our Founding Fathers most certainly did not intend the separation of God and government.

Jerry Falwell, *Listen, America!*, 1980.

One of the treasures of America is the treasure that Tocqueville called the "civil religion" and that Jefferson called the "general religion." This is the national creed that distills values common to all sects, in all religions, from all cultures. Neither Tocqueville nor Jefferson could have anticipated the variety of faiths that would eventually find a home in America—more than three hundred denominations at last count. Much divides each of these denominations from the others—small questions of doctrine and large questions of revelation. But what is agreed upon is important. It has content and power. It infuses American life with a sense of transcendence. All profit from it, although none is forced to assent to it. And, as the Founders predicted, the constitutional order depends on it.

"Government support or endorsement of religious doctrine or institutions is a denial of religious liberty."

America's Identity Is Secular

John M. Swomley

In the following viewpoint, John M. Swomley argues that the only way to guarantee the freedom to worship as one wishes is for government to remain neutral toward religion, neither encouraging it nor discouraging it. He further contends that any encouragement government shows to religion will lead to preference toward a particular sect. Swomley is a retired professor of social ethics and the author of *Religion, the State and the Schools*.

As you read, consider the following questions:

1. According to the author, what is the difference between religious liberty and religious tolerance?
2. Why does the author believe that government encouragement of religion harms religion?
3. Why does Swomley believe that the government cannot encourage all religions without favoring particular sects?

Reprinted from *Religious Liberty and the Secular State*. Copyright 1987 by John M. Swomley with permission of Prometheus Books, Buffalo, New York.

A democratic society is a society whose major decisions are made either by the people or with the freely given consent of the governed. It is a society responsive to law that protects the rights of individuals and minorities to oppose the prevailing opinion and to express themselves in debate and action. Unless a free society is controlled by constitutional limitations placed upon government, there is nothing to restrain state absolutism.

Religious liberty is a crucial aspect of a free society. People must be free either to accept or to reject religion or particular expressions of religion. Otherwise, they have no freedom of choice to determine their beliefs and the institutions that embody their beliefs about the universe, human nature, peace, justice, and comparable matters.

Given the fact of strong religious conviction and competing religious groups, religious liberty can be guaranteed only in a secular state. A secular state is not hostile to religion. It can be defined as a state that is uncommitted to any religious institution or institutions or to religious beliefs and practices. Its basis for state authority is in civil and natural law, not in religious doctrine or in divine revelation. As the Supreme Court said in *Watson* v. *Jones* (1872): "The law knows no heresy, and is committed to the support of no dogma, the establishment of no sect."

Philip Schaff, a distinguished American church historian in the nineteenth century, wrote that the U.S. Constitution "is neither hostile nor friendly to any religion; it is simply silent on the subject, as lying beyond the jurisdiction of the general government."

Treat All Religions Equally

The idea of a secular American state came from two sources. The first source was religious leaders who believed in the inalienable right of conscience and also in the principle of voluntarism in religion. They believed that genuine obedience to God must be uncoerced. Coercion cannot produce inward conviction. Separation of church and state was required to prevent church use of state machinery to coerce as well as to prevent state interference with religion.

The second source was John Locke, a philosopher whose writing influenced early political leaders. Locke said that everyone is born with natural rights to life, liberty, and property. He believed that the authority of the state is derived from the consent of the governed who create the state for their own convenience and for the public welfare. Since the state is a human invention and the state's laws are human laws, there is no basis either for the deification of the state or for anything other than a secular state.

A secular democratic state is compatible with all of the different religious views of the universe and with all religious organizations precisely because it supports no religious faith, no religious institution, and no dogma. It can therefore treat all equally. This is a very important attribute of the state because the long history of church-state relationships is one of state support of churches that claim to have the true faith. When there is no separation of church and state and no secular society, there is more likely to be religious toleration than religious liberty.

Government Cannot Promote Religion

America does need all the just and compassionate religious input it can get. No mistake. But the government must not, indeed cannot, by its nature be the evangelist. In a constitutional democracy like ours, government, in whatever form, has no role in *promoting* religion. To be sure, government must do its best to avoid interfering with the free exercise of religion. By the same token, the religious community must not look to government to do its work for it. Government and religion can be friends, neighbors, but they must not try to share the same house and never, never should they get married.

Robert L. Maddox, *Separation of Church and State,* 1987.

Toleration means putting up with or enduring someone or something with whom or with which you disagree. Sanford Cobb's description is helpful: "Toleration assumes that all are not equal, that one form of religion has a better right, while for the sake of peace it consents that they who differ from it shall be allowed to worship as shall best please themselves. Toleration, then, is a gift from a superior to one who is supposed to occupy a lower station in the scale of rights."

Liberty, Not Tolerance

The idea that the United States is a Christian nation presumes tolerance of Jews and other non-Christians. The idea once held in the United States that we are a Protestant nation that permitted freedom of worship for Roman Catholics is also evidence of toleration. Tom Paine wrote: "Toleration is not the opposite of intolerance but the counterfeit of it. Both are despotisms: The one assumes to itself the right of withholding liberty of conscience, the other of granting it." Toleration is a concession; religious liberty is a right.

Genuine religious liberty involves not only freedom of choice, but also the equality of all, so that in matters of faith, and membership or nonmembership in religious institutions, there are no special privileges and no second-class citizens. Every person and every religious or nonreligious group should be equal before the law. Those religious groups that proclaim one Creator of all humans and, therefore, the brotherhood and sisterhood of all believe, at least theoretically, in the equality of everyone before God. Probably most religious groups would also publicly acknowledge equality before the law. However, some would negate it by political action designed to secure special benefits for their own institutions. . . .

No Aid to Religion

If the state tries to support all religions, it compels those who claim no religion to support what they do not believe—something that is not appropriate to the democratic process. Actually, it is impossible for the government to aid equally more than 300 religious organizations of varying sizes and differing projects. Therefore, aid to all religions is necessarily preferential aid to the most politically influential or to those with a larger number of church projects, such as hospitals, schools, and homes for children. Equality of all religious bodies before the law is possible only in a secular state.

The religious liberty of all necessarily requires that no church, synagogue, denomination, or combination of religious organizations have the power to direct the government, its policies, or actions other than through the process of persuading public opinion on the issues or principles they advocate.

It is also essential that the government not institute its own religious activity either as a supplement or as an alternative to the religious expression of individuals or churches and synagogues. If government officials believe private religious expression is not adequate, or that the general public needs to be exposed to state-sponsored prayer services or religious gatherings under public auspices such as in public schools or in connection with public sports events, such state activity would violate religious liberty. The mere fact of prayer authorized by law is a civil matter and therefore a secular rather than religious expression.

The use by the state (and even by secular business corporations) of religious services and symbols secularizes and profanes them. The Bank of the Holy Spirit in Lisbon, Portugal, does not differ from other banks in interest rates charged to the poor or in its employment practices. When the government takes over a religious holiday or sponsors religious displays, it endorses the appearance of religiosity without the ethical and theological substance of the religion it endorses. In this way, because government is not a community of faith, it waters down and secularizes the otherwise sacred symbols. Government sponsorship of religious services, holy days, and religious symbols is thus an additional enemy of religious liberty and of religion itself.

In democracies or republics such as the United States, government rarely engages in such violations of religious liberty because it intends to secularize or to damage religion. It does so at the request of or as the result of pressure from organized religious groups. There are religious groups that believe that the state should not be an impartial administrator of justice or promoter of the general welfare but an agency to promote the true religion, which they believe is not only Christianity, but their particular expression of Christianity. Such groups retain legal and public relations staff for the purpose of gaining government aid or government expression of their position. Although such efforts over a period of decades are often counterproductive, religious bodies have a right to engage in such activity and to hold such beliefs, as do those who oppose their sectarian proposals or who oppose all religion.

No Power To Aid or Inhibit

The Constitution and the First Amendment must be construed as giving the government no power whatsoever to aid or to inhibit religion. It is to be neutral with respect to religious matters, except that it must guarantee to everyone religious liberty and the free exercise of religion. This leaves the raising of money, the winning of adherents, and the determining of doctrines, programs, church government, and all other religious matters to each religious body.

John M. Swomley, *Religious Liberty and the Secular State,* 1987.

Religious liberty cannot be founded on restriction of groups seeking dominance for their doctrines or organizations or on restriction of opponents of organized religion. Such restriction is the negation of liberty. The secular state, however, is constitutionally restricted and forbidden to legislate or otherwise involve itself in religious matters. That is the genius of the American doctrine of separation of church and state and of a secular constitution. Theocratic government, or something short of it in the way of government support or endorsement of religious doctrine or institutions, is a denial of religious liberty. Only when the state is secular can it be impartial and therefore guarantee equally the liberty of all religious organizations.

Distinguishing Bias from Reason

When dealing with controversial issues, many people allow their feelings to dominate their powers of reason. Thus, one of the most important critical thinking skills is the ability to distinguish between statements based upon emotion or bias and conclusions based upon a rational consideration of the facts.

The following statements are taken from the viewpoints in this chapter. Consider each statement carefully. *Mark R for any statement you believe is based on reason or a rational consideration of the facts. Mark B for any statement you believe is based on bias, prejudice, or emotion. Mark I for any statement you think is impossible to judge.*

If you are doing this activity as a member of a class or group, compare your answers with those of other class or group members. Be able to defend your answers. You may discover that others come to different conclusions than you do. Listening to the rationale others present for their answers may give you valuable insights in distinguishing between bias and reason.

> R = *a statement based upon reason*
> B = *a statement based on bias*
> I = *a statement impossible to judge*

1. The United States is not a welfare state because Americans are so religious they are more concerned with the hereafter than with the worldly needs of others.

2. That America is most religious when it is most patriotic cannot be denied.

3. Protestant Christianity was never the official religion in the United States, in that there was never a Protestant Church of the United States supported by tax revenues.

4. People must be free either to accept or to reject religion or particular expressions of religion. Otherwise, they have no freedom of choice to determine their beliefs.

5. Our commitment to freedom of religious belief follows from the respect for human dignity fostered by religion among the majority of Americans.

6. One cannot consider Evangelicals to be marginal members of society when one considers that the last three Presidents have claimed to be Evangelicals.

7. Even many Americans who claim not to be religious operate according to the prophetic vision and dogma of a national religious tradition expressed in such rituals as the Pledge of Allegiance and the national anthem.

8. A Catholic or Jewish America would not have emphasized the importance of personal development and character formation as much as the America founded by the Puritans has.

9. Only a secular state can guarantee religious liberty.

10. Surveys show that Americans are more religious than members of other Western nations. While 76 percent of the British, 62 percent of the French, and 79 percent of the Japanese said they believed in God, 95 percent of Americans said they did.

11. Traditional religious observance declined in the 1960s, when, for example, attendance at Mass among American Catholics declined from 71 percent to 50 percent.

12. If the state tries to support all religions, it compels those who claim no religion to support what they do not believe.

13. Christians feel more strongly about love of country, love of God, and support for the traditional family than do non-Christians.

Periodical Bibliography

The following articles have been selected to supplement the diverse views presented in this chapter.

Mark Jacobson	"God Knows," *Esquire*, March 1988.
Kirk Kidwell	"Back to God," *The New American*, June 20, 1988. Available from: 395 Concord Ave., Belmont, MA 02178.
Everett Carll Ladd	"Secular and Religious America," *Society*, March/April 1987.
Delos B. McKown	"Religion and the Constitution," *The Humanist*, May/June 1988. Available from: 7 Harwood Dr., P.O. Box 146, Amherst, NY 14226-0146.
Martin E. Marty	"Public Religion: The Republican Banquet," *Phi Kappa Phi Journal*, Winter 1988.
The New American	"It's Curtains for Humanism," interview with Gary DeMar, April 25, 1988.
Daniel Rader	"Deism and American History," *The Churchman*, June/July 1987. Available from: 1074 23rd Ave. North, St. Petersburg, FL 33704.
W. Stanley Rycroft	"America—Secular or Christian?" *The Churchman*, March 1987.
Fran Schumer	"A Return to Religion," *The New York Times Magazine*, April 15, 1984.
Curtis J. Sitomer	"Religion in US: Many Beliefs, a Common Morality," *The Christian Science Monitor*, April 21, 1988.
George Weigel	"Religion and the American Experiment: Issues for the Third Century," *The World & I*, September 1987.
Richard Wentz	"Beyond Nationalism," *The World & I*, September 1987.
Robert Wuthnow	"Divided We Fall: America's Two Civil Religions," *The Christian Century*, April 20, 1988.

2 CHAPTER

Should Religious Values Guide Public Policy?

Chapter Preface

Americans' religious attitudes range from conservative fundamentalism to atheism. Such diversity in belief often creates disagreement among members of society, especially on public policy issues. These disagreements frequently spread to the political arena, raising the important question of whether religious principles should guide political decision making.

Abortion, for example, is a volatile issue that often divides along religious lines. Catholics and conservative Protestants have traditionally opposed abortion, while liberal Protestants and many other people believe abortion should remain a woman's choice. When politicians want to enact laws restricting or permitting abortion on demand, they face an important question: Should legislation be passed for all people on issues that clearly have no moral consensus? In a nation strongly influenced by religion yet dedicated to the separation of church and state, this question can be difficult to answer.

The diverse viewpoints in this chapter discuss this dilemma.

"It is religious belief, indeed, that has made the American democracy successful."

Religious Values Preserve Democracy

Russell Kirk

Russell Kirk is a resident scholar at The Heritage Foundation, a conservative research organization. He is the author of several books, including *The Assault on Religion* and *The Constitution's Conservative Character.* In the following viewpoint, he writes that religious belief is necessary for the preservation of democracy in America. Efforts to separate religion and politics, he warns, undermine America's heritage and endanger the social order.

As you read, consider the following questions:

1. According to Kirk, what is the correct interpretation of the religion clause of the First Amendment? What is the incorrect interpretation?
2. Kirk calls Americans a "religious people." What examples does he give to prove this?
3. According to the author, what is the alternative to religious belief in the civil social order?

Russell Kirk, "The First Clause of the First Amendment: Politics and Religion," a speech given at The Heritage Foundation on December 9, 1987. Published as #146 in *The Heritage Lectures* series by The Heritage Foundation.

"Original intent," a doctrine much debated in connection with the Constitution of the United States nowadays, is easily determined when the first clause (or clauses) of the First Amendment is discussed. That provision is simply and directly expressed: "Congress shall make no law respecting an establishment of religion, or prohibiting the free exercise thereof. . . ."

This "freedom of religion" right was so expressed by two eminent congressmen who disagreed considerably about several other matters: Fisher Ames of Massachusetts and James Madison of Virginia. Their motives in drawing up this guarantee of liberty of worship are readily ascertained. And yet this first clause, in very recent decades, has been interpreted by federal courts most extravagantly, so that some writers suggest a quite new signification for those few words: "freedom from religion.". . .

Some people persist in fancying that somehow or other the Constitution, or at least the First Amendment, or perhaps the Declaration of Independence, speaks of "a wall of separation" between church and state. But of course no such phrase appears in any American state paper. Those words about the hypothetical "wall," which have provoked so much controversy during the latter half of the 20th century, occur merely in a letter written in 1802 by Thomas Jefferson, addressed to an assembly of Baptists. All but three or four of the fifty-five delegates to the Constitutional Convention in 1787, incidentally, had been members of Christian churches. . . .

The Basis of Good Society

The general understanding of the Framers of the Constitution, and of the Congress that approved the First Amendment, was this: Christian teaching is intended to govern the soul, not the state. But also the leading Americans of 1787-1791 believed that religious convictions form the basis of any good society. They were aware that both Christianity and Judaism have coexisted with imperial structures, feudalism, national monarchies, aristocracies, republics, democracies. Religion, they assumed, is not a system of politics or of economic management: it is an attempt, instead, to relate the human soul to divine power and love.

Yet many people, judges among them, today maintain a very different view of the meaning of the first clause of the First Amendment; and much confusion exists concerning the relationships between religion and politics or between church and state. . . .

The Key to Democracy

Religion in America never has been a private concern merely. It is religious belief, indeed, that has made the American democracy successful; the lack of religious foundation has been the ruin of other democracies. Alexis de Tocqueville makes this point strongly in *Democracy in America*: "I do not know whether all Americans have a sincere faith in their religion," Tocqueville put it, "—for who can search the human heart?—but I am certain that they hold it to be indispensable to the whole nation and to every rank of society. . . . While the law permits the Americans to do what they please, religion prevents them from conceiving, and forbids them to commit, what is rash or unjust."

Religious concepts about order and justice and freedom powerfully influence the political beliefs of the large majority of American citizens. These convictions join us together as a people. Were it otherwise, we would be exposed to the merciless politics of ideology, and parties would become fanatic ideological factions like those that devastate much of the world today.

Closely Intertwined

From the beginning of American history, religion and the practice of democracy have been closely intertwined. This relationship, despite changes in structure and recurring tensions, shows no signs of breaking. "Of all the dispositions and habits which lead to political prosperity," George Washington said in his farewell address, "religion and morality are indispensable supports. In vain would that man claim the tribute of patriotism, who should labor to subvert these great pillars of human happiness, these firmest props of the duties of men and citizens." Most Americans continue to believe that Washington was right.

A. James Reichley, *Religion in American Public Life*, 1985.

Of course, religious belief is not confined to one party. It is to be expected that in the United States nearly all candidates for office will declare that religious assumptions underlie their political programs. But neither party can claim to know the will of God. In the words of Abraham Lincoln, "In great contests each party claims to act in accordance with the will of God. Both may be, and one must be, wrong. God cannot be for and against the same thing at the same time." Religious convictions do not confer political infallibility. But political action without religious restraints can bring on public ruin.

A Religious People

Those militantly secularistic liberals who would like to erase religious principles from political contests ought to be reminded of the opinion of that liberal Justice, William O. Douglas, in the *Zorach* case (1952):

> We are a religious people whose institutions presuppose a Supreme Being. We guarantee the freedom to worship as one chooses. We make room for as wide a variety of beliefs and

71

creeds as the spiritual needs of man deem necessary. We sponsor an attitude on the part of government that shows no partiality to any one group and that lets each flourish according to the zeal of its adherents and the appeal of its dogma. . . . To hold that government may not encourage religious instruction would be to find in the Constitution a requirement that the government show a callous indifference to religious groups. That would be preferring those who believe in no religion over those who do believe. . . . We find no constitutional requirement which makes it necessary for government to be hostile to religion and to throw its weight against efforts to widen the effective scope of religious influence.

We being "a religious people whose institutions presuppose a Supreme Being," it scarcely is surprising that our President should entertain religious convictions. To try to govern a country by religious dogma alone always has been a mistake. It is a mistake still worse to argue that politics comes first and that one's religion ought to be subordinate to political programs. . . .

There exists an evil substitute for religion in public affairs: fanatic ideology, which pretends to offer the people an earthly paradise, to be achieved through revolutionary politics. But all that ideology can create is an earthly hell. When such an ideology is intertwined with false religious notions, as in the "liberation theology" of Latin America today, a country may experience the worst excesses of political fanaticism and religious fanaticism combined.

We Americans stand in no clear and present danger of such a ruinous combination of two forms of intolerance. But those people—still happily a small minority—who would deny the President the right to let religious principles influence his public recommendations are no friends either to religious freedom or to the Constitution of the United States. . . .

Beyond Absurdity

In dread of any form of religious activity—even Bible study before school or at lunch, even voluntary prayer or (quite as wicked) a moment of silence during which pupils might be praying, even (in many school districts) the mention of religious teachings in a course in history or literature—"neutrality" about religious beliefs has been carried beyond absurdity to positive prohibition. Most textbook publishers thoughtfully omit from their manuals all but incidental references to religion, lest they lose school adoptions. Christianity and Judaism are becoming forbidden faiths, so far as public instruction is concerned, although there is more indulgence of non-Western religions as part of "global education."

Formal schooling was commenced by churches. Ultimate questions cannot be answered except by religious doctrines—unless we are prepared to embrace the dialetical materialism of the Marxists. The Bible has been the most influential book in half the world, for hundred of years. How nasty that some little wretches should wish to study it, and should be supported by their parents.

Resting on Religion

Although the Framers did not want a state church, they had no intention of altogether dissociating the Republic from religion or, more specifically, from the Judeo-Christian version of it. Witness the chaplains, Bibles to be sworn upon, and the many official prayers and expressions of trust and belief in God. Indeed, the Establishment Clause was as much meant to protect religion from political interference as it was meant to protect the government from ecclesiastical interference. Churches and the government were to thrive separately, but the mutual independence was not an expression of indifference, let alone hostility. On the contrary, the Framers felt that the republic rested on civic virtue which, they thought, rested largely on religion.

Ernest van den Haag, *Phi Kappa Phi Journal,* Winter 1988.

Congress has chaplains and engages in public prayer. The armed forces commission and pay chaplains, and support religious services. Every President of the United States has professed his belief in divine wisdom and goodness. Yet the American Civil Liberties Union and certain judges deny the right of young Americans to pray in the public schools—even as an act of "commencement" concluding their twelve or thirteen years of school.

The Quest of Spiritual Growth

If the federal Constitution were hostile toward religion, it would be hostile toward our survival. Aleksandr Solzhenitsyn touched on that memorably in his Templeton Address:

> Our life consists not in the pursuit of material success but in the quest of worthy spiritual growth. Our entire earthly existence is but a transition stage in the movement toward something higher, and we must not stumble or fall, nor must we linger fruitlessly on one rung of the ladder. . . . The laws of physics and physiology will never reveal the indisputable manner in which The Creator constantly, day in and day out, participates in the life of each of us, unfailingly granting us the energy of existence; when this assistance leaves us, we die. In the life of our entire planet, the Divine Spirit moves with no less force: this we must grasp in our dark and terrible hour.

So the great exile expresses the ineluctable need for religious understanding in the civil social order: the alternative is grinding servitude, soon or late, to the total state. So much, at the moment, for the second great error in current discussions of religion and politics: the notion that religion should be driven out of politics altogether. . . .

Striving for Liberty

The Church always has striven for liberty, justice, and peace; but throughout the centuries, the Church has known that man and society are imperfect and imperfectible, here below. The only possible perfection is perfection through grace in death. Christian teaching has endured because of its realism; because it does not mistake the City of This Earth for the City of God. In upholding the theological virtues of faith, hope, and charity, the Church has not neglected the cardinal virtue of prudence. And most of the time the Church has not endeavored to usurp the powers of the State. "Two there are by whom this world is ruled," said Gelasius I, saint and pope, in the 5th century.

The Church cannot confer upon the world immediate, perfect secular liberty, justice, and peace—any more than could the zealots of the French Revolution or the Russian. But Christian truth does offer this: the perfect freedom which transcends time and circumstance, that peace which passeth all understanding. The Church has known that liberty, justice, and peace are preserved and extended only through patient and prudent striving; that Providence moves deliberately, while the devil always hurries.

Christian faith may work wonders if it moves the minds and hearts of an increasing number of men and women. But if professed Christians forsake Heaven as their destination, and come to fancy that the State (which nevertheless they denounce in its present form) may be converted into the Terrestrial Paradise—why, they are less wise even than Karl Marx.

Saving the World from Suicide

Such distortions of Christian teaching rise again and again, through the centuries, among professing Christians. One such was the Lambeth Conference of 1930, which provoked T.S. Eliot into writing one of his more enduring essays. All times are corrupt, Eliot declared then, and in our time Christianity is dispossessed and divided. "The world is trying the experiment of attempting to form a civilized but non-Christian mentality," Eliot concluded. "The experiment will fail; but we must be very patient in awaiting its collapse; meanwhile redeeming the time; so that the Faith may be preserved alive through the dark ages before us; to renew and rebuild civilization, and save the world from suicide."

Just so. Although Church and State stand separate, the political order cannot be renewed without theological virtues working upon it. This consideration brings us back to the question . . . "Is there such a thing as a Christian polity? Does Christian doctrine prescribe some especial form of politics—and conformity by all communicants to that political model?"

If we know the history of the Christian Church, particularly in the West, we are aware that no, the Church does not prescribe some one particular civil social order. When the Church has presumed to decree the prudential policies of the state, the Church has failed, falling into dismal confusion. The political successes of the Church have occurred rather in limiting the claims of the State than in dictating courses to the captains and the kings.

Political Regeneration

All the same, it is conceivable that the Church may do a work of political regeneration in our bent age, rebuffing the totalist dominations that would convert man into a producing-and-consuming animal merely. Permit me to explain succinctly; I am not contradicting myself.

Christian belief works upon the political order in three principal ways, sometimes effectually. These three ways are faith's influence upon statesmen; faith's influence upon the mass of mankind; and faith's shaping of the norms of the social order. . . .

The Survival of Democracy

Responsible Christians are not seeking to establish a theocracy but to ensure the moral strength of a democratic nation.

And this, ultimately, is the heart of the matter. We know that religion can survive without democracy; look at the Soviet Union, look at Poland. But can democracy survive without religion? Can it survive, that is, without becoming something else—fascism, or totalitarianism? The answer to this question will influence how we as a nation treat the place of religion in American life, whether we wish to encourage it or exclude it. Christians, of all people, should be ready with the answer.

Terry Eastland, *Whose Values?*, 1985.

People sustained by Christian faith, hope, and charity form a "colony of Heaven"—a social order in which it is possible to strive together for the preservation and the advancement of justice and freedom and peace. Without the bond of a shared faith, any society begins to disintegrate; even a society governed by soldiers and secret policemen. As Charles Maurice de Talleyrand put it, "You can do everything with bayonets—except sit upon them." Religious sanctions lacking, it becomes difficult even for the total state to enforce even the most essential laws.

During the Cambodian campaign, I talked for an hour, in the White House, with President Nixon. He was disheartened. He spoke of a lack of purpose and public spirit in the United States, and then inquired of me, "Do we have any hope?" He repeated the question, emphatically: "Do we have any hope?"

I replied that it is all a matter of faith. If the people believe the prophets of despair, then indeed hope vanishes, for everyone seeks his private hidie-hole, endeavoring to content himself with petty ephemeral pleasures. But if the people, not believing the prophets of doom and their self-fulfilling prophecies, still retain faith in a transcendent order—why, then, indeed hope for the social order has not departed, for it remains possible for men and women to brighten the corners where they are and to confront together the difficulties of the time. Given hope, great renewal is possible. The thinking Christian does not indulge hopes of Lotus-Land; he knows that politics is the art of the possible; he understands that his ultimate destination is not here below. Also he knows that here below the race is not necessarily to the swift, nor the battle to the strong. Yet he is not easily beguiled by predictions of imminent dissolution. "The men signed of the Cross of Christ go gaily in the dark," in Gilbert K. Chesterton's brave line.

It is from religious belief that our norms for social order grow; and when faith decays, those norms are flouted. Then, order overthrown, squalid oligarchs seize power, and the Savage God lays down his new commandments.

"When religion is defined as the only source of morality, . . . we put our democratic tradition at risk."

Religious Values Undermine Democracy

Barbara Ehrenreich

Barbara Ehrenreich is a contributing editor to *Ms.* magazine and a prolific writer. Her most recent book is *The Hearts of Men*. In the following viewpoint, she warns that politically influential religious groups in America threaten democracy by prescribing what people should believe and how they should act. Ehrenreich urges Americans to place their faith in their own ability to govern rather than in God, lest they lose the individual liberties that make the United States a democratic nation.

As you read, consider the following questions:

1. What is Ehrenreich's religious background? How did she arrive at her attitude toward religion?
2. Why is the author more worried about the Christian right than the Christian left?
3. The author lists two ways in which religion is a threat to America's democratic tradition. What are they? Do you agree or disagree that religion threatens democracy? Why or why not?

Barbara Ehrenreich, "One Nation, Divided, Under God," *Vogue*, December 1985.
Courtesy Vogue. Copyright © 1985 by the Condé Nast Publications Inc.

Not so many years ago, the big news about God was that He had died. Clergy in mainstream Protestant and Jewish denominations watched their congregations ebb away; wise suburban priests rescheduled mass for early Saturday evening, so as not to interfere with the Sabbath's recreational opportunities. But the obituaries, as we know, were premature. Nowadays, almost daily reports detail God's opinions on foreign policy, abortion, federal spending, and the arms race. He is alive and well; although, since all the reports are secondhand, it is hard to be sure if He is a left-wing revolutionary, as some radical Catholics believe, or a middle-aged conservative, as the Moral Majority seems to think. Either way, His name has become a regular feature of American political debate—whether invoked by one side or, as happens increasingly, by both.

Credit for the resurrection of religiosity in American politics goes largely to the Christian right, a swelling network of electronic congregations, educational institutions, and lobbying organizations that wage special campaigns on everything from abortion to foreign policy. Fifteen years ago, the Christian right was an insignificant speck on the political landscape, referred to by complacent moderates as "the lunatic fringe." Now it is a major political force, ranging ideologically from Billy Graham, on what might be called the left, to paramilitary groups like the Christian Identity Movement, on the far, far right, which has reportedly urged white Christians to take up arms for the coming confrontation with Jews, nonwhites, atheists, and other "Satanic" elements. . . .

A Chilling Prospect

As an atheist, I find the revival of religion in politics chilling. I did not arrive at my atheism through adolescent skepticism or even through spiritual laziness; it's a matter of family tradition. My ancestors abandoned religion because it seemed to them to be unduly compromised by the hypocrisy and greed of its earthly representatives—all this long before the advent of TV preachers flashing out their toll-free 800 numbers. But as a child in the 'fifties, I learned to be guarded about my family's beliefs. In that intolerant decade, "atheist" meant "communist," and to confess to being one was to face, at the least, some nasty persecution on the playground. So when I hear the soaring rhetoric of religious evangelicalism, especially in its politically dogmatic forms, I start to feel like the proverbial atheist in a foxhole: I wish that I had it in me to pray for our quick salvation.

There is a religious left, too; on the whole, I feel more comfortable with its adherents, if only because they seem to have no plans for a second Inquisition. But viewed from either side of the political spectrum, there is something disturbing about what we might call the Christianizing (for Judaism is still very much a worried bystander) of politics and the politicizing of religion. It's not that all religious Americans have become politically polarized, or that everyone at the political poles has had a conversion experience, but we do seem to be heading toward a time when public policy will be a matter of scriptural interpretation, and when political debate will be a contest between Bible-thumping believers.

The Christian right sees nothing wrong with mixing religion and politics, if, in fact, its leaders even see a distinction between them. Lurking within right-wing Christian thought is the notion that America is, or ought to be, a "Christian Nation," governed by Biblical law. "The idea that religion and politics don't mix was invented by the devil to keep Christians from running their own country," Jerry Falwell has said. And Pat Robertson believes that "the minute you turn [the Constitution] into the hands of non-Christian and atheist people, they can use it to destroy the very foundations of our society." It is this ambition to run America as a "Christian republic" that most alarms Americans who do not happen to be Christian or who are unfavorably impressed by other theocracies, such as the Ayatollah Khomeni's Islamic republic.

But there is no denying that the Christian right has struck a responsive chord with a considerable segment, perhaps even an eventual majority, of the American public. How much of the ap-

What dangerous and subversive activity is most feared by the Moral Majority?

THINKING

Doug Marlette. *The Atlanta Constitution.* Reprinted with permission.

peal is spiritual and how much is purely political is hard to tell, especially since right-wing politics and conservative religion have both been enjoying revivals. Today, 40 percent of the adult population call themselves "born-again Christians," and another 20 percent count themselves as evangelical Protestants. Some twelve to twenty million people tune into the Christian broadcasting empire; and at least one million children attend Fundamentalist schools (many of which were founded as an alternative to integrated public schools—hardly a religiously pure motive).

This huge pool of believers has been a rich recruiting ground for the secular wing of the New Right: The Moral Majority was founded in 1979 at the suggestion of leading New Right strategist Howard Phillips, who had been impressed by Jerry Falwell's ability to get his TV congregation to write letters to their congressmen. In today's network of New Right organizations, religious groups like the Moral Majority, the Religious Roundtable (a lobbying group), and Christian Voice (which, in 1984, published the *Presidential Biblical Scoreboard*) are tightly linked to secular groups like the Conservative Caucus, to the evident profit of the latter. A cynic might conclude that religion is being used by the right as a nonprofit front for more conventional political ambitions.

But a cynic would be wrong to discount the genuine religious impulse that inspires many on the Christian right or, for that matter, the religious left. Why, in the era of microwaves and MTV, so many people are drawn to dogmatic versions of ancient beliefs is still a puzzle for the sociologists. But the reason why so many Americans have been "born again" is probably not too different from the reason why young Arabs have been taking to Islamic fundamentalism, or why some American Jews are returning to orthodox Judaism. As the recently religious say, religion provides rules, a ready-made community, and a sense of belonging to something more lasting than the swirl of consumer culture. Religion can also endow the rest of one's beliefs and opinions with an inarguable kind of sanctity, and this is as true on the growing religious left as on the religious right.

An Increasingly Religious Left

The religious left has no mighty network of organizations comparable to that of the religious right, but what there is of an organized American left—what's emerged after the dissolution of the "new left" of the 'sixties—has taken an increasingly religious form. Black churches, many of them as conservative in religious matters as those of the Christian right, have been a major liberal force since the Civil Rights movement, and they have already produced one presidential candidate, the Rev. Jesse Jackson. But perhaps the most surprising voice from the left has been the Catholic church, which entered the political fray in 1973 to oppose abortion but then parted company with the religious right over the issue of nuclear weapons. . . .

Both the religious right and the religious left claim to have God on their side, but it is the right that has powerful friends on earth. The activist wing of the religious left is a low-budget, grass roots effort that resembles, in spirit and daring, the early Christians under the Roman empire. An estimated ten thousand congregations (Jewish as well as Christian) support the sanctuary movement, which offers havens and a public forum to Central American refugees whose lives would be endangered if they were deported. One religious network sends lay people and clergy to camp out, almost literally, on the Nicaraguan borders, to discourage the U.S.-backed *contras* from attacking. Other groups encourage their constituencies to "bear witness"—nonviolently, but not necessarily legally—against the arms race, U.S. intervention in Central America, apartheid, and occasionally against abortion, which some of the religious left opposes almost as fervently as the right.

That Enemy Was Religion

As late as 1974 it was illegal in Wisconsin for any unmarried person to purchase contraceptives, and our laws were hostile to birth control even for someone properly married. Trying to change that law turned me into an activist for free-thought, because I learned who the enemy really was.

That enemy was religion. That enemy was those long lines of priests, nuns, and fundamentalists who came to the state capital to testify against contraception and abortion, even as Wisconsin women were having babies every year until they died from it, even as the world began to shudder from overpopulation. In working for women's rights I fought in a battle that would never end, because the root cause of the denial of those rights was religion and its control over government. Unless religion is kept in its place, all personal rights will be in jeopardy. This is the battle that needs to be fought.

To be free from religion is an advantage for individuals; it is a necessity for government.

Anne Nicol Gaylor, *Free Inquiry*, Summer 1987.

On the other side, the Republican party gave its stamp of approval to the Christian right by having the Rev. James Robison give the opening prayer at the 1984 Dallas convention. A somewhat rough-edged version of Falwell, Robison has said that "the nonChristian can't understand spiritual things," and once defined an anti-Semite as "someone who hates Jews more than he's supposed to." President Reagan is openly supportive of the Christian right, and at a 1984 gathering of (right-wing) religious broadcasters, he approvingly quoted singer Pat Boone to the effect that it would be better to have one's children "die now believing in God than live to grow up under communism . . . no longer believing in God." The President has also confided in a number of people, including Jerry Falwell and former California state senator James Mills, his belief that nuclear war is the Armageddon prophesied in the Bible, and is therefore inevitable.

The Wall of Separation

If we had to choose between the religious right and the religious left, most of us would probably have no trouble deciding with which side our sympathies lie. A deeper question may be whether this is a choice we want to have to make—and whether the Christianizing of politics is compatible with the democratic process.

The founding fathers evidently thought it was not, and took pains to build our Constitutional "wall" of separation between church and state. One reason that they did not, as the Christian right claims, establish a "Christian Nation" was that they respected the religious diversity of the young nation, and knew there would be trouble if the new government appeared to favor any particular sect or denomination. But there is another reason, which is seldom mentioned in history textbooks: The founding fathers did not make this a Christian nation because they were, for the most part, not Christians at all.

Thomas Jefferson, Benjamin Franklin, James Madison, and many of their co-revolutionaries, including, in all likelihood, George Washington, were deists, meaning they believed that God may have started the universe but had departed shortly after laying down the laws of nature. Some of them were overtly hostile to religion. Revolutionary war hero Ethan Allen wrote the first anti-Christian book published in America, entitled *Reason: The Only Oracle of Man.* Jefferson, who was, for all practical purposes, an atheist, believed that organized religion was universally "hostile to liberty." Although generally more discreet about his religious views, George Washington approved the 1797 Treaty with Tripoli that stated unequivocally, "The government of the United States is not in any sense founded on the Christian religion."

An Irreligious Tradition

Nor were the founding fathers alone in their beliefs, or lack of them. If there had been a bestseller's list in the early republic, it would have included the works of free-thinkers like Voltaire, Rousseau, and Thomas Paine (whose *Age of Reason* is said to have converted thousands of Americans away from Christianity). No one, therefore, seems to have thought it strange that the Constitutional Convention proceeded without any religious invocation or blessing, and that the Constitution itself makes only one reference to the deity—in the date, "Seventeenth Day of September in the

Year of our Lord one thousand seven hundred and eighty-seven."

America's irreligious tradition includes not only the founding fathers, but Andrew Carnegie, the steel magnate, and Eugene V. Debs, the early twentieth-century socialist leader. Throughout the otherwise deeply religious nineteenth century, "free thought" (or atheist) periodicals and organizations flourished, especially among poorer people like my ancestors and, as far as I can tell, many of their neighbors and co-workers in the Old West. Among America's better-known religious skeptics were Thomas Edison, Abraham Lincoln, and feminist leader Elizabeth Cady Stanton, who believed "the Bible and Church have been the greatest stumbling block in the way of women's emancipation."

Secular Neutrality

All of the founding fathers were privy to the theocratic beginnings of the original colonies. One of the principles foremost in their deliberations on the forming of a new government was the acknowledgment of the divisiveness of religion—which could be added to an already complex process. The very cornerstone of the principle of separation of state and church was a desire to foster the unity required for a group of colonies to separate themselves from a monarchy that had used religion as a tool of persecution on prior generations. . . .

Thomas Jefferson, above all, understood that a secular government could not only exist outside of religious doctrines and with a position of neutrality with respect to the divergent, religious-derived moral values drawn along denominational lines, but that the success or failure of the revolution he and his colleagues had initiated depended on that secular neutrality.

Jon G. Murray, *American Atheist*, April 1986.

It was only in the 1950s that nervous patriots began to equate religious faith with "Americanism." As Senator Joseph McCarthy saw it, "The fate of the world rests with the clash between the atheism of Moscow and the Christian spirit. . . ." In 1954, the phrase "under God" was inserted into the pledge of allegiance, apparently at the urging of President Eisenhower's pastor, who reportedly worried that the God-free version could "just as easily be repeated by little Muscovites pledging allegiance to the hammer and sickle." Two years later, "In God We Trust" was adopted as the national motto, without debate or a single dissenting vote in the House or the Senate. It was as if, in the global confrontation with communism, Americans wanted to be sure of being on God's home team.

Today's religious right is, in a number of ways, descended from the "Christian anti-communist movement" of the 'fifties, but until recently the Fundamentalists kept a chaste distance from the political fray. In the 'sixties, Jerry Falwell even criticized his fellow clergyman Martin Luther King, Jr., for becoming too involved in worldly matters. But a number of developments—the 1963 Supreme Court decision against school prayer, the Civil Rights movement and the resulting drive for integration, the perceived sinfulness of post-'sixties' America—finally goaded the (mostly white) Fundamentalists into battle with a hostile world. If they seem excessively belligerent about their political views, it is because they are used to thinking of themselves not as a "moral majority" but as a persecuted and excluded minority.

Whether the religious right succeeds in remaking America to suit its beliefs remains to be seen. In some areas, like their campaign against the teaching of evolution, they have lost ground; the California Board of Education decided that no available textbook for seventh- and eighth-grade science gives *enough* space to evolution. In other areas, they appear to have lost face. Certainly Jerry Falwell's outspoken advocacy of the white-minority government of South Africa has not increased his stature as a moral leader. Yet the institutions of the religious right—especially the schools that are preparing a new generation of the politically and spiritually committed—are thriving. The threat—or as some see it, the promise—of a Christian nation will be with us for some time to come.

Putting Democracy at Risk

Surely no one would insist that religious groups should have no voice in the political dialogue just because they *are* religious. Nor is it easy to quarrel with religious activists when they say that they are simply bringing morality into politics: We all make efforts—if only by writing an occasional letter to a congressman— to bring public policy into line with our personal sense of right and wrong. But when religion is defined as the only source of morality, and when a handful of religious leaders are in a position to define religious truth, we put our democratic tradition at risk, in at least two clear and obvious ways.

First, we potentially limit who can have a voice. It is no wonder that Jewish groups have been particularly outspoken in defense of church/state separation; in a "Christian Nation," Jews would have no place. Even defining our political tradition as "Judeo-Christian"—as many leaders of the Christian right now do—leaves out the millions of American adherents of minority religions, such as Islam, not to mention all of us who are atheists or undecided. If nothing else, we should worry about adopting politico-religious assumptions that would have excluded Lincoln and baffled George Washington.

Second, any set of convictions derived either from dogma or personal revelation is, by its nature, beyond discussion—and if there is anything that democracy requires of us, it *is* discussion. When one side says that God commands us to build more nuclear weapons, and the other side says God commands us to tear them down, then there is really nothing that the two sides can say to each other. As the Fundamentalist bumper-sticker says, "The Bible said it, I believe it, and that's all there is to it." Only when we ask, "What is best for the world?" without resorting to supernatural authority to foreclose the question, do we open up the possibility of truly democratic decision-making.

Faith in Democracy

It seems we are witnessing not so much a revival of faith in God as a decline of faith in democracy. We are deeply—and emotionally—divided over issues from abortion to federal spending, and we seem to have given up on the possibility of reasoning with each other. If God has endorsed our opinions, we are saved from the slow and demanding task of arguing our position and trying to convince our neighbors. We have only to invoke His name and rush to the barricades with banners proclaiming His support—secure in the knowledge that our adversaries are not only wrong, but probably damned as well.

Yet citizenship, in a democracy, means nothing if we are not willing to listen, to argue, to reflect, and sometimes to be persuaded of a new point of view. What we need most is not less faith, but more—faith in each other as reasonable people and rational citizens, and faith in the democratic process, imperfect as it is, that our infidel founding fathers left to us instead of a God.

====

*"The real . . . world [is] inhabited by both
businessmen and bishops."*

====

Religious Leaders Should Challenge Public Policy

James Gaffney

On November 13, 1986, the US Catholic bishops published a pastoral letter titled "Economic Justice for All: Catholic Social Teaching and the US Economy." The pastoral proved controversial not only because it criticized some Reagan administration policies, but because many people believed that religious leaders have no right or expertise to comment on economic policy. In the following viewpoint, James Gaffney, a professor of religious studies at Loyola University in New Orleans, defends the bishops' pastoral. According to Gaffney, religious commentary on public policy is appropriate because public policies have a moral dimension.

As you read, consider the following questions:

1. According to Gaffney, what are the US bishops' qualifications to comment on the economy?
2. Why is the author bothered by criticisms of the US bishops' pastoral letter?
3. According to the author, how does the "fundamental principle of Christian morality" affect economics?

James Gaffney, "Our Bishops and Our Economy," *America*, January 24, 1987. Reprinted with the permission of America Press Inc., 106 W. 56th Street, New York, NY 10019. 1987 All Rights Reserved.

Proverbially, it has been said that a conservative is one who is unwilling to assume that his great-grandfather was much stupider or much wickeder than himself. I wish to adopt and commend that sort of conservatism in recalling—what we are never allowed to forget for very long—that ordinary and respected people in decisive numbers among our own great-grandparental ancestors maintained a social system that has occasioned deeper and more persistent shame than any other single aspect of our social history. I refer, of course, to the infamous business of slavery. And I share the common assessment of that business as a colossal instance of something that can happen any time, and which, in subtler forms, is happening all the time: the attenuation and obliteration of traditionally acknowledged moral values by prevailing economic interests. The sacrifice of life, liberty and the pursuit of happiness to the exigencies of commercial and industrial profit is something of which we know our forefathers to have been capable. And I am unaware of any evidence whatsoever that my own generation is endowed with a quality of effective conscience superior to that which perpetrated, aided or acquiesced in that atrocity.

I begin with this somewhat gloomy candor partly to clarify my own position, but also because of something I find disquieting about the climate of opinion that much of the discussion of the Catholic bishops' new pastoral letter appears to illustrate. I should have to describe it as a preemptive pose of innocence, establishing an atmosphere of resolute moral complacency, a genial consensus that, while our socioeconomic arrangements may fall short of technical perfection, our hearts are unquestionably in the right place, and our differences pertain always to the efficacy of our means, never to the rectitude of our purposes.

The Bishops' Critics

Among many signs of this attitude, some of the most eloquent were early professions of immediate surprise and eventual cynicism over the presumptuousness of such people, as bishops are assumed to be, in offering any criticism at all of economic behavior. The most grotesque example was provided by the editors of Fortune, who could find no explanation for the bishops' intervention other than a self-serving desire to intrude officiously upon the world of business by advocating socialism, which "gives them a role to play, while capitalism—reliance on impersonal market forces—leaves them in the cold." Thus, the editorial inconsequentially concludes, "the church will be driven to depict economics as ethics and economic policy-making as an exercise in distributive justice." In the same mood, but achieving a style of unsurpassable pomposity, the mock-prayerfulness of Forbes: "From sermonizing prelates, making up in presumption what they lack in knowledge of economic affairs, O Lord, deliver us!" Without multiplying examples, I venture to suggest that statements so naive, from sources so sophisticated, are not readily attributable to anything more amiable than hypocrisy. But, whether disingenuous or merely obtuse, such statements go far to demonstrate the importance, as well as the difficulty, of the bishops' undertaking.

Pride in Catholic Social Teaching

We do not count ourselves among those who think that, in speaking of economics, the bishops are overstepping their proper authority. On the contrary, we take pride in Catholic social teaching. We welcome the bishops' constructive contributions to that unfinished tradition.

The Lay Commission on Catholic Social Teaching and the US Economy, *Liberty and Justice for All*, 1986.

Pervading this bilious rhetoric is a portrayal of the bishops as soft-headed, censorious busybodies, intruding incongruously upon the private domains of hard-headed practical businessmen who wonder aloud, with mingled annoyance and amusement, what people like that could possibly find to interest them in places like this. Somehow, the implied scenario recalls an episode I heard in childhood from my grandfather, a New York newspaperman in the early days of that city's reform era—of how a group of uniformed members of the newly activated vice squad were met at the door of a discreet Manhattan brownstone by an attendant who asked, with completely sincere perplexity, "What are you guys doing here? This is a whorehouse!"

Capitalism and Morality

Far be it from me to press that analogy beyond the decent limits of satire. But it is no more fantastic to depict the capitalistic marketplace as a complacent brothel than to represent it as a realm of "impersonal forces," functioning under the refined surveillance of dispassionate scientists. The fantasy of capitalism's impersonality, naturalness and moral sterility is undoubtedly useful as a myth. It is exceedingly dangerous as a hoax. And it is restorative to turn from it to such common-sense observations as the following: "People of the same trade seldom meet together, even for merriment and diversion, but the conversation ends in a conspiracy against the public or in some contrivance to raise prices." Such remarks reconnect us with the real post-lapsarian world inhabited by both businessmen and bishops—who often, of course, are the same people. And it is especially comforting that the author of that truism was neither a businessman nor a bishop but an economist. Indeed, *the* economist—Adam Smith, who thought such things worth mentioning in *The Wealth of Nations*, even though obviously they would never get by censorship at the holy offices maintained by Fortune or Forbes. It is similarly comforting to borrow a summary reflection not from a religious periodical but from a columnist in The Wall Street Journal: "I'm always dubious about the self-righteous—including those who self-righteously proclaim that, alone among our citizens, those who stand in pulpits should keep silent!"

The attempt to discredit the bishops on the ground that they are not experts resurrects a familiar fallacy based on the absurd suggestion that talking intelligently about the economy means talking as a qualified economist or at least an experienced businessman. We remember the same sophistry from earlier pretensions that talking significantly about war means talking as a military strategist or tactician. It is like pretending only gynecologists could talk meaningfully about women, or pediatricians about children—or, for that matter, theologians about religion. Economics is, at least arguably, a science, but the economy involves immensely more than the subject matter, however generously defined, of that science. And an important part of what it additionally involves is morality. If the bishops' intervention did no more than remind us of that fact, it would serve an admirable purpose.

Bishops are, according to Roman Catholic understanding, the chief official teachers of a legacy of doctrine deriving from Jesus Christ. They acquire their distinctive role as moral teachers from the fact that Jesus' own teaching was essentially, though not, of course, exclusively, moral, and that the Christian Church's fidelity to Jesus is inseparable from commitment to that teaching. Let me attempt briefly to develop in my own way the connection between that episcopal duty of keeping Christ's morality alive among Christians and some of the general positions adopted in the pastoral letter. . . .

Christian Morality: Plain and Public

In the first place, the fundamental principle of Christian morality is as plain and public as any principle of any morality in recorded history. Its most familiar formulation, cited by Jesus from the Scriptures of His own religion, Judaism, is "Love your neighbor as yourself." The Christian Scriptures are at pains to remove any doubt that what is here meant by "love" is no inert affection, but a disposition to act, beneficially and protectively, deliberately bringing to the interests of one's neighbor the sort of positive, practical concern one spontaneously brings to one's own interests. And the same Scriptures leave no room for doubt that what is here intended by "neighbor" is simply anyone who requires or can provide kindness, anyone occupying any place in the whole vast scheme of social interdependence. "Love your neighbor as yourself" is thus one of several classic formulations of a moral principle that has, more often and more widely than any other, been regarded as fundamental: the so-called Golden Rule, whereby we are enjoined to treat others as we think it would be right for others to treat us if we were in their circumstances.

Something To Offer

Among many economists and social observers it has become almost commonplace to observe that the American and world economies are in the midst of a profound structural transition that calls into question not only traditional techniques for managing economic affairs, but also for conceptualizing the workings of both the economy and government. . . . Precisely because this situation has such profound effects on the everyday lives of so many people, and because of the basic choices with which it confronts us, it has also raised serious moral questions that involve our basic understanding of human nature—the individual, the family, community and society—and of human purpose, what we are called to become individually and collectively. More and more people inevitably are coming to see that the wisdom of their different religious traditions has something to offer in the debates and conflicts over the best responses to alternative policy choices, precisely because these policies seriously affect the lives of us all—our material well-being as well as our motivations and fears, hopes and desires.

Thomas M. Gannon, *The Catholic Challenge to the American Economy*, 1987.

This fundamental principle of Christian morality, shared by many other moralities professing no allegiance to Christianity, immediately implies the fundamental moral importance of a certain conception of justice. For treating others as one would approve of being treated by others means regarding others, for practical moral purposes, as essentially equal to oneself. According to a logic many of us first articulated in an elementary geometry class, things equal to the same thing are equal to each other. And by that familiar logic, the Golden Rule implies a universe of selves equal in some fundamental respect, despite the obvious diversity and changeability of their conditions. One may, if one wishes, postulate an inherent basis for this equality and call it human dignity, thereby clarifying a notion that, during the past century, Catholic literature has tended to overwork and underexplain. But the phrase really adds nothing to the argument, and the essential thing is that, at least for Christians, human equality in the sense indicated is not a moot point. Such human equality is not, God knows, a matter of observation. It is, however, a matter of obliga-

90

tion, implicit in the most basic of Christian moral principles. And since there is no logical way of dissolving the implication while preserving the principle, Christianity is finally inseparable from an egalitarian conception of justice.

What this means practically is that any notable differences in how people are treated must always be justified—and may sometimes be required, by corresponding differences in their conditions or circumstances. The rich man of Jesus' parable, in Luke 16, is condemned because his treatment of the afflicted Lazarus at his gate was outrageously different from the way he would obviously wish to be treated if their circumstances were reversed. The Samaritan, of Jesus' parable in Luke 10, is extolled, because his treatment of the man who fell among robbers was so perfectly like the way he would obviously wish to be treated if their circumstances were reversed. And those "sheep" and "goats" who go their separate ways to glory and perdition in Jesus' parable of judgment in Matthew 25 obviously owe their respective fates to the same standard—the persistent standard of Christian morality and, as many believe, the highest standard of rational morality, the standard of equal regard, of the Golden Rule.

The Good Samaritan in the Real World

However, even though these parables of Jesus clarify what might otherwise be misunderstood about His meaning of love and of neighbor, their artificial simplicity can occasion another kind of misunderstanding. The point can be made by artificially complicating them, with a particular sort of realism. Suppose, for example, that the Samaritan encountered on his journey not an isolated victim of robbers, but a whole throng of tattered, emaciated refugees from a distant area afflicted by drought. Since he is still the same "good" Samaritan Jesus envisaged, he will try to help, try to be, in Jesus' active sense of that word, a neighbor. Only now he must be neighbor to a multitude. The requisite help exceeds his private resources. Now, to give help, he must get help. And it must be organized and expeditious if it is to be really helpful. Add further realistic complications. Let him discover, from those to whom he applies for help, that the disaster he is coping with is not unique and that the drought which occasioned it is not accidental. A wealthy and influential vintner has diverted certain watercourses, originating on his private property, to obtain irrigation that increases the productivity and enlarges the profits of his vineyards—not to mention his subsidiary bottling plants and transport services. Our Samaritan appeals to the vintner, who assures him that, while he harbors no ill will for the famine-struck refugees, he is not prepared to frustrate the growth of a thriving business. On the other hand, he is willing to hire as migrant workers those of them who are able-bodied and who will settle for a modest wage. Appalled when he hears the amount of the wage, the Samaritan supposes such employment practices must be illegal. But a knowledgeable lawyer assures him that they are not. So he organizes an appeal to the legislature. We all have sufficient experience and imagination to continue that story through any number of subsequent connected episodes. And the only thing about it that might seem lacking in verisimilitude would be the Samaritan's continued perseverance. Nevertheless, no matter how the story is complicated, if that Samaritan remains in character, the story of his efforts will continue to be what the whole thing was about in the first place, Jesus' answer to the question, "Who is my neighbor?"

Let the Bishops Take No Guff!

I recall a conversation I once had with the late Justice William O. Douglas. He said, "If the Constitution which we're called upon to interpret had meant us to grant sovereign attributes to the market and thus to pure, economic efficiency, it would have been written differently. We're enjoined by the Constitution and the Bill of Rights to subordinate the claims for efficiency to the interests of human well-being." Justice Douglas's view, from the judicial standpoint, converges with the message of the bishops. So let the bishops take no guff!

Eliot Janeway, *Commonweal*, June 3, 1988.

The point, I assume, is obvious. As the compact little parable expands into something like a neorealistic scenario, the original teaching does not change its significance or lose its validity. It only displays its scope. The transition it illustrates corresponds to the contrast familiarly made between personal morality and social morality, private ethics and public ethics—if you like, microethics and macroethics. But the contrast remains essentially quantitative. With every new complication, it is still a question of loving one's neighbor as oneself—or not.

The Church's Task

Especially during the past century, the Catholic Church has tried repeatedly to widen the horizon of Christian moral vision in essentially the same way I have intimated by tampering with the parable. The main initiative has been papal. But in recent years, especially in South and North America, it has been taken up independently by regional groups of bishops, concentrating on problems predominating in their parts of the world. In the United States, the last few years have seen this task assumed with unprecedented energy and boldness, resistant to political pressure and popular prejudice, and with a topical relevance that has moved episcopal letter-writing from the inside pages of dioceasan weeklies to the front pages and prime time of world news media. . . .

If, then, one's moral judgment not only of individual actions but of social arrangements, including economic ones, is predicated on the Golden Rule and egalitarian principles, what kind of fact should attract one's critical attention? Obviously, the fact of there being in one's society people whose condition one would, in their place, find decidedly painful. Aware of such facts, the socially moral Christian looks, not for a culprit, but for an explanation. Is the suffering caused, or could it be alleviated by the actions of others? If so, what actions and what others? Individual or collective, random or systematic? None of these questions are, as yet, ethical questions, and correct answers to them need not disclose any ethical obligations. Nevertheless, there is an ethical obligation to entertain such questions earnestly and to answer them honestly. To discover that, whereas I am relatively happy, you are decidedly miserable, does not imply that I, or anybody else, is obliged to do anything about you. But it does raise that question, as one that it would be wrong to ignore. If I hear a cry of pain, I am not thereby obliged to undertake a rescue, but I am obliged to take a serious, practical interest. That is the very least that is demanded by the Golden Rule, by Christian morality, by egalitarian justice. By the same token, it is the very least that is involved in what the bishops cite as their main guiding motif, a "preferential option for the poor"—attending first to those who are most obviously hurting. And, to give at least minimal credit and discredit where they are due, let me say that the U.S. bishops, having heard cries of pain, have taken a serious practical interest, whereas a great many of their critics quite plainly have not.

"The larger concern . . . is that the clergy . . . focus on the first priority of bishops—evangelization and spiritual care of the parish."

Religious Leaders Should Not Challenge Public Policy

Dinesh D'Souza

Dinesh D'Souza is a senior policy analyst in the Office of Policy Development at the White House. In the following viewpoint, he criticizes the US Catholic bishops for writing pastoral letters on the economy and on defense. According to D'Souza, the bishops have no expertise in these matters. He concludes that religious leaders should focus on spiritual issues and leave public policy to the experts.

As you read, consider the following questions:

1. What were some reactions to the bishops' pastoral letters, according to the author?
2. What does D'Souza think is the cause of the bishops' increased political activism in the '80s?
3. What is the Vatican's attitude toward the bishops' pastorals, according to D'Souza?

Dinesh D'Souza, "The Bishops as Pawns, Behind the Scenes at the U.S. Catholic Conference," *Policy Review*, Fall 1985. Reprinted with permission of *Policy Review* a quarterly publication of The Heritage Foundation.

For most of this century, ecclesiastical proclamations by the American Catholic bishops dwelt on such subjects as "Field Education in the Catholic Seminary," "The Homily in the Sunday Assembly," "Rite of Penance," and "Liturgical Music Today." Response from the Catholic community was tepid, and the national media were understandably indifferent. Then in the late 1960s and early 1970s, the bishops entered the political arena, with increasingly frenetic denunciations of U.S. foreign policy and calls for redistribution of income. Even these statements, however, remained obscure to most people. Now the bishops have synthesized their political vision with two pastoral letters that challenge the basic tenets of U.S. defense and economic policy. And the reaction has been explosive, both inside and outside Catholic circles. Acres of press commentary have been devoted to praising or damning the pastorals, countless seminar participants have cogitated on the theological and policy implications, and even the Reagan Administration has been taken by the lapels and forced to respond to the bishops' criticism.

The pastoral on nuclear weapons, approved almost unanimously by the bishops in May 1983, urges the United States to move away from deterrence toward a peace based on disarmament and "mutual trust" with the Soviet Union. The bishops declare that "deterrence is not an adequate strategy as a long-term basis for peace; it is a transitional strategy justifiable only in conjunction with resolute determination to pursue arms control and disarmament." The argument of the pastoral is that "good ends such as defending one's country and protecting freedom cannot justify immoral means," such as threatening to wreak massive destruction on the Soviet Union. Thus the bishops demand progressive disarmament of superpower arsenals beginning with "immediate bilateral agreements" that "halt the testing, production, and deployment of new strategic systems." Even while depleting its missile stockpile, the United States should "under no circumstances" aim its nuclear deterrent at Soviet population centers, whether they house Soviet silos or not. Nor should the United States ever contemplate the first use of nuclear weapons—or issue such a threat. Without arms control efforts seeking "deep cuts" in nuclear arsenals, the bishops assert that the defense strategy of the free world cannot be morally justified.

Reactions to the Pastoral

The first draft of the letter on the U.S. economy, released in November 1984, proclaims that "Society has a moral obligation to take the necessary steps to ensure that no one among us is hungry, homeless, unemployed, or otherwise denied what is necessary to live in dignity." Labeling the welfare system "woefully inadequate," the bishops call for an "experiment in economic democracy," which would evaluate all fiscal and economic policies primarily in terms of their material impact on the poor. Dismissing criticism of two decades of failure of federal handouts as evidence of "a punitive attitude toward the poor," the pastoral urges greater transfers of resources to the indigent and the unemployed. The bishops fault trade policies in the West for poverty in the Third World, and propose an expansion of loans and foreign aid to rescue the beleaguered economies of Africa and Latin America. . . .

One immediate result of the two pastorals has been a switch of constituencies for the bishops. The people who once ridiculed and caricatured the theology of the bishops, and their pronouncements on settled Catholic teaching on abortion and artificial birth control, now speak their names solemnly, almost reverentially, invoking of all things the bishop's Authority. Even groups such as People for the American Way (PAW), which greeted the activism of evangelicals and Archbishop (now Cardinal) John O'Connor's comments about abortion with apocalyptic warnings

By Toles for The Buffalo News

Tom Toles. Universal Press Syndicate. Reprinted by permission.

about mixing God and politics, now throw confetti at the Catholic clerics as they march, in their hats and long robes, into the public policy arena. John Buchanan, president of PAW, calls the bishops' recent politicking "valuable" and "encouraging."

By contrast, the bishops' foray into partisan politics has prompted criticism from individuals, organizations, and journals usually supportive of the church hierarchy. Theologians such as Michael Novak of the American Enterprise Institute, Ralph McInerny of Notre Dame University, and Fr. James Schall of Fordham University, and publications loyal to the magisterium, such as the *National Catholic Register* and *Catholicism in Crisis,* have worried aloud about the bishops jeopardizing their theological credibility by attaching their name to dubious, or at least controversial, political causes.

No Expertise

As American citizens, the Catholic bishops certainly have a right to participate in the policy discussion. An entirely separate issue is what expertise the bishops have to tackle these issues. Foreign and economic policy data and analysis are not part of the curriculum at Catholic seminaries. So if the clergy wish to offer serious policy critiques which go beyond broad moral claims ("We must say no to nuclear war," "Bread before bombs") they must become familiar with the concepts and the terms of the debate.

In their pastoral letters the bishops do not confine themselves to general moral assertions. Indeed the reader is struck by the depth and specificity with which the bishops seek to dissect concrete policies and propose remedial action. In the letter on war and peace, the bishops call for a "no first use" declaration by NATO [North Atlantic Treaty Organization], for the United States to abide by arms control treaties including SALT II [Strategic Arms Limitation Talks], for abandonment of missiles such as the MX which "possess a prompt hard target kill capability," and for a counter-force as opposed to counter-value strategy. The draft letter on the economy condemns flat-tax proposals, sets the maximum permissible unemployment rate at three to four percent, demands more soft loans through the World Bank to underdeveloped countries, endorses comparable worth legislation and "judiciously administered" affirmative action, and invites consideration of a New International Economic Order.

Uninformed Indignation

I contacted several rank-and-file bishops to find out how much they know about defense and economic policy matters. These bishops were selected randomly to represent the mainstream of the American hierarchy. After all, the two pastorals are not intended, and are not being promulgated, as the view of a handful of bishops on a committee or a small crew of advisory staffers, but rather as the collective moral and political judgment of the American hierarchy. So it is fair to ask how competent the average bishop is to evaluate national policies and domestic policy.

Interviews with these bishops suggest that they know little or nothing about the ideas and proposals to which they are putting their signature and lending their religious authority. The bishops are unfamiliar with existing defense and economic programs, unable to identify even in general terms the Soviet military capability, ignorant of roughly how much of the budget currently goes to defense, unclear about how much should be reallocated to social programs, and innocent of the most basic concepts underlying the intelligent layman's discussion of these questions.

Nonsensical Dialogue

The lack of economics in the Bible is something that should be taken seriously. I suspect that there are no proper (or possible) biblical critiques or defenses of modern economies. All such criticisms and defenses are arguments of anachronism. Biblical writings are rooted in a set of social and moral assumptions that, in the context of to-day's society, are *pre*-economic. Dialogue between theologians and economists may be as nonsensical as a musical critique of the Dow Jones industrials.

George Dennis O'Brien, *Fortune*, December 8, 1986.

Bishop Edward O'Donnell of St. Louis is perplexed about terms such as "frictional unemployment" and "hard target kill capability" which appear in the pastoral letters bearing his name. He has no idea what percent of our budget is spent on defense; "I have to look it up." He wants an "adequate non-nuclear defense" to protect Europe against a possible Soviet invasion, but is alarmed at the information that conventional weapons cost more than nuclear weapons. Immediately he says that a conventional buildup "doesn't call for more spending on our part"; let the Europeans pay their own way. How many troops does the United States have in Europe? Bishop O'Donnell "just can't say." He does feel that "our whole strategy of fighting World War II was unjustified" because innocent civilians were targeted and killed. How else to defeat Hitler? "You know," says Bishop O'Donnell, "I don't have the answer." . . .

No Idea

Hartford bishop Peter Rosazza, who initially proposed the pastoral on the economy, has "no idea" how much the United States spends on defense. But "it's astronomical," he says. "It seems clear we're going for superiority." He condemns the MX missile and the B-1 bomber but is especially vehement about

98

strategic defense. "That's out. Out. To me, there's no question. It's a quantum leap in the arms race." Asked how poverty increased in the United States even while the amount spent to eliminate it by the federal government multiplied several times, Bishop Rosazza said, "Wow, that's a tough one."

One bishop who freely admits his lack of knowledge is Nevin Hayes of Chicago. "I'm not that well informed," he says. "Just how many nuclear and conventional weapons we have, I'm not sure." How can the United States deter a Soviet invasion of Europe without the threat to use nuclear weapons? "I don't know." Bishop Hayes condemns the "big monsters" for "putting the mom and pop stores out of business" in this country. He is flabbergasted when asked about marginal tax rates. "Marginal what? This is where I'm way over my head." At this point, it was probably hopeless to ask him whether he knew anything about the principle behind supply-side economics, Say's Law. "How do you spell that?" Bishop Hayes wanted to know. "Is it like Murphy's Law?"

The problem the bishops get into when they leave their ecclesiastical domain and try to be professionals on other matters has been commented on before. During the debate on the war and peace pastoral, Archbishop Philip Hannan of New Orleans accused his colleagues of not having "the faintest idea of what you are doing." And it is hardly new; in 1976 when the bishops passed a resolution calling on the Carter Administration to negotiate a new treaty with Panama, Cardinal John Carberry of St. Louis told the *New York Times* he knew "nothing at all" about Panama and felt foolish casting an uninformed vote on such an important foreign policy issue.

The reason the bishops boldly press ahead in their political activism is their abiding trust in the people who write their pastorals—the policy staff of the United States Catholic Conference (U.S.C.C.). Although most have no formal training as defense strategists or economists, the U.S.C.C. staffers greatly enjoy tackling public policy matters, and submitting lengthy analyses that the bishops assume are a correct application of Catholic principles. . . .

A New Catholic Militancy

In the late 1960s . . . the newly-formed U.S.C.C. began to hire an increasingly militant set of officials who were not content with what they considered vague formulations of Catholic principles and a narrow emphasis on individual and family behavior. The U.S.C.C. staff urged the bishops to be more specific about Catholic social doctrine, and place more emphasis on collective sins and collective (i.e. governmental) solutions. The result was an explosion of highly politicized U.S.C.C. pastorals.

In the 1970s, the bishops demanded that the United States

withdraw from Vietnam; opposed the bombing of Cambodia ordered by President Nixon; called for amnesty for draft evaders; supported a Panama Canal treaty; opposed capital punishment; advocated strict handgun control laws; denounced human rights violations in Chile and Brazil; supported the SALT treaties; declared the right of Palestinians to a separate state; opposed an anti-ballistic missile system for the United States; called for the United States to cut off all aid to El Salvador; supported increased U.S. aid to the Marxist regimes of Angola and Mozambique; and insisted on full employment, a guaranteed national income, and participation by the poor in welfare policy-making boards—to name a few policy positions of the U.S. Catholic Conference.

A Lack of Competence

The Bishops are blowing it by moving off terrain where they can speak knowledgeably and authoritatively, i.e., on traditional Catholic teaching on morality and ethics, and venturing into areas—like the impact of SDI on Soviet strategic planning and the wisdom of raising the minimum wage—where their lack of competence is manifest.

Patrick Buchanan, *The Wanderer*, May 12, 1988.

Individual bishops no doubt share the sentiments of concern for the poor and horror of war that underlie these pastorals, but they are not the ones who come up with the analysis or the specific recommendations. Martin McLaughlin, a former official at the Agency for International Development (AID), . . . says that even the bishops delegated to the pastoral committees "rewrite very few sentences" that the U.S.C.C. staff draws up; only "if they egregiously do not like something, they change it." The team working on the pastorals consists of men with a political agenda and intensity that is not shared either by the bishops or by the vast majority of American Catholics. Professor Brian Benestad, author of *Pursuit of a Just Social Order,* an authoritative study of U.S.C.C. statements, maintains that there is "no political diversity" on the staff, and that the U.S.C.C. "thinks it is more important to issue partisan policy statements than to communicate the principles of Catholic social doctrine." Russell Shaw, secretary for public affairs at the U.S.C.C., says that his colleagues are "probably more liberal" than the bishops, and "unrepresentative of the Catholic population.". . .

The men behind the activism of the American hierarchy are, like the bishops themselves, deeply moved about our social problems. But they seem only slightly better informed about the reality of those problems and the difficult choices that a society must make—choices that involve trade-offs. They seem to believe that we can have everything: peace without deterrence, deterrence without the threat to use nuclear weapons, adequate conventional defense without spending more on the military, more federal spending without raising taxes or the deficit, expanding social programs which do not curb incentive or increase inflation. That sort of perfection is not known to obtain in this world. . . .

Rooted in Discontent

The bishops' latest activism is rooted in their discontent with previous, largely unsuccessful battles to uphold orthodox Catholic teaching; and in their emerging struggle with Rome to control the agenda of American Catholicism. Through most of the 1960s, under a relatively conservative hierarchy, the bishops stressed evangelization over politics—their minimal lobbying was reserved mainly for issues such as abortion and school prayer. But now, says Russell Shaw of the U.S.C.C., the bishops may be punch-drunk from "the weary struggle" first to prevent and then to reverse *Roe v. Wade* and *Engels v. Vitale*, as well as to uphold *Humanae Vitae*, the encyclical forbidding artificial birth control on which the bishops have "largely given up." In comparison to these protracted and thankless endeavors, the bishops have discovered how pleasant it is to air progressive passions. And the accolades from the networks and the major newspapers more than compensate for the criticism of a Michael Novak or a William Simon.

In Rome, however, there are raised eyebrows over the bishops' activism. Monsignor Joseph Whalen, who is on the staff at the Apostolic Nunciature, says "Rome is not totally opposed" to the bishops' pastoral letters but notes that if his office had produced the documents "they would have been different." Indeed, the Vatican exercised leverage to moderate the nuclear weapons pastoral; shortly after the second draft was released, the Catholic press reported that Pope John Paul II sternly chastised Cardinal Bernardin for permitting what he considered irresponsible criticism of the defense policy of the free world. Hoping to offset a similar embarrassment, Archbishop Rembert Weakland, chairman of the committee overseeing the economics pastoral, went to Rome to give the Pope a briefing on the first draft and solicit his comments. . . .

The larger concern in the Vatican, however, is that the clergy stay away from these frontal attacks on the systems in the West that have ensured the church survival and prosperity, and focus on the first priority of bishops—evangelization and spiritual care of the parish.

"There is no Church teaching that mandates the best political course for making our belief everyone's rule."

Politicians Should Not Promote Their Religious Values

Mario Cuomo

Mario Cuomo is the governor of New York and a popular and often controversial political figure. In the following viewpoint, excerpted from a speech delivered at the University of Notre Dame, he uses the issue of abortion to explain why he believes politicians' religious beliefs should not dictate their political positions. According to Cuomo, Catholics and others opposed to abortion may hold strong religious beliefs but must recognize that in a pluralistic society other people believe differently and should not be made subject to a church's creed.

As you read, consider the following questions:

1. Why is abortion a divisive issue, according to the author?
2. To what historical controversy does Cuomo compare abortion? What point is he making?
3. What does Cuomo believe is the responsibility of the Catholic church?

Mario M. Cuomo, "Religious Belief and Public Morality: A Catholic Governor's Perspective." A paper delivered to the Department of Theology of the University of Notre Dame, September 13, 1984.

As a Catholic, I have accepted certain answers as the right ones for myself and my family, and because I have, they have influenced me in special ways, as Matilda's husband, as a father of five children, as a son who stood next to his own father's death bed trying to decide if the tubes and needles no longer served a purpose.

As a Governor, however, I am involved in defining policies that determine *other* people's rights in these same areas of life and death. Abortion is one of these issues, and while it is one issue among many, it is one of the most controversial and affects me in a special way as a Catholic public official.

So let me spend some time considering it.

I should start, I believe, by noting that the Catholic Church's actions with respect to the interplay of religious values and public policy make clear that there is no inflexible moral principle which determines what our *political* conduct should be. For example, on divorce and birth control, without changing its moral teaching, the Church abides the civil law as it now stands, thereby accepting—without making much of a point of it—that in our pluralistic society we are not required to insist that *all* our religious values be the law of the land.

Abortion is treated differently.

Prudent Political Judgment

Of course there are differences both in degree and quality between abortion and some of the other religious positions the Church takes: abortion is a "matter of life and death," and degree counts. But the differences in approach reveal a truth, I think, that is not well enough perceived by Catholics and therefore still further complicates the process for us. That is, while we always owe our bishops' words respectful attention and careful consideration, the question whether to engage the political system in a struggle to have it adopt certain articles of our belief as part of public morality, is not a matter of doctrine: it is a matter of prudential political judgment.

Michael Novak put it succinctly: "Religious judgment and political judgment are both needed," he wrote. "But they are not identical."

My church and my conscience require me to believe certain things about divorce, birth control and abortion. My church does not order me—under pain of sin or expulsion—to pursue my salvific mission according to a precisely defined political plan.

As a Catholic I accept the Church's teaching authority. While in the past some Catholic theologians may appear to have disagreed on the morality of some abortions (it wasn't, I think, until 1869 that excommunication was attached to all abortions without distinction), and while some theologians still do, I accept

103

the bishops' position that abortion is to be avoided.

As Catholics, my wife and I were enjoined never to use abortion to destroy the life we created, and we never have. We thought Church doctrine was clear on this, and—more than that—both of us felt it in full agreement with what our hearts and our consciences told us. For me life or fetal life in the womb should be protected, even if five of nine Justices of the Supreme Court and my neighbor disagree with me. A fetus is different from an appendix or a set of tonsils. At the very least, even if the argument is made by some scientists or some theologians that in the early stages of fetal development we can't discern human life, the full potential of human life is indisputably there. That—to my less subtle mind—by itself should demand respect, caution, indeed . . . reverence.

More than the State Should Grant

When bishops ask the state to criminalize abortion or the sale of contraceptive devices, they demand more than a democratic secular state should grant. The state must not make something illegal because God or the Pope forbids it. To ask the state to enforce church doctrine is to confuse church and state.

John M. Swomley, *The Churchman,* March 1987.

But not everyone in our society agrees with me and Matilda.

And those who don't—those who endorse legalized abortions— aren't a ruthless, callous alliance of anti-Christians determined to overthrow our moral standards. In many cases, the proponents of legal abortion are the very people who have worked with Catholics to realize the goals of social justice set out in papal encyclicals: the American Lutheran Church, the Central Conference of American Rabbis, the Presbyterian Church in the United States, B'nai B'rith Women, the Women of the Episcopal Church. These are just a few of the religious organizations that don't share the Church's position on abortion.

Certainly, we should not be forced to mold Catholic morality to conform to disagreement by non-Catholics however sincere or severe their disagreement. Our bishops should be teachers not pollsters. They should not change what we Catholics believe in order to ease our consciences or please our friends or protect the Church from criticism.

But if the breadth, intensity and sincerity of opposition to Church teaching shouldn't be allowed to shape our Catholic morality, it can't help but determine our ability—our realistic, political ability—to translate our Catholic morality into civil law, a law not for the believers who don't need it but for the disbelievers who reject it.

And it is here, in our attempt to find a political answer to abortion—an answer beyond our private observance of Catholic morality—that we encounter controversy within and without the Church over how and in what degree to press the case that our morality should be everybody else's, and to what effect.

Church Teaching and Politics

I repeat, there is no Church teaching that mandates the best political course for making our belief everyone's rule, for spreading this part of our Catholicism. There is neither an encyclical nor a catechism that spells out a political strategy for achieving legislative goals.

And so the Catholic trying to make moral and prudent judgments in the political realm must discern which, if any, of the actions one could take would be best.

This latitude of judgment is not something new in the Church, not a development that has arisen only with the abortion issue. Take, for example, the question of slavery. It has been argued that the failure to endorse a legal ban on abortions is equivalent to refusing to support the cause of abolition before the Civil War. This analogy has been advanced by the bishops of my own state.

But the truth of the matter is, few if any Catholic bishops spoke for abolition in the years before the Civil War. It wasn't, I believe, that the bishops endorsed the idea of some humans owning and exploiting other humans; Pope Gregory XVI, in 1840, had condemned the slave trade. Instead it was a practical political judgment that the bishops made. They weren't hypocrites; they were realists. At the time, Catholics were a small minority, mostly immigrants, despised by much of the population, often vilified and the object of sporadic violence. In the face of a public controversy that aroused tremendous passions and threatened to break the country apart, the bishops made a pragmatic decision. They believed their opinion would not change people's minds. Moreover they knew that there were southern Catholics, even some priests, who owned slaves. They concluded that under the circumstances arguing for a constitutional amendment against slavery would do more harm than good, so they were silent. As they have been, generally, in recent years, on the question of birth control. And as the Church has been on even more controversial issues in the past, even ones that dealt with life and death.

Moral Truths and Political Realities

What is relevant to this discussion is that the bishops were making judgments about translating Catholic teachings into public policy, not about the moral validity of the teachings. In so doing they grappled with the unique political complexities of their time. The decision they made to remain silent on a constitutional amendment to abolish slavery or on the repeal of the Fugitive Slave Law wasn't a mark of their moral indifference: it was a measured attempt to balance moral truths against political realities. Their decision reflected their sense of complexity, not their diffidence. As history reveals, Lincoln behaved with similar discretion.

The parallel I want to draw here is not between or among what we Catholics believe to be moral wrongs. It is in the Catholic response to those wrongs. Church teaching on slavery and abortion is clear. But in the application of those teachings—the exact way we translate them into action, the specific laws we propose, the exact legal sanctions we seek—there was and is no one, clear, absolute route that the Church says, as a matter of doctrine, we must follow.

Respecting the Beliefs of Others

Religious citizens have every right, it should go without saying, to believe for sectarian reasons that abortion is murder. But religious history isn't behind them on this one. Neither is the First Amendment, which requires us to respect the religious beliefs of others.

Betty McCollister, *Free Inquiry,* Winter 1986/87.

The bishops' pastoral letter, "The Challenge of Peace," speaks directly to this point. "We recognize," the bishops wrote, "that the Church's teaching authority does not carry the same force when it deals with technical solutions involving particular means as it does when it speaks of principles or ends. People may agree in abhorring an injustice, for instance, yet sincerely disagree as to what practical approach will achieve justice. Religious groups are entitled as others to their opinion in such cases, but they should not claim that their opinions are the only ones that people of good will may hold."

A Pluralistic Country

With regard to abortion, the American bishops have had to weigh Catholic moral teaching against the fact of a pluralistic country where our view is in the minority, acknowledging that what is ideally desirable isn't always feasible, that there can be different political approaches to abortion besides unyielding adherence to an absolute prohibition.

This is in the American-Catholic tradition of political realism. In supporting or opposing specific legislation the Church in this country has never retreated into a moral fundamentalism that will settle for nothing less than total acceptance of its views.

Indeed, the bishops have already confronted the fact that an absolute ban on abortion doesn't have the support necessary to be placed in our Constitution. In 1981, they put aside earlier efforts to describe a law they could accept and get passed, and supported the Hatch Amendment instead.

Some Catholics felt the bishops had gone too far with that action, some not far enough. Such judgments were not a rejection of the bishops' teaching authority: the bishops even disagreed among themselves. Catholics are allowed to disagree on these technical political questions without having to confess. . . .

The Church's Responsibility

In the end, even if after a long and divisive struggle we were able to remove all medicaid funding for abortion and restore the law to what it was—if we could put most abortions out of our sight, return them to the backrooms where they were performed for so long—I don't believe our responsibility as Catholics would be any closer to being fulfilled than it is now, with abortion guaranteed by the law as a woman's right.

The hard truth is that abortion isn't a failure of government. No agency or department of government forces women to have abortions, but abortion goes on. Catholics, the statistics show, support the right to abortion in equal proportion to the rest of the population. Despite the teaching of our homes and schools and pulpits, despite the sermons and pleadings of parents and priests and prelates, despite all the effort at defining our opposition to the sin of abortion, collectively we Catholics apparently believe— and perhaps act—little differently from those who don't share our commitment.

Are we asking government to make criminal what we believe to be sinful because we ourselves can't stop committing the sin?

The failure here is not Caesar's. This failure is our failure, the failure of the entire people of God.

Physician, Heal Thyself

Nobody has expressed this better than a bishop in my own state, Joseph Sullivan, a man who works with the poor in New York City, is resolutely opposed to abortion and argues, with his fellow bishops, for a change of law. "The major problem the Church has is internal," the bishop said in reference to abortion. "How do we teach? As much as I think we're responsible for advocating public policy issues, our primary responsibility is to teach our own people. We haven't done that. We're asking politicians to do what we haven't done effectively ourselves."

I agree with the bishop. I think our moral and social mission as Catholics must begin with the wisdom contained in the words "Physician, heal thyself." Unless we Catholics educate ourselves better to the values that define—and can ennoble—our lives, following those teachings better than we do now, unless we set an example that is clear and compelling, then we will never convince this society to change the civil laws to protect what we preach is precious human life.

Better than any law or rule or threat of punishment would be the moving strength of our own good example, demonstrating our lack of hypocrisy, proving the beauty and worth of our instruction.

We must work to find ways to avoid abortions without otherwise violating our faith. We should provide funds and opportunity for young women to bring their child to term, knowing both of them will be taken care of if that is necessary; we should teach our young men better than we do now their responsibilities in creating and caring for human life.

Through Practice of Love

It is this duty of the Church to teach through its practice of love that Pope John Paul II has proclaimed so magnificently to all peoples. "The Church," he wrote in *Redemptor Hominis* (1979), "which has no weapons at her disposal apart from those of the spirit, of the word and of love, cannot renounce her proclamation of 'the word . . . in season and out of season.' For this reason she does not cease to implore . . . everybody in the name of God and in the name of man: Do not kill! Do not prepare destruction and extermination for each other! Think of your brothers and sisters who are suffering hunger and misery! Respect each one's dignity and freedom!"

The weapons of the word and of love are already available to us: we need no statute to provide them.

"If a person really does accept the Church's teaching on abortion . . . there would be no question about what the legal status of such an act should be."

Politicians Should Promote Their Religious Values

Christopher Wolfe

In the following viewpoint, Christopher Wolfe criticizes Catholic politicians who do not promote church teaching on abortion. He writes that politicians who claim to be religious have a moral obligation to support laws which reflect their beliefs. Arguments that religious political leaders in a pluralistic society should respect the beliefs of others are merely excuses for moral apathy. Wolfe teaches in the political science department at Marquette University.

As you read, consider the following questions:

1. Why does the author find it difficult to understand Catholics who do not support anti-abortion legislation?
2. What point does Wolfe make by comparing abortion to the slavery issue in the nineteenth century? The author of the opposing viewpoint makes a similar comparison. How do their conclusions differ?
3. What does Wolfe call Catholics who will not support legal prohibition of abortion?

Christopher Wolfe, "Abortion and Catholic Politicians." Reprinted with permission from the October 1984 issue of *Catholicism in Crisis*, PO Box 1006, Notre Dame, IN 46556.

There is a growing number of Catholic politicians who put distance between themselves and the teaching of the Church on abortion. . . . The existence and increasing influence of such "Catholic pro-choice" politicians cannot but help exacerbate the problems over Church authority in the U.S. Inevitably, push is going to come to shove on the issue at some point.

In dealing with this new phenomenon, it is necessary to distinguish between two apparently very different kinds of positions. There is the Catholic politician who, like some Catholic theologians, claims that it is possible to be Catholic without accepting the teaching of the Church, even on very important issues such as abortion. Then there is another Catholic politician who claims to accept Church teaching, but adopts the position: "While I am personally opposed to abortion, I think that the law should allow people to choose for themselves whether to have an abortion."

A Rejection of Catholicism

I understand the first position. Basically it is a rejection of Catholicism. Whatever the reason why such people want to retain their identification as Catholics, they are explicitly rejecting one of its fundamental and irrevocable principles, namely, the authority of the Church (through its hierarchy) to teach and command in matters of faith and morals.

The second position I find much more difficult to understand. These individuals deny that they are rejecting the teaching of the Church, and claim that they only want to refrain from imposing the Church's teaching on others.

Normally one would assume that if a person really does accept the Church's teaching on abortion—that it is an unspeakable crime—there would be no question about what the legal status of such an act should be. Taking the life of an innocent human being would have to be prohibited by law. And yet there are Catholics in politics who strongly deny that reasoning. What is the counter-logic of their positions?

The Pluralism Argument

Position No. 1: I think that one would have to rule out one possible line of argumentation. Pro-abortion Catholic politicians (that is, "pro-choice ones"—the only relevant meaning of "pro-abortion" or "pro-choice" is that one advocates that abortion should be legal) cannot mean something like this: "I know that, as the Church teaches, abortion is an unspeakable crime against unborn human life, but we live in a pluralistic society, so it is not right for us to impose this principle on others through law." The problem with this argument is obvious if one simply substitutes other moral principles, as for example "I am opposed to breaking Jewish or Negro skulls, but others in our society disagree with me and therefore I do not feel that I can impose this principle on them." We would obviously have to reject such an argument, not just because of the Jewish and black voting blocs, but because there are a certain number of minimum obligations we all would agree the law must fulfill, one of which is protecting innocent human beings from those who would deprive them of life.

Thus, there must be some difference between "killing Jews or Negroes is wrong" and "killing unborn children is wrong." Which brings us back to the question of what the pro-abortion Catholic politician means when he says "I am personally opposed to abortion."

A Moral Evil

Position No. 2: We can also rule out another extreme, I think, that goes something like this: "Abortion is a terrible thing and it should not be necessary; we all look forward to the day it can be eliminated." What this might very well mean is merely that the speaker prefers contraception to abortion (abortion is a "last resort" after "failed contraception" in the case of those who are "irresponsible," ignorant, or unlucky). Abortion might be "terrible" not in the sense that it is a terrible moral evil, but in the sense that it is a kind of personal trauma: moral, but still ugly. For example, many people would think it terrible if the Humane Society had to kill a lot of cats, because killing cats is not a pleasant thing. Abortion is like that, only very much worse because there is "a part of a woman herself" involved (one which a surprising number of women having abortions refer to as "my baby"). That is, some people who would call abortion a terrible thing, would not be opposing abortion in the relevant sense, i.e., they would not be morally opposed to it, but merely find it an extremely "unpleasant" thing.

An Untenable Position

Most Catholics profess to think that abortion is indeed an evil, yet not only are they willing to tolerate it, they even urge that the government pay for it. They could scarcely hold such a position if they really believed it to be what it is—the deliberate snuffing out of preborn human life, often by brutal and painful means.

James Hitchcock, *The Human Life Review,* Winter 1986.

This too would put the speaker in the first category of people who simply reject the teachings of the Church. It would be a rejection of the teaching that abortion is a terrible *moral* evil.

Position No. 3: Another possible defense of the Catholic pro-abortion politician's position would focus on the question of subjective sincerity: "Abortion would be morally wrong for me, but I recognize that if other people have different moral positions, it might not be wrong for them." But that line of reasoning would be a defense of not prosecuting Nazis or white supremacists who liked to crack Jewish or Negro skulls. Sincere Nazis and racists who do such things should be punished for doing so, however sincere they might be in their moral views. Likewise, if abortion is objectively wrong, then those who perform it should not be exempted on the basis of sincerely held moral views.

Incompatible with Catholic Teaching

Position No. 4: Perhaps what is meant by "I am personally opposed to abortion, but . . . " is the following: "Abortion is obviously a very unfortunate thing, which no one really wants; in fact it's morally wrong, I think. But I'm not entirely sure, and so I should not impose what is merely my opinion on others." But a statement of this sort is not compatible with Catholic teaching. Rather than being an assent to the proposition that abortion is morally evil, it is merely an assent to the different, lesser proposition that abortion might be, or even that it *probably* is, evil.

Of course, even if a person sincerely believed that abortion might be or probably is killing an innocent human being, elementary morality should lead such a person to oppose the legalization of abortion. If somebody else were about to commit an act of murder, we would be obliged to do what was in our power to prevent the act. Likewise if someone were about to perform what might be an act of murder, we should stop him if we could. (Not to do so would suggest that we don't really believe that a possibly or probably evil act is being done.)

Position No. 5: Another position of the pro-abortion Catholic politician might be this: "Abortion in general is wrong, but sometimes what is wrong can become the right thing to do if it is necessary in order to avoid a greater evil; I'm not sure that I'd ever say that abortion is the lesser evil, but other good and sincere people, with their viewpoints, might balance various conditions differently and decide to have an abortion."

This position too is incompatible with the Church's teaching (though it is exactly what some theologians are saying). It is the position of consequentialism, which says that it is sometimes right to do (a moral) wrong in order to avoid another (physical or nonmoral) evil. (For example, abortion might be justified in order to avoid the supposedly greater evil of the pain and trauma of a rape-caused pregnancy.) In fact, this is to deny the Church's teaching that abortion is always wrong and that circumstances cannot make it right.

Position No. 6: A final argument, which may at first glance seem to explain "Catholic pro-choice" politicians, is this: "Abortion is a terrible moral evil; but many people (at *least* a very large minority) disagree with us, and an attempt to impose our views on them would be likely to have horrible results: widespread civil disobedience and a real 'fracturing' of our body politic. Therefore, we should not impose our views."

In the first place, though, this is not an accurate statement of the position of most (probably all, in fact) pro-abortion Catholic politicians. It is difficult to detect any anguish in their saying that we cannot successfully "impose" our views that unborn human life should be protected, reflecting a genuine belief that many lives are being destroyed. They do not say that we are simply *unable* to impose our views, but that we *should* not impose them—a very different thing. (This is especially obvious in the case of those who favor abortion funding.)

Standing by Their Convictions

It is sad to see politicians abandon their convictions, especially when the issue involved is one of life or death. A little expediency on something like tariffs or farm subsidies may be understandable. But when politicians do not draw the line where human life is involved, where can they draw it? What is left of their principles, and why should anyone trust them?

Mary Meehan, *The Human Life Review,* Winter 1984.

I do not contest that in some cases Catholic politicians, having vigorously enunciated the correct moral principle and fought strenuously to have it realized, may have to vote for compromises which fall short of full protection of the unborn, pending the day on which achievement of what elementary morality demands becomes possible. But the Catholic politicians we are talking about are not those in the forefront of the battle to limit abortion—they are generally in the ranks of those who fight to expand abortion "rights."

A Necessary Risk

One must also ask whether this position reflects a genuine belief in the terrible evil of abortion, if one looks at other positions obviously associated with it. How many of those who adopt this position would have made the same argument about slavery in the 1850s? Stephen Douglas's position on the issue—"popular sovereignty," i.e., letting the people of the territories decide on slavery for themselves, without Congress imposing one view—was, after all, closely paralled to the "pro-choice" view (although the perfect parallel would be letting individuals decide for themselves whether to have slaves). Was Lincoln right to "fracture" American political life with his demand that slavery be prohibited in the territories, so that it would eventually die out? (Yes!) For that matter, didn't the Supreme Court risk fracturing America over segregation and civil rights in *Brown v. Board of Education* (1954) and later cases—decisions "pro-choice" politicians would certainly applaud? Sometimes, on fundamental moral issues, it is necessary to risk fractures. (I would jump two stories from a burning building to avoid death, despite the risk; and I would risk damage to the body politic on issues such as slavery and abortion.)

Finally, the dangers of "imposing" our views are limited because we are unlikely to obtain more than the country will tolerate. The very fact that stringent limits on abortion could be obtained in our political system would show that there was broad consensus supporting (or at least tolerating) it. There might be a significant minority opposed, of course, but not one so great as to fracture our society beyond healing.

The lamentable corollary to this argument is that it will take an enormous effort to change the prevailing mores to achieve elimination of abortion. Right now, the consensus of society makes possible only a partial limit on abortion (though certainly greater than what the Supreme Court has allowed). At the same time, it is very implausible that abortion on demand (the "pro-choice" position) is the only position which will prevent fracturing the nation. There is a general consensus for *some* limits on abortion. This suggests that fears about "fracturing" the nation are really a cover for something else, i.e., at least a qualified acceptance of abortion itself.

Political Apostates

I have not yet been able to come up with another explanation of what is meant by "I am personally opposed to abortion, but I do not think the law should prohibit it." Some of the above positions are obviously untenable (e.g., that sincerity should exempt one from legal restraints, or that one can never enforce moral principles in a pluralistic society), while others are tenable only on the basis of a rejection of Catholic teaching. The net effect is to make it very clear that those who say they are opposed to abortion, but will not legally prohibit it, are not really "opposed" to it as Catholics are opposed to it.

Thus, to be honest, we must say that there are not two kinds of pro-abortion Catholic politicians, those who reject the Church's teachings outright and those who accept the teachings but are unwilling to "impose" them on others. There is just one single category of those Catholic politicians who abandon the moral principles of their faith in the conduct of their political duties: what might be called the category of "political apostates."

114

Recognizing Deceptive Arguments

People who feel strongly about an issue use many techniques to persuade others to agree with them. Some of these techniques appeal to the intellect, some to the emotions. Many of them distract the reader from the real issues.

Below are listed a few common examples of argumentation tactics. Most of them can be used either to advance an argument in an honest, reasonable way or to deceive and distract readers from important issues that may weaken the author's arguments. It is helpful for critical thinkers to recognize these tactics in order to evaluate rationally an author's ideas.

    a. *bandwagon*—the idea that "everybody" does this or believes this

    b. *personal attack*—criticizing an opponent *personally* instead of rationally debating his or her ideas

    c. *scare tactic*—the threat that if you don't do this or believe this, something terrible will happen

    d. *slanter*—trying to persuade through exaggerated and inflammatory language instead of through reason

    e. *strawperson*—distorting or exaggerating an opponent's arguments to make one's own seem stronger

    f. *testimonial*—quoting or paraphrasing an authority to support one's own viewpoint

The following activity will allow you to sharpen your skills in recognizing deceptive arguments. The statements are derived from the viewpoints in this chapter. *Beside each one, mark the letter of the type of deceptive appeal being used. More than one type of tactic may be applicable.*

1. Catholic politicians who refuse to oppose legalized abortion are heretics who will burn in hell.

2. Those who oppose the Bishops' pastoral on the economy believe instead that the proper attitude to take toward the poor is that of benign indifference.

3. Those who endorse legalized abortion are ruthless, callous and anti-Christian.

4. If our government and society does not promote religious values, then the entire country will become one big Atlantic City: shabby, amoral, impoverished.

5. The Catholic bishops should not speak on such technical matters as economics and disarmament because they do not know what they are talking about.

6. If we allow Christians to gain political power, public policy will be dictated by scriptural interpretation rather than reasoned debate.

7. Conservative Christians want to establish a "Christian Nation" governed by Biblical law.

8. Editors of such respected Catholic publications as the *National Catholic Register* and *Crisis* worry aloud that the bishops are weakening their theological credibility by supporting dubious political causes.

9. The Catholic bishops are soft-headed, censorious busybodies intruding upon the private domains of hard-headed practical businessmen.

10. Politicians who say they are opposed to abortion but don't want to impose their views on others are in fact proponents of abortion.

11. No less of an authority than former Secretary of the Treasury William Simon has called the bishops' pastoral on the economy a naive and misguided document.

12. Those people who bring their religious convictions to politics have only to invoke God's name and rush to the barricades, secure in the knowledge that they are right and that those who disagree with them are damned.

13. Political action without religious restraints will bring public ruin.

Periodical Bibliography

The following articles have been selected to supplement the diverse views presented in this chapter.

Robert N. Bellah — "Resurrecting the Common Good: The Economics Pastoral, A Year Later," *Commonweal*, December 18, 1987.

James Montgomery Boice — "Five Basics for Political Involvement," *Eternity*, September 1987.

David Glidden — "Prophets and Politics: When True Belief Differs from Belief in Truth," *Los Angeles Times*, December 28, 1986.

Joshua Haberman — "America's Safety Belt in the Bible Belt," *The Washington Times*, October 6, 1987.

Terry Muck — "The Wall that Never Was," *Christianity Today*, July 10, 1987.

Jon G. Murray — "Religion and Democracy," *American Atheist*, April 1986.

National Review — "The Bishops and the Economy: Round Two," December 31, 1986.

Richard Neuhaus — "The Fear of Holy Fanaticisms," *The Washington Times*, April 11, 1986.

Michael Novak — "Advocacy of Religious Left Is Out of Step," *Los Angeles Times*, December 10, 1986.

George Dennis O'Brien — "The Christian Assault on Capitalism," *Fortune*, December 8, 1986.

Anthony M. Pilla — "How To Implement 'Economic Justice for All,'" *America*, January 31, 1987.

A. James Reichley — "When Religion and Politics Should Not Mix," *The Wall Street Journal*, November 25, 1985.

Peter Steinfels — "Understanding the Reactions to the Economics Pastoral," *Origins*, June 11, 1987.

US Bishops — "Economic Justice for All: Catholic Social Teaching and the US Economy," *Origins*, November 27, 1986.

James M. Wall — "Preacher-Bashing and the Public Life," *The Christian Century*, April 15, 1987.

Does Religious Discrimination Exist in America?

RELIGION IN AMERICA

Chapter Preface

There is an ongoing debate concerning under what circumstances government should restrict religious beliefs and practices. Some limits are accepted with little controversy. The line can become more blurred, however, when the government must deal with issues where there is no social consensus, even in matters of life and death.

The viewpoints in this chapter examine two issues on which there is disagreement concerning freedom of religious practice: rejection of children's medical treatment for religious reasons, and prayer in public schools. At the heart of these arguments is the question of how to balance the right of personal religious belief with the duty of government to protect the rights of all.

"God has become so terrible a word that all the legal talent in the country must be mustered to exclude it absolutely from the public schools."

Banning School Prayer Is Religious Discrimination

George Goldberg

In 1962 the Supreme Court ruled that public schools could not authorize moments of prayer or compose prayers for students. In the following viewpoint, George Goldberg argues that banning official school prayer is discrimination against the majority of parents who want their children to participate in some kind of religious observance during the school day. He believes that banning prayer in public schools limits the free exercise of religion. Goldberg is an attorney and author of several books on legal topics.

As you read, consider the following questions:

1. According to Goldberg, why is it unfair and unrealistic to expect all religious instruction and observance to be carried out solely by families?
2. Why does the author believe a constitutional amendment is necessary to allow public schools to hold religious observances?
3. Why does Goldberg believe that holding religious observances in public schools is not a violation of the rights of non-believers?

George Goldberg, *Church, State and the Constitution*. Lake Bluff, IL: Regnery Gateway, Inc., 1987. Reprinted with permission of the publisher.

The arguments in favor of school religious exercises boil down to a belief that spiritual values must be inculcated in our children and that the home and the church are unequal to the job. The principal argument against them is that religion in our pluralistic society is essentially divisive and must be kept out of the public schools, which have been a major vehicle for creating a cohesive society.

I think the proponents of school prayers expect too much from them, and the opponents fear them too much. Both sides exaggerate the significance of what inevitably must be a rather formal exercise necessarily drained of deep meaning by the requirement of sectarian neutrality. Nevertheless, a major literature could be created from the eloquence and passion with which the issue has been discussed. It evidently means a lot to many people, and in a democracy, that matters.

But the issue must be discussed against the background of the First Amendment, not, as is too often the case, in a vacuum. The idea that secular or "humanistic" ideals are entitled to the same constitutional consideration as religious principles, or that agnosticism and even atheism must be given equal constitutional billing with traditional religion, is simply false. All forms of expression enjoy constitutional protection under the free speech and press clauses of the First Amendment, but religion enjoys something more: the free exercise thereof. The argument that to give nondiscriminatory aid to all religions is to discriminate against irreligion has as its effect, if not its purpose, the emptying of the free exercise clause of any meaning whatsoever.

Restricting the Exercise of Religion

But the basic weakness of the strict separationist position on school prayers is that it is not honest. It is fascinating how the same people who on certain occasions profess great sympathy for minorities and poor people turn into Marie Antoinette when confronted with school prayers: let them go to private school, or let their parents teach them religion. How can a person who in the context of aid to dependent children cites statistics of broken homes, rodent-infested apartments crowded beyond imagination, and children roaming the streets untended, in the context of school prayers conjure up warm families sitting around the fireside listening to the paterfamilias (50 percent of minority children in the United States live in fatherless homes) recite verses from the Bible with appropriate commentary?

But middle-class children from two-parent families may not receive much more religious training at home than ghetto children. The image of the patriarchical family reading the Bible (or anything else) around the hearth is nearly as fanciful in the suburbs as in the central city. Only judges of venerable age and

Flash: The U.S. Supreme Court removed D, G and O from the alphabet because when arranged in a certain way they foster religion.

Wayne Stayskal. Reprinted by permission: Tribune Media Services

advanced myopia can suppose that there is time and occasion in the modern middle-class home for morning prayers. . . .

With what in their lives can our middle-class children, much less our ghetto children, compare the moments of face-splitting joy, the perpetual epiphanies, they see on TV? When have they known the pure bliss of the prize winners, the gum chewers, or the beer drinkers? They may not need a refrigerator or a microwave oven, they have chewed truckloads of gum with little effect on anything but their teeth, and if they're old enough to drink beer they know that Lowenbrau was turned into just another American beer when Miller bought the ancient German name. But they can imagine one day wanting a refrigerator or anyway a Corvette, they can readily imagine ingesting something which will provide great joy (doubtless they can find purveyors of things more powerful than gum in the schoolyard—the feds are much better at stopping prayers than drug peddlers), and they can surely hope to find a better beer when they are up to that. What they know now, and know in the vitals of their being, know as firmly as a Jew or a Christian or a Moslem knows there is a God, is that happiness, health and friendship come from *things*.

That, your Honor, is what children learn at home. Perhaps religious faith is a sham, "a chronic disease of the imagination contracted in childhood," the opium of the people. Perhaps

Charlie's angels have more to offer than those Billy Graham writes about. But if you think so, why not say so? To pay lip service to the "spiritual needs of our young people" and then tell them that they must seek their fulfillment at home and only at home, is ignorant or dishonest or both. . . .

God Absolutely Excluded

But what about prayers? The Court has now held that prayers may be said at the beginning of legislative and judicial sessions and one may suppose that the executive enjoys equal rights; and every President from Washington to Reagan has invoked divine assistance at his inauguration. It has also held that students at a state university have a *right* to hold prayer meetings on school premises, and at least four Justices would extend that right to public high school students. But, largely as a result of Chief Justice Warren Burger's tripartite establishment clause test, prayers are still banned from all public elementary and high schools in the country.

It should be understood that the ban is virtually total. For example, in 1982 the Tennessee legislature was considering a bill to allow (not require) public schools to set aside time for—well, for whatever the courts would allow. It had before it a statute drawn up by the Georgia legislature according to which a school could set aside up to three ten-minute periods a day—before school, after school, or during the lunch break—where students who so desired could use an empty classroom for prayers or silent meditation. The attorney general of Tennessee advised the legislature that the statute was unconstitutional. After several tries the legislature finally agreed on one minute of silence at the beginning of the school day and included a warning that teachers were not to suggest what the students should be thinking about during that minute. Even this statute was submitted to the attorney general for an opinion. He reviewed the cases, noted that "It is well-settled that the Establishment Clause forbids the state from requiring or even condoning perceptible religious exercises in public schools," and said that as long as the teachers did not encourage the students to say prayers during the minute of silence, the statute was constitutional. The Supreme Court's subsequent decision in the Alabama silent-prayer case shows that the Tennessee attorney general's warnings were well taken.

But isn't it ridiculous? Any attempt to restrict the availability of obscene, racist novels in public school libraries is immediately attacked as Nazism in the making; public school students are held to have a constitutional right to select their dress and hairstyles and to demonstrate in class against governmental policies of which they disapprove; but *God* has become so terrible a word that all the legal talent in the country must be mustered to exclude it absolutely from the public schools.

It is true that America's religions did not always live together in peace and harmony. The Puritans were not known for their tolerance of dissenters, anti-Catholic agitation once disfigured a large part of our public life, and no one named Goldberg is unaware of the history of anti-Semitism in America. But it is equally true that the tables have turned 180 degrees, and shields have been transformed into swords. In the words of a Jesuit scholar:

> There has been a full and truly vicious circle, from religious persecution, intolerance and church establishment to benign tolerance; to disestablishment; to equality of all faiths before the law; to equality of belief and nonbelief before the law; and now to the secularists' and the religious dissenters' intolerance of religious belief in public law. The wry irony is that this is being done in the name of and for the sake of religious liberty.

Atheistic Schools

The public schools in the United States are more rigidly atheistic than the schools in any Eastern Bloc nation, other than the Soviet Union. In Poland, crosses still hang in the classroom. In Hungary the 10 Commandments are still displayed on the school walls— something that would today be unthinkable in our government schools. . . .

Because a whole generation or two has grown up in this atheistic school environment, Americans have to varying degrees accepted the fallacy that the "separation of church and state" rules out any consideration of religion, religious principles, God, or prayer in all of our public policies and public arenas.

William Murray, *The New American*, June 20, 1988.

The Supreme Court's abuse of the establishment clause over the past forty years has generated a national conflict of epic proportions—precisely what the Founding Fathers designed the First Amendment to avoid. "The Court's misinterpretation of the establishment clause," writes Richard E. Morgan, professor of constitutional law at Bowdoin College and chairman of its department of government, "is now an open scandal." But as the Court of Appeals for the Eleventh Circuit held in the Alabama silent prayer case, "If the Supreme Court errs, no other court may correct it." There is only one way of correcting the Supreme Court: by amending the Constitution, even if only to add the words "and we mean it."

Polls consistently show that 80 percent or more of the American people want religious exercises in their public schools. Accordingly, proposed constitutional amendments have been introduced in Congress, such as H.J. Resolution 279:

> Nothing in this Constitution shall be construed to prohibit individual or group prayer in public schools or other public institutions. No person shall be required by the United States or by any State to participate in prayer. Neither the United States nor any State shall compose the words of any prayer to be said in public schools.

Neither this proposed amendment nor any other has yet been voted on by either House but there is mounting pressure for something to be done. It would be most unfortunate if an amendment should prove necessary, for it will only usher in another generation of conflict over interpretation and application.

Proposed Amendment

For example, H.J. Resolution 279 does not require that prayers in public schools must be nondenominational or that if sectarian that various religious groups are entitled to recognition. There is no limitation as to time, and whereas a school is not permitted to compose the words of a prayer, there is no express prohibition on it engaging the services of a priest or a rabbi to do so, and to conduct the exercises. The proposed amendment would seem to permit a Catholic priest to celebrate the Mass at a public school or a rabbi to conduct an entire Passover seder there. Can anyone doubt that such an amendment should be subtitled *Constitutional Lawyers' Relief Act?*

But we are a democracy and the overwhelming majority of Americans want religious exercises in their public schools. If the Constitution must be amended for their desires to be respected, then I would suggest a much simpler formulation:

> Nothing in this Constitution shall be construed to prohibit public schools from conducting or permitting a brief nondenominational prayer at the start of each school day.

Intolerance is ugly, no matter who practices it. When a minority practices it, it is also foolhardy, for intolerance breeds more intolerance, and minorities naturally suffer the most from an atmosphere of intolerance. With tolerance for the beliefs and practices of others, however foolish they may seem, and enlisting the aid of the courts not to prevent others from doing what they want but only to enforce one's own right to equal time, the issue of prayers in public school could be resolved tomorrow.

Nearly a century and a half ago, New York's Superintendent of Schools, faced with this very issue, put the solution in terms I think cannot be improved upon:

> Both parties have rights; the one to bring up their children in the practice of publicly thanking their Creator for His protection, and invoking His blessing; the other of declining in

behalf of their children, the religious services of any person in whose creed they may not concur, or for other reasons satisfactory to themselves. These rights are reciprocal, and should be protected equally; and neither should interfere with the other. Those who desire that their children should engage in public prayer have no right to compel other children to unite in the exercise, against the wishes of their parents. Nor have those who object to this time, place or manner of praying, or to the person who conducts the exercises, a right to deprive the other class of the opportunity of habituating their children to what they conceive an imperious duty. Neither the common school system, nor any other social system, can be maintained, unless the conscientious views of all are equally respected. The simple rule, so to exercise your own rights as not to infringe on those of others, will preserve equal justice among all, promote harmony, and insure success to our schools.

"Government has no business composing official prayers for any group of Americans."

Allowing School Prayer Is Religious Discrimination

Robert L. Maddox

In the following viewpoint, Robert L. Maddox contends that by conducting official prayer services, public schools impose religion upon students. Allowing official school prayer, he argues, discriminates against students who do not share the religious views reflected in the prayers. Maddox is a Baptist minister and the executive director of Americans United for Separation of Church and State.

As you read, consider the following questions:

1. According to Maddox, what was the Supreme Court's reason for ruling school prayer unconstitutional?
2. Proponents of prayer in public schools often argue that such prayer would still be voluntary. Why does Maddox disagree?
3. Why does Maddox think that official school prayer contributes little to the spiritual lives of students?

From *Separation of Church and State: Guarantor of Religious Freedom*, by Robert L. Maddox. Copyright © 1987 by Robert L. Maddox. Reprinted by permission of The Crossroad Publishing Company.

Of all the church/state cases decided by the U.S. Supreme Court in modern times, probably none created an uproar like the 1962 and 1963 rulings on prayer (*Engel v. Vitale*) and Bible reading in public schools (*Schempp v. Abington School District; Murray v. Murray v. Currlett*). Both of these cases have received monumental misreading and misunderstanding by many Americans. I have to suspect that some of the confusion has been deliberately generated by those who want to gain political points by stirring up the public.

In 1951 the New York State Board of Regents, charged with running the state's educational system, recommended that the local public schools begin their day with the following prayer: "Almighty God, we acknowledge our dependence upon Thee, and we beg Thy blessings upon us, our parents, our teachers and our country." A number of local school boards adopted the prayer and made recitation of the prayer a required part of the schools' programs.

Right away, the parents of ten pupils in New Hyde Park, most of whom were members of various religious groups in the community, brought suit against the practice, saying that it violated the First Amendment's "no establishment of religion" clause.

Violating the Constitution

The U.S. Supreme Court agreed with the parents, ruling that state government-sponsored school prayer indeed violated that clause of the First Amendment. Justice Black wrote the prevailing opinion; he rejected the state's claim that the prayer was simply part of its program of moral instruction. Black declared that prayer is a part of religion, of religious exercise. The prayer program established the religious beliefs embodied in the prayer. When government attempts to promote, support, establish, or use religion in any way, both church and state suffer. Justice Black went on to say that the founders of our government regarded religion as "too personal, too sacred, too holy, to permit its 'unhallowed perversion' by the civil magistrate." Governmentally established religion and religious persecution go hand in hand. Justice Black insisted that government has no business composing official prayers for any group of Americans. Great danger to liberty comes when the government places "its official stamp of approval upon one particular kind of prayer or one particular form of religious service." The First Amendment stands "as a guarantee that neither the power nor the prestige of the Federal Government would be used to control, support or influence the kinds of prayer the American people can say."

Black declared, as the court had done all along in its rulings on church/state cases, that the decision indicated no hostility toward prayer or religion. "It is neither sacrilegious nor anti-religious to say that each separate government in this country should stay out of the business of writing or sanctioning official prayers and leave that purely religious function to the people themselves and to those the people choose to look to for religious guidance.''

Justice William O. Douglas, who agreed with the majority, took the occasion of the *Engel* decision to give some profound thoughts on religious freedom. He said:

> The price of religious freedom is double. It is that the church and religion shall live both within and upon that freedom. There cannot be freedom of religion, safeguarded by the state, and intervention by the church or its agencies in the state's domain or dependency on its largess. The great condition of religious liberty is that it be maintained free from sustenance as also from other interferences by the state. For when it comes to rest upon that secular foundation it vanishes with the resting.

Justice Potter Stewart dissented. The prayer program did not violate the Constitution. In his opinion, the justice declared prayer to be part of the national heritage. If children did not pray, they missed out on a major piece of Americana. Justice Stewart, like

Tom Toles. Universal Press Syndicate. Reprinted by permission.

so many before and after, evinced a utilitarian view of religion. Religion exerts positive good for the state and should, therefore, be encouraged by the state. In all the hullabaloo that followed the *Engel* decision in 1962, many in the country have overlooked the fact that the Supreme Court never even attempted to "outlaw" prayer in public schools. Justice Black and the others who voted with him recognized the complete inability of government to stop anyone from praying whenever the person chooses to pray. In fact, the ruling simply dealt with prescribed prayer and did not mention spontaneous and voluntary praying in public schools.

Voluntary Prayer Not Outlawed

As a practical matter, the court did not rule out spontaneous, voluntary prayers that teachers or students might feel persuaded to offer at special times. Of course, a student or teacher could not disrupt the class with some kind of aberrant religious outburst, but no court is going to slap a teacher in jail who mentions God or religion or has a moment of prayer for some special reason. In our own time, on January 28, 1986, when the space shuttle *Challenger* exploded, many thousands of students and school officials offered prayers, individually and collectively, for the astronauts and their stricken families. The crucial element in school-prayer controversy is the role of the government—the school board—in promoting or requiring the religious exercises.

Proponents of school-sponsored prayers say that dissenting youngsters can leave the room during the prayers or simply sit quietly while the class prays. Do you remember when you were seven or eight years old, or even fifteen or sixteen? Did you like to feel estranged from the rest of the class? It is patently unfair to ask children to attend public schools, paid for by their parents' taxes, and then be made uncomfortable at the most sensitive of all points in one's existence: religion.

Remember how cruel we could be to each other as youngsters? If someone came to school wearing something different or looking different, we could make him or her feel miserable. Teasing, chiding, jeering, even physically attacking our fellow classmates was not unheard of, if they demonstrated sufficient "differentness" from the rest of us. Not in every instance, but in far too many to be permissible, children whose faith did not permit them to participate in the school's established religious exercise had to leave the room, or simply sit in non-participation frequently receiving cruel treatment from their peers. For the dubious benefit of rote prayers, we should not subject youngsters to that kind of pressure—ironically, in the name of religion.

On the heels of the *Engel* decision, school boards and administrators across the country issued their own guidelines, effectively outlawing spoken prayers on their campuses for any reason and under all circumstances. They overreacted out of concern lest their schools become arenas for angry confrontation between pro- and anti-school prayer partisans. School officials overlooked the fact that the court did not forbid individuals praying on campus. The court really did not outlaw occasional, spontaneous prayers in such cases as the crash of the *Challenger*.

How widespread was the practice of school prayer? A survey by Professor R.B. Dierfield of Macalester College found that, in 1962, only approximately half of American public school districts, mostly in Southern and Eastern states, had some form of mandated prayer. And even in those parts of the country that called for religious exercises, the actual practice was spotty. Certainly the tradition of opening the school day with prayer, Bible reading, and a pledge to the flag goes back to the earliest days of the common school. But, as we have seen, these exercises quickly took on the garments of civil rather than biblical religion. Many defenders of school prayer stuck up for the devotional time more from a concern for the stability and well-being of the country than out of concern for the spiritual welfare of the youngsters, harking back to the utilitarian view of religion held by many of the country's Founding Fathers.

Official Sponsorship Is the Problem

Official sponsorship, not prayer itself, is the constitutional mischief, whether the result is a "harmless" silent prayer that no one else can hear or something truly egregious, such as the forced recital of Hail Marys by little Alabama Baptists. (Now there's a thought to jolt that great vent of hot air, Jerry Falwell!)

Experiments in official religious indoctrination, no matter whose doctrine is involved, often portend trouble—sometimes bloody, tragic trouble. Without the First Amendment restraints, a nation of our degree of sectarian variety could be especially vulnerable to it.

Edwin M. Yoder Jr., *Los Angeles Times*, June 11, 1985.

When the Supreme Court declared state-sponsored religious exercises unconstitutional, many people in the country felt that something basic to the nation's self-understanding went by the board. The hue and cry arose not so much over the loss of prayers as over the shift in the way the nation viewed itself. . . .

Why did the decisions on prayer and Bible reading create such an on-going shock wave? The United States, as we have noted in other places, likes to regard itself as a deeply religious nation. Much of this popular religion is a form of civil religion with little biblical or theological content, but still we draw comfort, of sorts, from this fuzzy, amorphous, "God, motherhood and apple pie" feeling. When the Supreme Court demanded the removal of these ingredients of state religion, they struck at something in the national psyche of many Americans. The justices created a *disease* in the way we viewed ourselves. Today, even supporters of required prayer and Bible reading concede that the exercises have little or no religious content, but the presence of the rituals support morality and Americanism.

One has to wonder how Old Testament prophets like Jeremiah or Amos would regard such routine religious practices.

"The constitutionally protected freedom of religion should not permit children to be endangered by the religious practices of adults."

Government Should Override Personal Belief

Arthur Caplan and Anthony Shaw

Christian Scientists believe that physical ills can be cured through focused steadfast prayer. They often use this approach instead of seeking medical treatment. In recent years several Christian Science parents have been charged with child neglect after their children died. In the following two-part viewpoint, Arthur Caplan and Anthony Shaw call for prosecution of parents who for religious reasons do not provide medical care to their seriously ill children. They further argue that laws recognizing spiritual healing as a legitimate alternative to medical care should be abolished. Arthur Caplan is the director of the Center for Bioethics at the University of Minnesota. Anthony Shaw is a pediatric surgeon in Los Angeles.

As you read, consider the following questions:

1. According to Caplan, why does the government have the right to intervene in cases where parents refuse medical treatment for their children?
2. Why does Shaw believe that state laws which provide religious exemption from medical treatment are confusing?

Arthur Caplan, "Parents Have No Right To Rely on Prayer Alone," *St. Paul Pioneer Press Dispatch*, May 23, 1988. Reprinted with permission.
Arthur Shaw, "Children Are Suffering As Faith Healers Hide Behind Religious-Exemption Shield," *Los Angeles Times*, March 23, 1988. Reprinted with the author's permission.

I

Robin Twitchell died on April 8, 1986. He was 2 1/2 years old and had suffered from a high fever and sluggishness for at least five days before his death. While Ginger and David Twitchell were very concerned about their son, they did not take him to a doctor or hospital. Even when, a few hours before his death, Robin developed convulsions and lost consciousness, no medical assistance was sought.

The Twitchells are Christian Scientists. Their church teaches that spiritual healing is the appropriate response to disease or disability. As a result, they sought to help Robin through prayer rather than medicine. But a grand jury took a dim view of their faith in spiritual healing. The Twitchells [went] on trial for manslaughter in a Boston court on June 1, [1988].

Sacrificing Children

I think the ethical principles that govern situations in which people do not seek or refuse medical care are crystal clear. As long as someone is competent and rational, he or she has the absolute right to refuse any and all forms of medical care. One can do so on religious grounds, as Christian Scientists might. Or one can do so for reasons that have nothing to do with religious beliefs.

The ethical principles governing medical care and minor children are equally clear. Adults have every right to risk death in the name of their faith, but they do not have the right to sacrifice their children to their religious convictions.

The law, however, lags behind morality in this area. Ordinarily, if a child has a life-threatening medical condition, parents are held liable by the state for seeking competent medical assistance for the child.

Exceptions are in Massachusetts and a number of other states, which have enacted laws recognizing spiritual healing or faith healing as legitimate alternatives to medical treatment. Massachusetts enacted its law in 1971. The Massachusetts law recognizes the legitimacy of spiritual healing when conducted under the auspices of an established church as a legitimate alternative to medical care.

Robin Twitchell died as a result of this law. He had an obstruction in his bowel. Surgery might have saved him. Legislators who encourage people to avoid seeking medical care for their children when they are very sick may win votes, but they deserve condemnation.

A Child's Right to Life

Public policy cannot allow parents to treat the lives of their children as tests of faith. God may call various Abrahams within American society to place their Isaacs on the altar, but state laws must not encourage them to do so. Laws permitting spiritual healing as a legitimate alternative to medicine in situations in which children are concerned are unethical, unconstitutional and unacceptable.

No child is merely the property of its parents. The state has a legitimate interest in doing what it can to preserve and protect the lives of those who are helpless to protect themselves. If this means overriding sincerely held religious beliefs, then so be it. Those who believe in the power of prayer to fight obstructed bowels must be forced to yield to the coercive authority of the state when doctors know they can do better with surgery.

According to our Constitution, no persons can be deprived of the right to life by another. Children have this right, too. Laws that fail to recognize their rights, as the Massachusetts statute surely does, flout the very essence of our constitutional protections.

Required Medical Care

We as a society can establish in law that parents have a duty to provide medical care for children without exceptions for religious belief and that something that calls itself a health care system has duties to both the state and its patients.

Rita Swan, *Free Inquiry*, Spring 1984.

And what in the name of God is meant by laws that recognize spiritual healing or faith healing as alternatives to medicine when conducted under the auspices of "an established church"? Can Lutherans or Orthodox Jews pray their way to health if a sufficient number of Americans think their religious views respectable? What of the Moonies? How about Scientologists? Or those inside the Washington beltway with a keen faith in astrology?

Is it only the prayers issued from the mouths of reputable church-goers that legislators think will catch God's ear? Are those on the fringes of American religious life or whose numbers are so small that they have not yet held an annual convention simply ineligible for religious rights? Did the legislators who enacted these laws intend to respect freedom of religion or only to heed the political clout of established religions?

Alternative Treatment Laws Are Wrong

The Robin Twitchells of the future deserve to have the state take their lives seriously, regardless of their parents' church affiliation. The Twitchells should be put on trial. Not to punish them; no punishment a secular state can dream up will rival the death of their child. The aim of the trial should be to insure that laws recognizing prayer, spiritual healing or faith healing as alternative forms of treatment for life-threatening medical ailments are unconstitutional, awful as public policy and just plain immoral.

The Twitchell case follows on the heels of a long series of heated debates about the care due infants born with disabilities. Many liberals argued that the state ought to respect parental wishes concerning decisions about whether newborns should receive medical care. Many conservatives and those in the disability rights movement argued that it was wrong to withold care from a child simply because it was born with Down's syndrome or spina bifida.

The conservatives won. Federal and state laws—the Baby Doe statutes—were enacted and mandate care for all newborns, except those born dying or with irreversible, terminal illnesses.

I once thought the conservatives were on the wrong side of the Baby Doe argument. I now think they were correct to protest the practice of allowing children to die simply because they have disabilities.

The Twitchell case and others in which faith healing or spiritual healing are tolerated by law as reasons for avoiding or refusing medical care for children are exact analogues of the Baby Doe cases. Prayer can be just as much a form of child neglect as bias against those born with disabilities. Those who fought against policies that permitted discrimination against the handicapped should now join the fight against allowing children to die as a result of religious discrimination.

II

It has been four years since 4-year-old Shauntay Walker of Sacramento succumbed to bacterial meningitis after a 17-day ordeal during which her only treatment consisted of bedside prayer by a religious healer.

Now the California Supreme Court will decide whether her mother is subject to prosecution for manslaughter and felony child endangerment or, as Laurie Walker's lawyers contend, whether she is protected by a provision in the California Penal Code that exempts from the definition of child neglect "treatment by spiritual means through prayer alone in accordance with the tenets and practices of a recognized church or religious denomination by a duly accredited practitioner thereof."

Sporadically, over the past few years, the media have reported tragic cases similar to Shauntay's in which young children with curable life-threatening conditions like bacterial pneumonia, meningitis or intestinal obstruction died after decisions by parents to substitute spiritual for medical treatment.

This religious-exemption clause in California's child-abuse and neglect-reporting law was incorporated into the laws of all 50 states during the mid-1970s as a condition of eligibility for protective-services grants under the federal Child Abuse Prevention and

Treatment Act of 1974. Although the federal law has been amended to eliminate this statutory requirement as a condition of federal funding, California remains one of 43 states to retain this confusing, unfair and harmful exemption in its child-abuse and neglect-reporting law and in recently amended juvenile-dependency provisions of the Welfare and Institutions Code.

Exemption Laws Are Confusing

The inherently confusing nature of the religious exemption is highlighted by the current legal controversy over Walker's culpability. California's child-abuse reporting law says that a child "receiving treatment by spiritual means . . . by a duly accredited practitioner" or "not receiving specified medical treatment for religious reasons . . . shall not *for that reason alone* be considered a neglected child." This vague language leaves unclear whether those responsible for choosing spiritual over medical treatment may be held legally responsible if harm comes to a child under such circumstances.

Depriving Children of Life

Should the government recognize religious practices as legal health care for children? I feel strongly that such recognition should be given only to state-licensed, secular health care. A child's right to live supersedes a parent's right to practice religion.

Today a wide variety of religions may cause injury to children. Many children have recently been beaten to death because of a belief that beatings promote obedience to divine will. Children have been maimed and killed because of belief in demon-possession. There is no question that the state will file charges in such cases, sometimes even against the church leaders who counsel the parents. So why should our laws suggest that it is all right to deprive children of lifesaving medical care in the name of religion?

Rita Swan, *Free Inquiry*, Spring 1984.

The recently enacted child-dependency legislation does permit the juvenile court to assume the jurisdiction of a child under "spiritual treatment through prayer alone" if it is "necessary to protect the minor from suffering serious physical harm of illness." But these supposed safeguards are undermined by the ambiguities, vagueness and contradictions in the reporting requirements that in effect exempt faith healers from the provision that requires reporting of medical neglect by *all* "health practitioners," which includes by definition "a religious practitioner who diagnoses, examines or treats children."

Furthermore, the religious-exemption clause unfairly provides parents belonging to a "recognized" religion with immunity from prosecution for medical neglect—a status clearly denied to the larger number of negligent parents whose spiritual credentials are unrecognized, or whose denial of medical care to their children is not supported by any religious philosophy. Although the primary purpose of child-abuse reporting laws is to protect children, not to punish parents, the religious exemption, to the extent that it excuses a class of parents from legal accountability for an otherwise prosecutable offense, puts children of such parents at increased risk.

Don't Deny Medical Care

The American Academy of Pediatrics Committee on Bioethics recently argued against the religious-exemption clause, noting that it may protect "severe (even fatal) physical discipline, failure to seek needed medical care, or refusal of a proven efficacious treatment of a critically ill child."

In its published statement the committee added: "The opportunity to grow and develop safe from physical harm with the protection of our society is a fundamental right of every child. No statute should exist that permits or implies that denial of medical care necessary to prevent death or serious impairment to children can be supported on religious grounds."

The constitutionally protected freedom of religion should not permit children to be endangered by the religious practices of adults.

One can acknowledge the constructive role that religion may play in the lives of families and still agree that the religious exemption is bad law. No attempt to amend or modify it is likely to make it less confusing, unfair or harmful. Nothing short of total expungement of this clause, which permits harm to children under the shield of religious exemption, will do.

"Despite this continuing (and obvious) evidence of healing, Christian Scientists' right to continue relying on spiritual treatment in caring for their children is being challenged."

Government Should Not Interfere with Personal Belief

Nathan Talbot

In the following viewpoint, Nathan Talbot argues that Christian Science techniques have been proven successful and deserve to be a legally available alternative to medical treatment. Government should respect Christian Scientists' religious beliefs, he contends, because laws against spiritual healing would deny religious freedom. Talbot is the manager of the Committees on Publication of the First Church of Christ, Scientist in Boston.

As you read, consider the following questions:

1. Why does Talbot believe that physicians' criticism of Christian Science spiritual healing is unfair?
2. According to the author, what is the real reason for prosecuting Christian Science parents?
3. Why does Talbot believe that Christian Science should receive legal recognition as a form of treatment?

Nathan Talbot, "Spiritual Healing: A Responsible Alternative," 1988. This article was written specifically for *Religion in America: Opposing Viewpoints*.

Perhaps the most common stereotype of Christian Scientists is reflected in the comment, "Oh, those are the people who don't go to doctors," or even "Those are the ones who refuse to give their children medical care." If that's all the information one has to go on, questions like "Do parents have the right to deny their children medical care?" can seem pretty rhetorical. Who doesn't want children to get the care that they need? . . .

The question "Do parents have the right to deny their children medical care?" implies that the only options are medical care or denial of medical care—and that all responsible parents necessarily choose medical care. To ask this question of parents who are known for abusing or neglecting children would be understandable. But to address the same question to responsible, law-abiding parents who obviously love their children, and who have a strong past record of caring for them devotedly and well, is more problematic.

Alternative Forms of Care

If the only two options for care *were* medical treatment or no treatment, Christian Scientists like others would undoubtedly choose medical treatment. Based on long experience, though, they've found that the choice is not actually limited to those options. For well over a century, Christian Scientists have been relying on spiritual healing for their families—and they've seen extensive healing results, in many instances after medicine could do no more.

Everyone agrees that children need responsible care. In light of Christian Scientists' experience, the real question is: Should parents be obligated to give their children medical care, or is there an alternative way to care for children responsibly?

The word "care" has many connotations. For purposes of this discussion, perhaps we can define "care" or "responsible care" simply as a consistent form of treatment which regularly and effectively meets the needs and maintains the well-being of recipients.

This definition doesn't limit care to medical care alone. But it does distinguish between merely subjective, isolated, or chance success in healing and a more uniform and dependable standard of treatment (e.g., one wouldn't want to generalize that lime jello was a responsible treatment for chicken pox just because one individual appeared to get better after eating it or because one "healer" consistently recommended it!).

Conversely, no matter how logical or scientific a method of treatment appears, it would hardly be a responsible method if the majority of those who received it were not benefited. Nor would it make sense to pan a whole method of treatment as irresponsible because of an occasional loss, however tragic. For example, although over 60,000 children between the ages of two and four die each year while under medical care, one does not therefore dismiss the responsible efforts of doctors.

Is Spiritual Healing Rational?

For Christian Scientists, reliance on disciplined prayer is a way of life deeply rooted in reason and love—not merely a religious dogma. They see this approach to healing as based on uniform spiritual law governing the whole of life rather than an arbitrary belief in "God's will" for a particular person. Hence Christian Scientists' conviction that spiritual healing can be practiced systematically, even "scientifically," though this practice involves heartfelt devotion to the work of understanding God rather than the usual experimental detachment of a research lab. . . .

It Works

State laws accommodating the practice of Christian Science healing are consonant with First Amendment guarantees of the "free exercise" of religion.

But there is a more basic reason that parents must be free to use spiritual means to help their children: It works.

The Christian Science Monitor, May 6, 1988.

Christian Scientists believe that the healings that have been so much a part of their experience aren't random or exclusive. When a Christian Scientist turns to God in prayer, he is not pleading with God to make an exception in his case and heal him. Rather, he is turning more wholeheartedly to God to perceive the underlying spiritual law which rules out illness and inharmony in proportion as it is understood.

Christian Scientists see specific, consistent prayer not merely as a vague help (i.e. like a placebo) but as a definite form of treatment. In trying to understand what such treatment is, it may be helpful to clarify several things it is not. Specifically:

• It is not positive thinking, nor is it based on the belief that healing results from some form of "mind over matter." True prayer involves something much deeper—a heartfelt yielding to God's presence and power.

• It does not ignore illness or injury nor dismiss it blithely as "an illusion." Christian Scientists like other responsible parents love their children far too much to ignore suffering, or the need for comfort and healing.

• It is not a form of "faith healing" or "miracle" in the usual sense of those terms. Nor is blind faith something that Christian

141

Scientists see as particularly helpful in any area of life.

• It is not something forced on people. Christian Scientists deeply respect each person's ability to discern what is right in a given instance. Those who choose Christian Science treatment even in difficult situations are likely to do so—not out of any peer pressure—but because they've found from previous experience that it has effectively and reliably met the need. . . .

The Evidence of Spiritual Healing

Healings through prayer in Christian Science are not a once-in-a-lifetime experience. They are natural everyday occurrences which involve far more than physical healing, however necessary and welcome that is. In fact as one writer put it, "In looking back on a healing, the Christian Scientist is likely to think, not 'That was the time I was healed of pneumonia,' but 'That was the time I learned what real humility is,' or 'That was the time I saw so clearly that all power belongs to God.'"

Perhaps because genuine spiritual healing usually includes a quiet change of heart or understanding, one isn't as likely to hear about them on the evening news nor read about them in one's local paper or the latest medical journal. But that alone doesn't make the healings any less real. In fact, although some critics try to dismiss the evidence of Christian Science healing as merely "hearsay" or "anecdotal," that kind of labeling seems pretty irrelevant to a father whose young daughter is happily bounding around after being healed of dysentery or the family whose loved ones have been healed of serious injuries sustained in a car accident.

The most abundant evidence for spiritual healing isn't reams of medical records but the living proof of those individuals and whole families that have relied on Christian Science treatment to meet all their needs, in many cases for four and five generations. Over 50,000 testimonies of healing have appeared in the Christian Science periodicals since the turn of the century. These represent only a small portion of the healings in Christian Science families which have been witnessed by friends, neighbors, colleagues and in many cases confirmed by medical evidence.

Christian Scientists don't live in isolation. They're familiar with medicine and medical personnel because they live and work and raise their families alongside those of differing beliefs. In contrast to the stereotypes, they don't "hate doctors," but respect their work and dedication and are grateful that good medical care does exist for those who desire it. They cooperate with health authorities and have their babies with the help of midwives or physicians as required under the law. While Christian Scientists don't normally seek medical attention, thousands of healings have been documented by required medical diagnoses and examinations for school, employment and insurance purposes or in other circumstances.

As an article in *The New England Journal of Medicine* noted, an examination of the 4000 healings that appeared in the Christian Science periodicals "during the single decade 1971 to 1981 shows 647 testimonies concerning illnesses that had been medically diagnosed, in some cases both before and after a healing. The figure also includes 137 pediatric cases. These disorders include leukemia and other neoplasias, both malignant and benign; diphtheria; gallstones; pernicious anemia; club feet; spinal meningitis; and bone fracture, among numerous others." A further sampling of medically documented healings are included in a recent booklength exploration of the implications of spiritual healing in a high tech world, *Spiritual Healing in a Scientific Age* by Robert Peel.

Protecting an Effective Healing Method

There would be no statutes recognizing spiritual healing if spiritual healing was not being proven to be responsible, safe, reasonable and effective in the public trenches of day-to-day living. Reasonable spiritual healing came first, then the statutes, which were intended to be neither preferential nor discriminatory, but to protect a religious method of healing that had proven effective. . . .

Children die from physical diseases, not from laws permitting a responsible healing practice. Although Christian Scientists have compiled a significant record of spiritual healing over more than 100 years, we do not claim an infallible record. Is modern medicine practiced without failure or tragedy? Is it ethical to judge responsible spiritual healing by a standard of infallibility that modern medicine itself cannot meet?

James D. Van Horn, *St. Paul Pioneer Press Dispatch*, June 28, 1988.

This evidence, however extensive and valid, is not the clinical data and laboratory proofs some doctors feel are requisite. But then again, it isn't intended to be. Spiritual healing is hardly some new invention or fly-by-night discovery. It is Biblically rooted in both the Old and New Testaments and was practiced by Jesus and the early Christians for several centuries. Christian Scientists' practice began in the late 1800's with the work of a New England woman, Mary Baker Eddy—one of the few women religious leaders in her era.

While those uncomfortable with religion or unfamiliar with spiritual healing may feel it has been outmoded by the technological breakthroughs of the past century, Christian Scientists feel that it has an immense contribution to make to the world—and that, far from being outmoded, it is only just beginning to be understood. The practice of spiritual healing within families has been recognized legally for many years in most states. Most major insurance companies offer coverage for Christian Science treatment in lieu of medical care precisely because of its long (and continuing) history of reliable care. These healings continue to restore full health and hope in serious as well as less serious situations. One of the most moving healings documented in Robert Peel's book, for example, involved a severely handicapped child unwanted by others who was adopted by Christian Science parents.

Legal Challenges to Spiritual Healing

Despite this continuing (and obvious) evidence of healing, Christian Scientists' right to continue relying on spiritual treatment in caring for their children is being challenged in several states by some doctors and public officials who feel medical care should be the only viable treatment. In the last five years, there have been several court cases brought against Christian Science parents who have lost a child. The question raised in these cases is the one on which this article has focused: Is there a responsible alternative to medical care? The court cases also raise the corollary question: Is it fair or just to equate "responsible care" with "infallible care" in the case of Christian Scientists when the rest of society does not hold itself to the same standard?

Naturally, no one grieves over the loss of a dearly loved child more than the parents. But it hardly seems reasonable to further penalize parents for such a loss solely because they chose an alternative to medical care for that child. While some claim in hindsight that the children would have been healed through medicine, issues of children's health-care simply aren't that simple or straightforward. The fact is at this point no form of treatment, however responsible, has an infallible record. And the consequences to society of this sort of unprecedented reaction based on a few isolated instances are enormous. As Eugene D. Robin, one member of the Stanford University Medical School faculty, noted in a recent article: ". . . the present trend of prosecuting Christian Scientists in medically dubious cases poses a threat to medicine. Suppose every physician who committed an error in judgment were brought to trial. Our already overburdened court system would be taxed to the limit."

Dr. Robin's conclusion goes farther than most physicians' probably would. But many people would agree with the observation that there is a much larger issue at stake than just one denomination's right to rely on a longstanding spiritual alternative to medical care in the treatment of their children. It really boils down to a question of perspective. Are we as a country ready, despite more than a century of evidence to the contrary, to say that it is in the best interest of our children to have only one form of treatment legally available to them? Are we as a society willing to say that medical and technological advances alone are enough to sustain and satisfy man and meet the challenges ahead of us? Or, are we willing to affirm—on the basis of those children who have been healed, or who someday may need healing—that there is room for more than one legitimate and responsible answer to the sickness and other challenges we face?

Distinguishing Between Fact and Opinion

This activity is designed to help develop the critical thinking skill of distinguishing between fact and opinion. Consider the following statement as an example: "The first Christian Science church was chartered by the state of Massachusetts in 1879." This statement could be easily verified as true by checking government records. But consider this statement: "Christian Science is a legitimate alternative to medical care in the treatment of physical ailments." There are many physicians who would dispute this, and Christian Scientists who would assert that it is true. This statement is an opinion.

When investigating issues it is important to be able to distinguish between statements of fact and statements of opinion. It is also important to recognize that not all statements of fact are true. They may appear to be true, but some are based on inaccurate or false information. For this activity, however, we are concerned with understanding the difference between those statements which appear to be factual and those which appear to be based primarily on opinion.

The following statements are related to topics covered in this chapter. Consider each statement carefully. *Mark O for any statement you believe is an opinion or interpretation of facts. Mark F for any statement you believe is a fact. Mark U if you are uncertain.*

If you are doing this activity as a member of a class or group, compare your answers with those of other class or group members. Be able to defend your answers. You will discover that others come to different conclusions than you do. Listening to the reasons others present for their answers may give you valuable insights in distinguishing between fact and opinion.

O = *opinion*
F = *fact*
U = *uncertain*

146

1. Robin Twitchell died on April 8, 1986.

2. The idea that atheism must be given equal constitutional billing with traditional religion is simply false.

3. Over 60,000 children between the ages of two and four die each year while under medical care.

4. The overwhelming majority of Americans want religious exercises in their public schools.

5. The New York State Board of Regents recommended that the local public schools begin their day with the following prayer: "Almighty God, we acknowledge our dependence upon Thee, and we beg Thy blessings upon us, our parents, our teachers and our country."

6. Governmentally established religion and religious persecution go hand in hand.

7. As long as someone is competent and rational, he or she has the absolute right to refuse any and all forms of medical care.

8. The attorney general of Tennessee advised the legislature that the "moment of silence" statute was unconstitutional.

9. Laws permitting spiritual healing are unethical, unconstitutional and unacceptable.

10. The American Academy of Pediatrics Committee on Bioethics argued against the religious-exemption clause of the Child Abuse Prevention and Treatment Act.

11. Christian Scientists hate doctors.

12. The Supreme Court has ruled that prayers may be said at the beginning of legislative and judicial sessions.

13. Christian Science nurses provide physicial care and support to those relying on spiritual treatment.

14. Prayer can be a form of child neglect.

15. Over 50,000 testimonies of healing have appeared in the Christian Science periodicals since the turn of the century.

16. The government has a right to force parents to seek medical care for their children.

Periodical Bibliography

The following articles have been selected to supplement the diverse views presented in this chapter.

James E. Brodhead	"Atheists Are Guaranteed Freedom, Too," *Los Angeles Times*, June 4, 1986.
Edd Doerr	"Religion in Public Education," *The Humanist*, November/December 1987. Available from: 7 Harwood Dr., P.O. Box 146, Amherst, NY 14226-0146.
Barbara Ehrenreich	"Give Me That New-Time Religion," *Mother Jones*, June/July 1987.
Thomas J. Fleming	"Pluralism and Public Schooling," *The World & I*, July 1987.
Carl Horn	"Religion in the Schools: A Model Policy," *A.L.L. About Issues*, February/March 1988. Available from P.O. Box 1350, Stafford, VA 22554.
Jill L. Kahn	"Church-State Relations in America: Is the Wall Crumbling?" *USA Today*, May 1984.
Martin E. Marty	"Challenging the Private Sector," *The Christian Century*, October 7, 1987.
Larry Martz	"Keeping God Out of the Classroom," *Newsweek*, June 29, 1987.
The New American	"America Without God," interview with William Murray, June 20, 1988. Available from 395 Concord Ave., Belmont, MA 02178.
Richard N. Ostling	"Threatening the Wall," *Time*, July 6, 1987.
Peggy L. Shriver	"Reassessing Religion and Public Education," *Education Digest*, December 1987.
Nathan A. Talbot	"Spiritual Healing: Still in Court After Eight Decades," *Los Angeles Times*, May 1, 1988.
Cal Thomas	"Get Ready for Another Season of God-Bashing," *Los Angeles Times*, November 30, 1986.
Kenneth L. Woodward	"The Graying of a Church: Christian Science's Ills," *Newsweek*, August 3, 1987.

Is Television
Evangelism Positive?

RELIGION
IN AMERICA

Chapter Preface

In 1987, television evangelist Jim Bakker was removed from his post at PTL Network for sexual indiscretions and financial mismanagement. Around the same time, Oral Roberts extracted millions of dollars in donations from loyal followers by claiming that God would cause his death if he failed to raise more money for his ministry. Then, in 1988, Jimmy Swaggart, another well-known television evangelist, confessed to soliciting a prostitute and stepped down temporarily from his position in the Assemblies of God church. These television evangelist scandals cast doubts on the credibility of religious broadcasters.

The evangelists caught in these scandals had aggressively condemned the very sins they committed. Whether the scandals will reduce these evangelists' popularity is far from clear, however. Bakker, Roberts, and Swaggart have loyal followings and their disciples are far less critical of the evangelists than the rest of the public is. Many born-again Christians credit their renewed religiosity to these leaders. In addition to evangelists' ability to inspire them, these Christians point to the good works evangelist leaders have done—building schools, providing counseling and other social services, and establishing missions.

The following chapter examines the impact of television evangelism. As controversy continues, it is clear that the questions surrounding TV evangelism will not be resolved easily.

"I do pastor people whose lives have been changed by the gospel . . . presented by many television evangelists."

Television Evangelism Is Legitimate

Steve Wright and Dawn Weyrich

In the following viewpoint, a pastor and a journalist defend television evangelists. In Part I, Steve Wright, the senior pastor of Wesleyan Community Church in Oak Lawn, Illinois, gives several examples of parishioners who have been helped by television ministries. In Part II, Dawn Weyrich, a journalist who has been published in *Conservative Digest* and *The Washington Times,* describes successful charitable ministries of some leading television evangelists. Both authors write that media attacks on these evangelists are illegitimate.

As you read, consider the following questions:

1. According to Wright, who do television evangelists reach with the gospel? Why are they sometimes more effective than churches?
2. What successful ministries of television evangelists does Weyrich list? According to her, why do the media ignore these examples of true Christian charity?

Steve Wright, "Good News for the Disenfranchised," *Christianity Today,* March 18, 1988. Reprinted with the author's permission.
Dawn Weyrich, "When the Media Attack Christians," *Conservative Digest,* July/August 1987. Reprinted with permission.

I

Rarely do I watch Christian television programs. When I do, I get angry and embarrassed. I feel like I am watching "Begging for Dollars" or "Top My Testimony."

But I do pastor people whose lives have been changed by the gospel so imperfectly presented by many television evangelists. Their lives temper my generalized judgments and display the sovereignty of God.

Changed Lives

Standing near me in the baptistry, she testified how her spiritual pilgrimage had led her from an anti-evangelical church to a ladies' Bible study to praying to receive Christ with the host of "The 700 Club." It was neither Pat Robertson's theology nor his politics but the power of the Holy Spirit drawing her to believe that she, too, could know Christ.

At a luncheon, a businessman unsympathetic to evangelicalism startled me after I finished speaking apologetically about the recent TV scandals. "My mother-in-law left all her jewels to this TV evangelist," he said. "The family was very angry. I told them— she did the right thing. For more than 15 years, the family seldom visited her, and her church never did. She looked forward every day to her hour with this TV evangelist. That was her time of inspiration. She had hope, joy, and was not afraid to die. He earned his pay!"

They lived together in the city far from our suburban church. Unmarried. Bisexual. Promiscuous. Addicted to alcohol and drugs. He visited our church at the invitation of a friend. She refused to attend. He accepted Christ. She did not. They separated over his desire for a changed life. Two years passed—I met them again. Married. Soon to be new parents. Free from addiction and immorality. Alone she had listened soberly to a TV evangelist preaching in a perspiring rage. Every sin he named she had committed. She prayed to the Christ who receives sinners, convinced that he would accept her. Their lives will never be the same.

I Want To Be Baptized

At 82, she visited our church for the first time. "I want to be baptized," she said trembling. We talked. "Have you ever been baptized?" I asked. "Why, no, Pastor! I'm not even saved. But I want to be." In asking her how she became interested in becoming a Christian, she told me about the TV evangelist whose name she could not remember, who urged his audience to find a nearby church where someone could help them grow as Christians. She prayed for such a church. She drove through the neighborhood until she saw our building. That night I had the joy of watching her receive the Christ she sought. At 94, she still inspires everyone

152

she meets with her vibrant faith.

Ever since God first chose people to be his, those people have sought for some way to franchise salvation. Seldom have "the chosen" accepted taking the Good News outside traditional forums.

Yet the Good News really belongs to the disenfranchised. The blind beggar, the leper, the harlots, the fishermen, the tax collector, the demoniacs, the centurion, the common people, and the Gentiles—all heard the Good News outside the local franchise.

We make noble talk about reaching the unevangelized in America, but we are quite selective about the sinners we minister to. We like our sinners clean and acculturated to the importance of our style and traditions.

A Natural Entry Point

But a large and growing oral communication culture exists in America, and it does not fit nicely into our pews. Its members respond best to communications media that are narrative, oral, contemporary, and visual. They are suspicious of our traditions, for we resemble the Judaizers in our attempts to convert them. We regard their culture as secular and ours as so spiritual. Television is a natural entry point for the gospel into their lives. It gives them a private opportunity to hear the gospel.

Feeling Close to God

Viewers of religious programs are drawn by content they cannot find elsewhere on television. In fact, their dissatisfaction with the "prevailing moral climate" (much of which, of course, comes to them through and from television) may be one of the most distinctive bonds between religious programs and their viewers. The sermons, the preaching, the music, the experience of "having your spirits lifted" and "feeling close to God" are frequently expressed satisfactions that viewers derive from religious programs.

George Gerbner, *New Catholic World*, May/June 1987.

An excellent case exists for convicting Christian television of many abuses. An even better case exists for indicting the church on those same charges. Merchandising, marketing, fund raising, immorality, fraud, and heresy have found great homes in Christian publishing, parachurch ministries, mission ministries, and the local church itself.

Those who mismanage funds with sinister motives have always existed in the church. They even existed right under the nose of Jesus Christ in the Twelve. We would do well to study how he illustrated that the sovereignty of God cannot be thwarted by such perversion. He is the Lord of the whole harvest, of both tares and wheat.

I do not intend to become a Christian TV groupie. But neither will I discount the place of television ministry. I know there are devoted men and women of God in broadcast ministries. I also know that the gospel—and neither the messenger nor the medium—is "the power of God for salvation to everyone who believes."

II

Early spring [1987] was jackpot time for the liberal press. The sudden fall of television evangelists Jim and Tammy Bakker heartened the enemies of traditional values and was splashed on the front pages of newspapers nationwide, even making the covers of *Time, Newsweek,* and *U.S. News & World Report.* Not only could the Bakker tragedy be used to bash Christians but it contained all the appealing elements. Sex. Drugs. Misused money. It was a chance for the liberal media to reinforce to the public what they've held true for decades—that religious leaders and their ministries are storefronts for the sort of lust, greed, and corruption Sinclair Lewis imagined in *Elmer Gantry.*

Such attacks were meant to leave us wondering. The same press had for decades published hardly a line about anything good to have come from these evangelical efforts. Either they are traps for fools, tens of millions of fools, or Christian love and generosity don't sell newspapers and magazines like adultery and betrayal. *Conservative Digest* went looking, and what we found was very different from what was being headlined.

Responsible Charity and Committed Faith

What we found, in fact, is that millions of American Christians contribute their time, money, and goods to worthy ministries in our own country and around the globe. The name of televangelist Jerry Falwell often comes to mind whenever the combination of responsible charity and committed faith are discussed. Dr. Falwell's huge ministry supports more than 600 missionaries in 65 countries and includes a home for unwed mothers as well as the 7,500-student Liberty University. It is Dr. Falwell who has been asked to step in to try to save the PTL television ministries in the wake of the Bakker scandals, and he has done his best to do so with both Christian charity and candor.

Other names which come immediately to mind are those of televangelists D. James Kennedy and Pat Robertson. Still others who raise fund for Christian works which they administer are known only in their own towns or neighborhoods. That these good people should be subjected to harassment and smear by liberal media that are looking only for an opportunity to attract attention by bashing conservative Christians is a national shame. Here, for instance, are some stories you haven't seen reported by the liberal press. . . .

James Kennedy

First Step is but one of a dizzying number of social outreach programs for which senior minister Dr. D. James Kennedy and the 7,500-member Coral Ridge Presbyterian Church are responsible. The church opened its doors 28 years ago, and now has an annual budget of $4 million, the bulk of which goes into support of social and evangelistic ministry.

Dr. Kennedy believes in mixing charitable work with religion, recognizing that God calls His people to bring His work into everyday life. "Social programs are not the main task of the church; the main task is conversion," Dr. Kennedy told me. "But it is often converts who lead the agencies that help the needy."

An Unfair Media

Jim Bakker confessed to an unfortunate affair seven years ago and it has made front-page headlines for 90 days. But there is a very popular liberal minister in Dallas, Texas, who is now suspected of murdering his wife, yet the story appears on Page 15 of the front section of the *Tulsa World*. It would seem that the alleged murder of one's wife is more tolerable to the liberal news media than a Bible-believing gospel preacher who has committed an indiscretion seven years ago. All of this doesn't make sense to me unless you agree that the national news media is not wholeheartedly against liberal preachers. They are viciously against fundamentalist preachers who believe in the deity of Christ, the Virgin birth, the death, burial and resurrection of Christ, and inspiration of the Scriptures.

Billy James Hargis, *Christian Crusade*, Vol. 34, No. 7, 1987.

Coral Ridge has provided many thousands of dollars to homes for troubled boys and girls; provided large sums of money to help the hungry in Africa; conducted religious services for convicts and the immobile elderly; given financial assistance to runaways on the beaches, and talked them into returning home; counseled substance abusers through the church's Christian Addicts Anonymous; provided free employment counseling for those down on their luck; and, has sent 135 families to teach the Gospel and help the needy help themselves in miserably poor countries around the world.

This just skims the surface. Dr. D. James Kennedy, of course, is one of the nation's leading television evangelists, with an annual TV budget of $15 million. That is an awful lot of money to raise for spreading the good news, and the current anti-Christian blitz suggests that those who raise such funds have little time or interest left to engage personally in Christian charity. The experiences of Coral Ridge Presbyterian and Dr. Kennedy indicate that just isn't so.

Bear in mind that Dr. Kennedy's TV evangelism is *separate* from his church. All the television funds are channeled back into the ministry, and mainly used to purchase airtime to spread the good news about Jesus Christ. The hour-long program, "Coral Ridge Pulpit," reaches TV stations in 20,000 cities and towns; and 120 radio stations in America and 25 foreign countries.

But Kennedy accepts no salary from Coral Ridge or its ministries. If he were an entertainer he would command an income in seven figures. Dr. Kennedy lives in a $74,000 home. "And I drive a three-year-old Mercury," he laughed. "Quite contrary to the picture painted of greedy evangelists.". . .

Pat Robertson Helps

Kenneth Johnson was unable to read or write for the first 33 years of his life. Diagnosed with cerebral palsy at age four, he spent most of his first-grade schooling—the crucial time for learning basic reading skills—in and out of surgery. Because of the prolonged hospital visits, Kenneth didn't return to school again until the seventh grade. He attended classes through the tenth grade, but left the system still unable to read.

"Always wanting to know what something was in print, and not being able to figure it out, I felt like a fish out of water. It was very frustrating always having to ask for help," Kenneth told me. But . . . he heard a radio advertisement for the "Heads Up" program run by Dr. Marion G. "Pat" Robertson, the Christian broadcaster. Classes were being held to teach the illiterate to read, and Kenneth Johnson decided to try again. It took Johnson about eight months to learn basic reading skills. Though it was a struggle, he repeatedly emphasized to us that completing the program has changed his life. "Sometimes my 12-year-old daughter would give me papers from school that she could read and I couldn't. I never knew what grades were on them. Now she can't get away with the things she could before," he joked.

Heads Up started in Los Angeles in 1985, and has since become a national program. With chapters in approximately 700 communities across the United States, it has taught some 110,000 people—adult and child failures of the school system—how to read. The program is strictly volunteer and is sponsored by groups such as the Y.M.C.A. and local churches. Pat Robertson's Christian Broadcasting Network (CBN) has put $700,000 into materials and teacher training, and funding has also been raised on the local level. There has thus been no cost for people serious about overcoming their handicap.

Lee R. Newsome, 23, has been unemployed since the Kentucky mine he worked for went bankrupt in the fall of 1986. He had been receiving Food Stamps from the government, but Lee and his wife now rely on their large backyard garden for food. They are able to do so because Newsome received seeds and compost donated by Dr. Pat Robertson's "Operation Blessing" program.

Since its inception in 1978, this private relief outreach has given an estimated $138 million to 24 million needy throughout America and in thirteen foreign countries. Last year it disbursed $8.2 million in cash, and donations of goods and services brought the total to $48.2 million, benefitting 6.3 million people.

Operating with a $50 million annual budget from CBN funds donated specifically for this program, Operation Blessing has provided medical examinations for the homeless; sent food and clothing to suffering Christians in Poland; and, given referrals and fielded prayer requests. This ministry has also helped to rehabilitate villages in South Lebanon; delivered hay to farmers during severe drought; fed the poor in inner cities; sent disaster relief to earthquake victims in Mexico City and Guatamala; and, drafted six National Football League teams to deliver rice to the needy. Its staff of 45 full- and part-time workers and countless volunteers operates 45 counseling centers in 38 states, and its services are distributed by members of 1,300 cooperating churches. One half of one percent of the annual budget goes into overhead— the rest is used for the needy.

Christian Ministries

Dr. Robertson meanwhile runs the Christian Broadcasting Network, which owns two commercial television stations and a radio station. This cable network has 9,000 affiliates in 16,000 cities, reaching 35 million households. According to fourth-quarter 1986 Neilson ratings, Robertson's CBN had the highest share of viewers among the cable networks.

Is Dr. Pat Robertson bleeding all of this for his own benefit? Not on your life. His salary of $60,000 a year comes from the network, but last year the broadcaster gave $90,000 back to his ministry. He even gave CBN the $400,000 house he had paid for himself. Though running CBN is a full-time job for Dr. Robertson, he considers it part of his Christian ministry. The satellite ministries that teach and feed the poor are other indicators of his Christian belief. "We do this because we're trying to obey the Bible," he explains. "To please God, you must give bread to the hungry; if homeless, you must bring them into the house. It's nothing less than Biblical charity."

Why do you suppose we are not reading about any of this in *Time, Newsweek,* and *U.S. News & World Report?*

"The televangelists' programs are on the screen and are successful . . . because they trade in 'matters of faith and salvation.'"

Television Evangelism Is Not Legitimate

Henry Fairlie

Henry Fairlie is a contributing editor to *The New Republic*, a weekly news and opinion magazine. In the following viewpoint, he attacks television evangelists for hypocrisy and greed. According to Fairlie, these evangelists use their influential positions and a warped version of the Christian gospel to exploit the poor and amass fortunes for themselves. In Fairlie's opinion, they have no authority to speak on spiritual matters.

As you read, consider the following questions:

1. Which of the seven deadly sins does Fairlie attribute to the television evangelists?
2. According to Fairlie, why are television evangelists able to exploit people without getting caught?
3. What effects have the television evangelists had on religion in America, according to the author?

Henry Fairlie, "Evangelists in Babylon," *The New Republic*, April 27, 1987. Reprinted by permission of THE NEW REPUBLIC, © 1987, The New Republic, Inc.

Since no one's god would pick his pocket or break his leg, said Jefferson, it did not matter to him if someone believed in one god or in many. But the Rev. Oral Roberts has flagrantly put God to work as a pickpocket, eventually lifting a $1.3 million off one Jerry Collins, the owner of two dog-racing tracks in Florida. This earned Roberts, as *Time* put it, "a surprise stay of execution." Roberts then announced that God insisted his life be saved at a cost of $8 million every year, payable to Roberts, which is evidence enough for a grand jury to indict God for running an extortion racket. Since evangelicals regard gambling as a sin, Roberts can claim that he merely relieved Collins of some of its wages—in short, that he is an instrument of divine redistributive justice in this life, a communist of sorts: "From each according to his gullibility. To me according to my greed," which might also be the text of the other big televangelists. They are all beginning to look as if they came out of Fagin's kitchen.

Except for some titillating and tawdry details, the revelations have hardly told us anything we could not have realized for some time. Anyone who has watched or listened to the programs of the star evangelists must have felt his nose twitch at the odor of all the (fairly far advanced) corruptions the flesh is heir to, and of at least four of the Seven Deadly Sins: Avarice, Envy, Gluttony, and Lust. The *Charlotte Observer*, circulating where Jim Bakker built his Heritage USA, has tried persistently for ten years to uncover the truth about his operation; and the *Tulsa Tribune* published a series of articles that were the result of a year's investigation into the empire of Oral Roberts. These papers are subject to immediate commercial pressure, such as the withdrawal of advertising, and, as the metro editor of the *Observer* says, when they publish a story in the morning, the evangelists are on the air by eleven to retaliate. . . .

Matters of Faith and Salvation

What is the story? John Corry, the television critic of the *New York Times*, begins a cretinous article about the evangelists' "mastery of the medium" by saying, "Put aside now matters of faith and salvation." Where this leads him may be seen in this passage displaying his rigorous critical standards:

> For sheer amiability, Mr. Bakker and his wife, Tammy Faye, had a quality all their own . . . ; the Bakkers were just Jim and Tammy. This viewer remembers with pleasure a program that Mrs. Bakker ran on her own. There she was in the middle of the big auditorium at the Heritage USA theme park in South Carolina, surrounded by the audience. The camera came in close. Tammy wanted everyone to see her high-heeled boots; they had little flowers stuck on them. "Aren't these silly," she said and giggled. Then she read a poem about Abraham Lincoln and cried. Scoff if you must, but . . .

Pat Crowley. Copley News Service. Reprinted by permission.

A scoff would hardly seem adequate.

The televangelists' programs are on the screen and are successful not because of their mastery of the medium, but precisely because they trade in "matters of faith and salvation." Beyond the sleaziness and titillation in the current revelations, there is a story that interests us only because it goes to the core of the connection between the avowed beliefs of the evangelicals and the moral precepts they say follow from these beliefs. We would be reading only about some petty corporate scandals if it were not for the radical and disturbing questions the story raises about the correctness of the evangelists' reading of the Bible; the source and nature of the inspiration or motives of their beliefs; the sincerity with which the televangelists hold these beliefs; and their understanding of sin, its place in human life, and even in the ultimate design of God.

Exploiting the Poor

Above all, the story asks us to consider the lengths to which the televangelists are ready to go to inveigle (the "Jim and Tammy Show"), manipulate (Jerry Falwell's "Old Time Gospel Hour"), and intimidate (the "Jimmy Swaggart Hour") the vulnerable, the anxious, the largely ignorant, the lost, the afraid, and all too often

160

the poor into believing that they will find consolation and even salvation in their message, if only they contribute, week by week, money they can ill afford, and in many cases they cannot afford at all. The *Washington Post* reported on April 4 [1987] that Jerry Falwell is considering returning $79,000 contributed bit by bit by an 82-year-old woman in a North Carolina retirement home who has Alzheimer's disease. And social workers in Altoona, Pennsylvania, found that a 67-year-old woman who was about to have her heat turned off for not paying the gas bill had sent $55 to Oral Roberts out of her Social Security check in response to one of his pleas to save his life.

Knowing that such cases can be multiplied countless times, and that those who contribute are on average older and poorer than those who do not contribute, it is hard to avoid concluding that these top televangelists are heartless people. Yet David R. Gergen, the editor of *U.S. News and World Report* (who formerly served Nixon, Ford, and Reagan in the White House), writes an editorial telling the media to lay off what he twice dismisses as the "squabbling" of the preachers. The media should "keep quiet" like Billy Graham. But for years Billy Graham has denounced the greed of the new breed of televangelists, and in 1979 he took the initiative in setting up the Evangelical Council for Financial Accountability. This body today has 354 members. Not one of the top ten televangelists is among them, and they are consistently in breach of its code.

Free of Authority

That is not the only license they enjoy. Most of those involved in the present scandals are subject to almost no authority in their ministries beyond their own professed beliefs, rationalizations, fancies, and appetites. They are singularly free of any church with the authority to watch what they preach, and discipline them for their transgressions. Falwell calls himself an independent Baptist, and has no ties to the Southern Baptist Convention. Pat Robertson has vague ties to it, but when he said he was speaking for it on the issue of school prayer, he was publicly rebuked by its leaders. Roberts is a layman of the United Methodist Church, but it has never granted him the standing of a minister. Robert Schuller is a wholly freewheeling minister of the Reformed Church in America. As for the Assemblies of God (the denomination that ordained both Jim Bakker and Marvin Gorman), Richard Mouw of the Fuller Theological Seminary in Pasadena, California, told Marjorie Hyer of the *Washington Post* that it "doesn't have a very strict authority structure." Pastors of the church "have a tendency to set up local power bases, and TV becomes just another of these ecclesiastical structures. . . . Those of us who don't like the Vatican telling a priest what he can teach at a Washington university wish there were somebody in the church that could tell Jim Bakker what he could preach in the name of Christ."

Beyond these current examples, religion in America leaves one (especially a European) with the impression that in place of churches there are only Do-It-Yourself God Kits. Or as a professor at Calvin College in Michigan said, referring to today's turmoil: "Americans don't want religion. They want God." Accompanying this is the weakness of theology in this country's religions. Where there is no theology there is no religion. There is only personal faith, which is no more religion than the secular humanism that has been eccentrically elevated to that status. Theology may seem designed to uphold only the one true faith of a church. But its continuing task is to prevent the proliferation of countless false personal faiths. One of the best cases for this task is put by an unbeliever, George Bernard Shaw, into the mouth of the Inquisitor in *St. Joan.* Joan heard bells in her head. She chose to believe that God spoke to her through them. What would happen if all the people who heard bells in their heads believed that God was speaking to them (like the Son of Sam, one might add)? What was more, Joan's bells told her that France must take up arms in a nationalist war against England. If there were countless Joans, the world would go down in "a welter of war."

I'll Show You a Charlatan

Honoré de Balzac said that "behind every great fortune there is a crime." I say show me a television evangelist with much more than a cloth coat and I'll show you a charlatan.

The fact is that television evangelism is a deceptive way to make a fast buck. It pays well and it pays consistently. No statement, no matter how ridiculous or audacious, fails to produce results.

William B. Michaels, *The New York Times*, April 2, 1987.

The main spur on all sides in the "unholy war" among the televangelists is greed: staking a claim to the rich bounty that is there to be wrested from media proselytizing. There is an endemic financial insecurity built into each operation. A spokesman for one of the televangelists said that the programs are so expensive that if the contributions begin to fall off you are quickly in trouble. The contributions have been falling off (those to Oral Roberts dangerously, hence the desperateness of his appeals), partly because of the fierceness of the competition, and partly because the age group that has given most is now being winnowed by the Grim Reaper.

But beyond the greed, the savagery in the televangelists' war is also due to the fact that they have no authority, no certainty, to which they can appeal. Like all people in a weak position, they can argue only by accusing. When challenged, they have no justification but that which they have chosen to say God has told them to speak. And though not all the evangelicals interpret the Bible as literally as does the fundamentalist Jerry Falwell, insofar as one can trace an ultimate source of what they preach, it is to be found in their personal reading of "what the Bible says." It might be thought that by taking the Bible literally, the fundamentalists are giving it an unchallengeable authority. But they are doing the opposite. They are stripping it of authority. For what they are saying is that anyone may interpret the Bible as he or she wishes. There is no established and authoritative interpretation that stands behind their ephemeral readings.

The televangelists' Bible is not the book to which I listened in the Presbyterian Church of Scotland in my boyhood and youth. That book had been strengthened by centuries of interpretation by many of the best and most devout minds in Western civilization. The evangelists leave the Bible with no more authority than is provided by the credentials of Ann Landers.

Distorting the Doctrine of Sin

So when they speak of sin—which is at the heart of the current story—it is impossible to know what they are speaking of—beyond what any individual may happen to dislike, fear, and envy in the behavior of other people. The exposition of the Seven Deadly Sins in Christian theology is a mighty structure—intellectual, moral, and even psychological—that we have inherited from Gregory the Great. One reason the list has prevailed is that, as one commentator has said, the sins were so defined that they were "able to serve as a classification of the normal perils of the soul in the ordinary conditions of life." This is precisely what the evangelical view of sin does not do.

The teaching of the Seven Deadly Sins, and of the traditional Protestant and Catholic religions, is that sin is not only in us, but of us. It is part of our humanity, our human condition in this life. It reflects our free will, the rebellion in Eden. On these terms, it is something with which we can and should wrestle, with some reward. But the sin of the evangelicals is something that has gotten into us from outside. The devil, they say, is not part of our fallen natures, but an alien whom we let in at some weak moment and therefore can expel. The fundamentalists and evangelists do not talk much of Original Sin. They cannot. For that doctrine means precisely that sin is part of our natures. Representing the devil as this alien has its convenience. Jim Bakker and his staunchly loyal followers can say that his downfall is not his fault, but the "work of the devil."

That the gospel and example of Christ are used to exploit the poor and the meek (the very people in whose aid the gospel was preached) to create large fortunes; to build mighty pleasure domes greater than in Xanadu; to surround preachers with security guards so that their ill deeds shall not be investigated; to try to intimidate all opposition; to offer high-heeled boots with flowers stuck on them in place of the crucifix; to build a prayer tower when it was enough for Christ to sink to his knees in Gethsemane; to do nothing in the name of Christ unless they are highly paid for it; to offer a version of Christianity, both in preaching and by example, in which there is not a jot or tittle that recalls the lives, say, of St. Francis of Assisi, St. Teresa of Avila, and in our own time, of Mother Teresa of Calcutta, is a sinning almost beyond the imagination.

Borderline Ideologies

The power of the pulpit to embolden, enlighten and empower no longer rests in the heart and voice of local clergy who speak to their loyal constituency face to face for 20 minutes a week. It has been appropriated by a small cadre who have invented the electronic church to reach into millions of homes day and night with borderline-religious ideologies that often are far removed from biblical teaching but capable of generating millions of dollars.

Peter G. Kreitler, *Los Angeles Times*, March 18, 1987.

The only words we know that were spoken from the Cross search our hearts: "Eli, Eli, lama sabachthani. . . . My God, my God, why hast thou forsaken me?" The day one hears that forlorn cry from the prayer tower of Oral Roberts, or any of the other televangelists, then one may grant them some claim to speak in the name of their Lord. Meanwhile, count them among the servants of Mammon.

"Religious traditionalists who have embraced network color television . . . may have struck a mortal blow to exactly what they are trying to defend."

Using Television Weakens Fundamentalists' Influence

Harvey Cox

Harvey Cox is a professor of divinity at Harvard Divinity School and the author of many books on religion and ethics. In the following viewpoint, excerpted from his book, *Religion in the Secular City,* he condemns fundamentalists' use of the mass media. According to Cox, television and fundamentalism represent opposite ideologies. If Jerry Falwell and other television evangelists continue to rely on the mass media, Cox argues, they will so distort their message that they will cease to influence the very people they are trying to reach.

As you read, consider the following questions:

1. What kind of an ideology is fundamentalism, according to the author?
2. What medium for spreading fundamentalism would Cox prefer to television?
3. According to Cox, television is not a neutral tool. Why? Do you agree or disagree?

Fundamentalism is not only a theology and a subculture, it is also an ideology. It interprets and defends the perceived life interests of an identifiable social group. Jerry Falwell and Ed Hindson (using the familiar ploy by which blacks and gays and others have appropriated terms originally used as epithets against them) are largely correct to call fundamentalism "redneck religion." This also means that fundamentalism, like liberation theology, the religion of Native Americans, and some other theologies, is an *antimodern* ideology. For the small-town and rural poor who appropriated it, fundamentalism expressed their opposition to the powerful modern, liberal-capitalist world that was disrupting their traditional way of life.

An ideology is a cluster of ideas and values that provides a class or a nation or some human group with a picture of the world that can guide and inspire corporate action. As an ideology, fundamentalism contains an implicit image of what society should be like. Fundamentalists not only insist on preserving the fundamentals of the faith, they also envision a world in which these fundamentals would be more widely accepted and practiced. They want not only to "keep the faith" but to change the world so the faith can be kept more easily. . . .

A Destructive Romance

My . . . reason for doubting fundamentalism's influence on postmodern Christianity is its recent romance with the electronic media. Fundamentalism is a highly traditional religious expression. Television is a tradition-smashing phenomenon. Yet rarely has any religious movement embraced an artifact of modernity as enthusiastically and as uncritically. The top regular religious television shows (Rex Humbard, Pat Robertson, Jerry Falwell, Oral Roberts) are all more or less fundamentalist in orientation. Colleges and seminaries associated with the fundamentalist movement have some of the finest television equipment available to students anywhere. It is generally acknowledged that fundamentalist television is produced with a high level of technical competence. . . .

What happens when a profoundly antimodernist attempt to reassert the primacy of traditional values utilizes a cultural form that is itself thoroughly modern and antitraditional? This is the tension between content and form, between message and medium, that occurs when the Old Time Gospel Hour goes out on network television.

The Decay of the Aura

The German Jewish writer Walter Benjamin took up this issue in an influential essay first published in 1936, "The Work of Art in the Age of Mechanical Reproduction." Benjamin was writing about art, but his observation, as he himself says, is equally applicable to religion. He argued that the mechanical reproduction of any work of art profoundly alters its meaning, makes it different in ways its reproducers can never anticipate. It was Benjamin's conviction that "the technique of reproduction detaches the reproduced object from the domain of tradition." This leads ultimately to "the liquidation of the traditional value of the cultural heritage," what Benjamin called the "decay of the aura."

When one applies this analysis to religious phenomena, the change in meaning is particularly radical. For Benjamin, an essential feature of any work of art is the sense of distance and awe it elicits, a power he believed is also derived from the religious and spiritual purpose art originally served. It is this distance which gives it authority. Reproduction, in severing the object from its intended spiritual "location" and depriving it of its aura, at the same time robs it of its authority by making it too close, too

"You know . . . I actually used to believe in god, before we started watching these TV evangelists."

Edgar Argo. Reprinted with permission from the *American Atheist*.

available.

Jerry Falwell and other religious traditionalists who have embraced network color television, the ultimate form of modern mechanical reproduction, may have struck a mortal blow to exactly what they are trying to defend, the "old time Gospel" and traditional religion. The move from the revivalist's tent to the vacuum tube has vastly amplified the voices of defenders of tradition. At the same time it has made them more dependent on the styles and assumptions inherent in the medium itself. This explains the none too subtle shift one feels at Thomas Road Baptist Church when the adult Bible study ends, the big lights go on, and the entire congregation suddenly becomes the cast of a nation-wide network show. It is hard, despite Jerry Falwell's consummate skill at bridging the gap, not to feel that one has been pushed further into the modern world and moved a notch away from the "old time" antimodernist intent of the message.

Moving Toward Entertainment

Religious television moves toward entertainment. Jerry Falwell still appears behind the pulpit, but Pat Robertson uses a setting copied from late-night talk shows. A succession of splendidly dressed guests tell the audience how the Lord has brought them success, health, money, power. The Gospel is reduced to a means of achieving the same modern secular goals the evangelist began by opposing.

The German social critic Jurgen Habermas sees a battle shaping up between what he calls "communicative life-worlds" and the more formally organized systems based on power and money steered by the media. This is exactly the contradiction television-based political fundamentalism finds itself in today. In the contest between the System and traditional morality, Jerry Falwell and his followers fervently believe they are on the side of the angels. They believe they are defending the old-time moral values against the invasion of modernity. But the technical and organizational means they have chosen to fight the battle may be destroying precisely the religious resources most needed to save traditional morality.

Television, mass computer mailings, the latest marketing techniques are not neutral tools. Embedded in them are a set of attitudes and values that are inimical to traditional morality. They extend massification. As Habermas says, capitalist modernization transfers more and more "social material" from the "life-worlds" into realms of action controlled by large outside systems. This process previously left religion, education, the family alone, and concentrated instead on more overtly economic sectors like banks and factories. Now, "the system's imperatives," says Habermas, "are attacking areas of action which are demonstrably unable to perform their own tasks if they are removed from communicatively structured areas of action." Network television and computer mailings are not "communicatively structured areas of action." They are powerful anticommunicative forces, engaged in shoving more and more of those human activities which used to go on in small "life-worlds" into the insatiable maw of the modern system.

An Unavoidable Contradiction

The contradiction between traditional religion and the mass media seems unavoidable. The deepest contradiction lies in the question of the nature of a genuine religious community. One real strength of the newly emerging Christian base communities in Latin America and elsewhere is that they foster the face-to-face groupings human beings need so badly. The television evangelists do not. Despite their efforts to include viewers through letters, telephone calls, and a folksy style on camera, something essential is missing in a television congregation. By buying into the mass-media world so heavily fundamentalism may have unintentionally sold out to one of the most characteristic features of the very modern world it wants so much to challenge. If the devil is a modernist, the TV evangelists may have struck a deal with Lucifer himself, who always appears—so the Bible teaches—as an angel of light.

Failing To Reach the People

I believe the electronic church has failed miserably to adequately meet the needs of the people it has identified so accurately. It has failed for two reasons: because it has not taken seriously enough the demonic nature of general television, and because it has proceeded on an inadequate understanding of the nature of the Christian gospel.

William F. Fore, *Television and Religion,* 1987.

Just before I left Lynchburg [Virginia] I stopped in to visit the national headquarters of the Old Time Gospel Hour, in a converted warehouse next to a supermarket. Inside, rows of volunteers take incoming calls on banks of telephones. The atmosphere is brisk, friendly, efficient. Earlier in the day I was there Falwell had appeared on network television talking about President Reagan's decision to seek an amendment to the United States Constitution that would permit voluntary prayers to be said in the classrooms of public schools. He interviewed Senator Jesse Helms of North Carolina, a supporter of the amendment, and offered a "Kids Need to Pray" bumper sticker. He also asked viewers to call in their opinion on the subject to his toll-free number. The volunteers were receiving continuous calls, nearly all of them supporting the amendment. By calling and giving their names and addresses, of course, they were also supplying the Old Time Gospel Hour with thousands of prospective new donors. But some volunteers were also engaged in a kind of hi-tech counseling. Typists sat at word processors sending out a stream of prewritten letters to troubled and questioning viewers all over the country. The age of mechanical reproduction, I thought, has come not just to art but to prayer and the cure of souls as well.

The Last Defeat

In its nearly a century of life American fundamentalism has weathered many attacks. It has been a scandal to liberal intellectuals and a stumbling block to skeptics. But it has always been irascible, full of a certain feisty vitality. Beaten back into its corner on many occasions it has always emerged again, picking up stones to sling at the Goliath of modernism. But will the subtle whirr of computers and Neilsen ratings succeed where contempt, condescension, and even persecution have failed? Fundamentalists and other conservative Christians have something important to say to a world that has grown rightly sick of modernity. But there are very few people who want to live in a society in which the values of a particular subculture are unloaded onto all of us in the name of Jesus.

Fundamentalists have had a record of turning defeats into victories, and vice versa. When William Scopes was convicted for teaching evolution, it was a victory for fundamentalism. It quickly became evident, however, that because of the immense publicity the case received, it had not been a victory at all, but a defeat. After the trial fundamentalists retreated again. Now with television and computer mailings available they smell a new victory, much bigger than the one they achieved at Dayton, Tennessee. But for some of the same reasons this victory could turn into another defeat, perhaps this time for good.

"No other interest group has ever possessed so much access to media for the purpose of promoting an ideological perspective as do the Christian religious broadcasters."

Using Television Strengthens Fundamentalists' Influence

Jeffrey K. Hadden

In the following viewpoint, Jeffrey K. Hadden explores the influence of the church's use of mass media. According to Hadden, evangelical fundamentalists have discovered a medium for shaping the cultural and political future of America—television. Their access to television, he writes, will make them a powerful social movement well into the next century. Hadden is a professor of sociology at the University of Virginia and coauthor of *Prime Time Preachers: The Rising Power of Televangelism.*

As you read, consider the following questions:

1. According to the author, what elevated the evangelicals to a controversial position during the early 1980s?
2. How significant are the televangelists, according to Hadden? To what religious figure does he compare them?
3. What statistics does the author offer to show the influence of the Christian religious broadcasters? Why does he expect these numbers to increase?

Jeffrey J. Hadden, "Televangelism and the Future of American Politics," in *New Christian Politics*, David G. Bromley and Anson Shupe, eds. Macon, GA: Mercer University Press, 1984. Reprinted with permission.

While religious broadcasting has been with us for as long as man has had the capability to transmit his voice over the air, it was not until the beginning of this decade that most Americans became aware of the phenomenon which Ben Armstrong has called the "electric church." Armstrong, Executive Director of National Religious Broadcasters, sees the electronic church as having "launched a revolution as dramatic as the revolution that began when Martin Luther nailed his ninety-five theses to the cathedral door at Wittenburg."

This may sound like trade association boosterism, but I believe it would be a mistake to dismiss it as such. Armstrong's assessment of the significance of religious broadcasting is based on the belief that modern communications technology has provided an important tool for the fulfillment of the Scriptures. Evangelicals believe Christ's greatest commandment was "Go ye into all the world, and preach the gospel to every creature" (Mark 16:15). Electronic communication, some Evangelicals believe, is literally a gift from God which makes possible the fulfillment of this Great Commission.

It is not the success of televangelists in preaching the Gospel message, however, that has made the electronic church controversial. Rather, it is that a few of those who preside over electronic pulpits came to use airwaves as a means of transforming America politically. It was this shift in attitude toward politics by a few Evangelical and fundamentalist preachers that elevated the electronic pulpits into a position of great controversy during the early 1980s. . . .

A Burgeoning Social Movement

The New Christian Right is a burgeoning social movement. It is one of the most important social movements of this century. It may even signal a revolution of the order and magnitude of the revolution that Martin Luther's nailing of his ninety-five theses to the cathedral door in Wittenburg symbolized. The politically minded televangelists have been and will continue to be critical to this unfolding social movement. . . .

If we are experiencing the dawning of a new era, the New Christian Right is destined to play a major role in shaping its character. The reason this is so is that Evangelicals, who lean politically to the right, have developed unprecedented access to mass media. No other special interest group, save the interest of selling the products of our free enterprise system, has ever had so much unrestricted access to mass media. . . .

In *The Emerging Order*, Jeremy Rifkin argued that "the evangelical community is amassing a base of potential power that dwarfs every other competing interest in American society today." Rifkin's conclusion is based on his assessment of their access to mass media. Their television broadcasting, he believes, will provide the foundation for the infrastructure to "build a total Christian community." Rifkin is hopeful that this force will creatively address issues, like the environment, which liberals view as critical to the well-being of mankind.

In *Prime Time Preachers*, Charles Swann and I substantially agreed with Rifkin's assessment of the potential power base. We were less sanguine about the prospects that this emerging political force would creatively address issues considered important to liberals, although we did not rule out the possibility of changing political agendas with the rise to power.

Shaping America's Future

Forecasting has always been a precarious business, but there are several reasons why I believe that televangelists will play an important role in shaping America's future. My reasoning is grounded in the assumptions of the resource mobilization theory of social movements. The arguments are essentially structural in character.

Media personalities come and go. Jerry Falwell has a lot of talent, and a lot going for him, but I'm not certain that he will be the central figure of the New Christian Right ten or twenty years from now. In fact, my guess is that he will not. All social movements need charismatic leaders, but it takes more than leadership to produce a movement.

The Impact of Radio and Television

I believe one of the greatest factors in the religious resurgence in this country has been the impact of religious radio and television.

Billy Graham, quoted in *Christianity Today,* October 17, 1986.

After fifty years of elaborating on the combinations and permutations of liberal democratic philosophy, America is now in the process of reassessing its values and its government. Among other things, the struggle has much to do with the role of government in our lives—what it may and may not do, what it should and should not do, and what it must and must not do. These concerns create a mosaic that crisscrosses traditional liberal-conservative positions. It is likely that the resolution of many of these issues will not be easily labeled with traditional conceptions of liberal and conservative. Still, it seems quite likely that many issues will be resolved in terms more compatible with a conservative than a liberal philosophy.

I would identify . . . structural properties possessed by the New Christian Right that give them an edge over the New Right and

173

every other competing interest group in the struggle to reshape America.

Media Access. No other interest group has ever possessed so much access to media for the purpose of promoting an ideological perspective as do the Christian religious broadcasters. The latest figures reported by the National Religious Broadcasters show that there are 1,108 religious radio stations and 65 religious television stations in this country. There are currently three Christian networks broadcasting 24 hours a day which can be picked up via satellite nationwide and several other networks on abbreviated schedules.

The last Arbitron figures in 1983 showed that 83 syndicated programs were drawing 24 million viewers. While the total audience for religious television programs has been relatively stable for seven years, significant developments suggest we may anticipate sizable audience growth ahead. First, the number of syndicated programs has grown by approximately 40 percent during the last three years. This offers a significant pool of talent from which new leaders may emerge as some of the current televangelists advance in years and may be expected to retire. Second, Oral Roberts and Rex Humbard, the longtime leaders in the audience sweepstakes, have changed their formats and seem to be rebounding after having suffered serious audience losses in recent rating periods. Third, preliminary research suggests that as greater proportions of America become wired to receive cable television, religious viewing will increase significantly. This is so because the religious broadcasters have a firm foothold in satellite transmission.

Reaching Larger Audiences

Furthermore, as direct mail research has made abundantly clear, it is not the size of the audience that is critical, but the confluence of interests between what is promoted and the receiver of the message. Those who like what they hear from Jerry Falwell or Pat Robertson or James Kennedy will likely end up on mailing lists that will provide them with printed material which will reinforce commitment to the cause. Already the politically oriented televangelists are speaking to far larger audiences than Martin Luther King, Jr., for example, addressed when he was the unchallenged leader of the civil rights movement. . . .

Finances. Social movements can be launched by voluntary labor, but to become effective agents of social change, they need money. The televangelists could not survive without converting audience response into financial contributions to pay for air time. It takes over a million dollars a week to fund Falwell's "Old-Time Gospel Hour" and the various Liberty Baptist College projects he promotes on the air. He can't afford to lose "OTGH" contributions to the Moral Majority. But given time, he has the technical skills required to raise really significant sums of money for his political activities as well. So too do the other politically minded televangelists. . . .

They Haven't Disappeared

Whatever the outcome, one terribly important fact has been almost completely missed by the media and intellectuals. The "kooky fundamentalists," whom secular intellectual elites thought disappeared after the Scopes Trial, have already defined much of the agenda of this society for the foreseeable future and, thereby, already shaped the direction of American culture as we rush toward the twenty-first century.

"Communications and media must become valid, legitimate ministries in the church of the 21st century."

The Church Should Use Television

Jay Cormier

In the wake of scandals involving well-known television evangelists, many church members from mainstream denominations have questioned whether their local churches should use this media. In the following viewpoint, Jay Cormier, director of public relations at Merrimack College in North Andover, Massachusetts, argues that television can benefit the church. According to Cormier, local churches can use television much more wisely than Jimmy Swaggart, Jim Bakker, and other evangelists have used it. He believes churches can use television to reach a wider audience and support existing ministries.

As you read, consider the following questions:

1. How did the author react to the scandals involving Jim Bakker and Jimmy Swaggart?
2. What is lacking in local parishes, according to Cormier?
3. What suggestions does the author give for using television wisely?

Jay Cormier, "Cues from the Television Evangelists," *America*, March 26, 1988.
Reprinted with the permission of America Press, Inc., 106 W. 56th Street, New York, NY 10019. All Rights Reserved.

When I was a diocesan director of communications, more than one parishioner would ask me why we Catholics do not do what the Protestants (meaning the televangelists) do on television. With tongue firmly planted in cheek, I would say in mock disgust: "Well, if we didn't put so much money into churches and schools and hospitals, we could do what those ministers are doing on television."

If truth be told, we members of the "mainline" churches have taken an almost smug satisfaction in the "holy war" that has been raging for the past year in television evangelism—the Bakers vs. Jimmy Swaggart and Jerry Falwell, fundamentalists vs. charismatics, the Oral Roberts God-who-takes-hostages vs. the happy-thinking-hourly-powerful God of Robert Schuller.

The money-hustlers have been thrown out of the temple, we cheer. The charlatans have been exposed, we exult. The "electronic church," we chide, has been shown for what it is: expensive and glitzy, empty and shallow as are most shows on television.

Using Modern Communication

I cannot help but feel a certain vindication in all that has taken place since Jim Bakker's and Jimmy Swaggart's falls from grace; but I have also been struck by the challenge these events pose for us Catholics in realizing our vision of church and how we should—and should NOT— use the tools of modern communications.

The phrase "electronic church" is becoming entrenched in our lexicon; but whatever one wants to call the phenomenon of the "PTL Club," "Old Time Gospel Hour," "Hour of Power" and the others, the one thing it is NOT is an experience of "church." Church is as its most basic, a group of people, bound together by faith, supporting one another, not only through the good times, but also through the bad times, the painful times and the tragic times. That kind of community cannot be created or shared via the one-way medium of televison—especially in the sanitized, squeaky-clean televised ministrations we see on Sunday morning.

Harvey Cox, professor of divinity at Harvard University, explained on ABC-TV's "This Week With David Brinkley": "An audience is not a congregation. An audience is a mass of people who don't know each other, who can't really meet to be together, to support each other. . . . I think it would be much better if the people who have been attracted to [televangelists] would somehow return to [their local] church where there's a continuation of fellowship with other people . . . where there's ongoing life and prayer and gathering in spirit."

We Catholics have done a phenomenal job at building churches and schools. But what kind of job have we done at building community and fellowship within those walls? The growing number of Spanish-speaking, for whom the church has been home for centuries but who are now turning to the Protestant fundamentalist churches, are but one indication that perhaps our parish communities are not all they should be.

The Damage of Priest Horror Stories

Another indication: "priest horror stories." Everybody, it seems, has a tale to tell of an encounter with a pastor whose style was not that of the warm Bing Crosby in *Going My Way*. Some of those stories are funny memories of a sometimes eccentric church that, we pray, has grown up a great deal in the last 25 years. But these encounters are not yesterday's news. The friendly, accepting, welcoming image of the television minister is in sharp contrast to the clumsy, insensititve encounters many people continue to have with the Catholic Church.

Using These Tools

C.S. Lewis identified the missionary task of the church as presenting "that which is timeless (the same yesterday, today, and tomorrow) in the particular language of our own age." The dominant language of our own age continues to be the mass media, and our business continues to be to use these tools to communicate the good news of Jesus Christ.

Terry Lindvall, *Christianity Today*, October 17, 1986.

The Rev. William Fore, a United Methodist minister and Secretary for Communications for the National Council of Churches, is extremely critical of television evangelists "for providing trival and superficial religion, a quick fix to people's anxiety." But in his book *Television and Religion*, published by Augsburg Press, he credits them for bringing out the "spiritual hunger of millions" that is not served by the nation's mainline churches. "The television evangelists understand," Dr. Fore writes, "that people are hurting because they feel ignored and are not needed, because they are often treated like commodities."

There is no question that our priests are overworked, and most of them are good, kind, dedicated men. But, in view of the number of people turning away from the Catholic Church for other churches or for the television ministers, it must be asked if our emphasis on form and structure is costing us the sense of community and fellowship that the Gospel challenges us to build. . . .

There are those in religious communications who justify the high cost involved in such productions by saying that if Jesus or St. Paul were alive today, he would use television to reach the masses (and I must confess I used that line now and then, especially around budget time). But one would be hard-pressed to prove that the Saviour and His apostles would use the same approach as the television ministers.

It is also a myth to believe that millions of sinners out there turning their television channel selectors each week (probably on their way to the Playboy channel) and, discovering the "PTL Club," are instantly converted to Jesus Christ. Television religion does reach many people, but a very small percentage of the total viewing public (and that number, according to Nielsen and Arbitron, is shrinking).

And, as the saying goes, the television ministers are "preaching to the choir." Most of the people who tune in are already "saved." What about reaching those who are not seated in the television chapel on Sunday mornings but are out in the marketplace of "Dallas," "L.A. Law," "Wheel of Fortune" and "M*A*S*H" reruns? Good stewardship demands that churches confront the question of whether such expenditures are the most effective use of their resources.

The point is that television cannot instill a faith that is not there—faith cannot be instilled by simply watching television any more than simply watching Julia Child can make a viewer a gourmet cook. Television can nurture faith and can even make faith grow in a long fallow field; but television cannot plant the seed. That has to be done within a community of three-dimensional, breathing, loving human beings.

In other words, television cannot sow the seeds of faith, but it can water the garden.

Supporting Other Ministries

Should the church be on television? No doubt about it. But we should not be building "video kingdoms" on Sunday mornings. The limited resources that the church could devote to buying time on radio and television—the days of sustained or "free" public service time are long gone, neighbors!—should be tools to enable us to more effectively carry on our other ministries.

A few years ago, the Rev. Everett Parker of the United Church of Christ and Ellwood Kieser, C.S.P., producer of the Paulist television series "Insight," asked the Federal Communications Commission to consider a rule that would require television and radio stations to give free time regularly to air the messages of community service groups. In the current climate of deregulation, the proposal never saw the light of day. But the question they raised is still valid today, especially in the wake of televangelism: Shouldn't there be room on television and radio for the messages of churches that devote their resources to preaching the Gospel through their programs that feed the hungry, heal the sick and brokenhearted, educate children and build communities of faith that support and help its members to grow?

Churches with limited resources should realize the limitations of television and should target their messages accordingly. The one thing television does best is to deliver audiences to sponsors. That is not to suggest that faith be "packaged" like Big Macs, but that churches design short, effective messages inviting different people to be a part of the many ministries that we are about. That takes a commitment of time, talent, planning and, yes, money. But if done well, it can reap a rich harvest.

Marching On

We hear tragic stories of fallen pastors who had nothing to do with television. In all eras, great men of God have fallen because of moral weakness. This should not negate the use of television to preach Christ crucified. The Word of the Lord marches on.

Paul Crouch, *Christianity Today*, October 16, 1987.

The Sunday television Mass in many communities is an excellent vehicle for serving those who, for one reason or another, cannot participate in their parish celebrations. The Archdiocese of New York launched a "Come Home for Christmas" campaign, inviting people who had left the church or who had not been to church in some time to return, and telling them they would be welcomed. Like any good campaign, "Come Home for Christmas" relied on short 30- and 60-*second* radio and television spots rather than 30- and 60-*minute* programs.

Communicating to the Public

Every church ministry—from adult religious education and ministries to the poor to youth ministry—should earmark the necessary resources to communicate effectively its programs to its "public." Communications and media must become valid, legitimate ministries in the church of the 21st century.

There is another area of television that the church could take far more advantage of: television news. News directors and producers often look for church leaders—especially bishops—to speak on issues. But most bishops are loath to subject themselves to interview situations they cannot control. Their reluctance is, to a degree, understandable. One solution is to provide training for all bishops and church leaders in handling media interviews in order to articulate the church's positions and teachings with concise clarity, conviction and compassion—and without smugness, shrillness and condescension.

But first we have to make communications a priority in the church. It should strike us as strange that the church, whose mission from Christ is so dependent on communications, does not provide its ministers with better communications skills. We all know the overall state of preaching in the church—and there is some training in the seminary for that; but what about training in effective writing, interpersonal and leadership communications skills as well?

Carrying Out Our Mission

The fall from grace experienced by American televangelism is both a blessing and a curse to the mainline churches. We can remain aloof from the media and elect not to "demean" the Gospel by collaborating with the media types; or we can learn from the televangelists' mistakes and begin to use television as a means of carrying out our mission to all God's people. As with everything else we do as a church community, it begins with an act of faith.

"The particular contents of television . . . make it an especially pernicious antagonist to the Christian message."

The Church Should Not Use Television

Peter G. Horsfield

In the following viewpoint, excerpted from Peter G. Horsfield's book, *Religious Television: The American Experience,* the author explains his opposition to religious television ministries. Television, he writes, represents the values of the secular culture, not the values of Christianity. Thus it cannot be used to spread the teachings of Christianity. He suggests that churches resist the manipulation of the media and stay away from television. Horsfield has been the pastor of The Arlington Heights United Methodist Church in Massachusetts and The Gap Uniting Church in Brisbane, Australia. He has done doctoral work in theology and mass communications at Boston University Graduate School.

As you read, consider the following questions:

1. What two main arguments against mass media does the author give?
2. According to the author, how do religious broadcasters defend their use of television?
3. Why does Horsfield believe the church has been manipulated by the television industry?

From *Religious Televison: The American Experience* by Peter G. Horsfield. New York: Longman, Inc., 1984. Reprinted with permission of the author.

Each time a new mass medium has emerged, the church has been there and adapted the medium's use to the church's purpose. The first mass printing of a text was of the Bible in 1456; a regularly scheduled religious service appeared on radio only two months after regular radio programming began in 1920; and religious programs were among the first year's offerings on television in 1940. Within the church, there have always been the enthusiastic communicators who have tried to raise the church's sights to see the potential of mass communication.

But also within the church there have always been the critics who have cautioned against the hazards of greeting any new advance with unquestioning praise. These critics have not always been conservatives seeking to preserve an established domain nor the jealous attacking a successful project. In relation to the mass media, some of the strongest criticisms within the church have come from people actively involved not only in the mission of the church but in seeking the vision to encompass new developments in society. It is not accurate to seek to pass off such criticisms simply on the basis that other religious leaders "feel threatened" or that they express "resentment for another's success."

Criticisms of the use of mass media for religious communication center on two main arguments, the first based on philosophical and theological grounds, and the second based on the structural implications of the television industry itself.

A Contradiction in Terms

There has been a persistent body of people who question the use of mass media in religious communication as an inherent contradiction in terms. The essence of Christian communication according to many is its responsiveness, its service of human need, and its affirmation of the individual. To speak of "mass" communication is an impossibility. Theologian Harvey Cox has made the point that "you cannot communicate a message about love and reciprocity when you are telling someone with no opportunity of him/her talking back." What results in this case is a reduction of the gospel message to information and often carefully hidden coercive information. Such one way communication of a religious message eventually strips the message of its interactive, existential dimensions. Writer Virginia Stem Owens challenges this basic presumption underlying current religious mass media:

> Theologically (a Radio Church) is a contradiction in terms. In our rush to support modern man's spirituality in the style to which he had become accustomed, we had forgotten the one thing necessary for worship—total presence. . . . There are very few experiences where one must still be physically present to participate in them, so far has technology extended our nerve-endings. Birth and death, sex and liturgy, remain the holdouts.

183

None of these can be performed satisfactorily by proxy or long distance.

These criticisms suggest that the problem facing religious communicators is not just a matter of content but a questioning of the nature of the whole medium itself. The particular contents of television, however, aggravate the problem and make it an especially pernicious antagonist to the Christian message. Television's highly centralized, capital-intensive, hard-edged conceptualizations make it virtually impossible even for Christian content to remain intact. One of the most ascerbic critics in this regard has been the experienced mass-media practitioner, Malcolm Muggeridge. In his challenge of the use of mass media for religious communication, Muggeridge focuses on the question of the *illusion* created and presented by the mass media, particularly that of television: "Not only *can* the camera lie, it always lies. . . . The ostensibly serious offerings of the media, on the other hand, represent a different menace precisely because they are liable to pass for being objective and authentic, whereas actually they, too, belong to the realm of fantasy." Muggeridge who, late in life, became an active Christian, considers that the fantasy image of the television screen stands in direct contrast to the reality of Christ and therefore is totally unadaptable to the proclamation

Bob Englehart. Reprinted with permission.

of the Christian message.

> Now we, the legatees of Christendom, are in our turn succumb-
> ing to fantasy, of which the media are an outward and visible
> manifestation. Thus the effect of the media at all levels is to draw
> people away from reality, which means away from Christ, and
> into fantasy.

One defense against such criticisms offered by the paid-time
broadcasters is that these critics have failed to realize the significant difference between print media and electronic media. The
critics, in Marshall McLuhan's terms, are bound by the linear logic
of the written page. It is the electronic communicators who have
perceived the gestaltic logic of the electronic media and have applied that logic to the explication of the Christian message. It is
significant in this regard that most discussion about religious uses
of television takes place in print, while the actual practice continues in electronics. Editor James Taylor of the United Church
of Canada suggests that today the church is in a new Reformation, the significance of which for the life of the church may be
as dramatic as the Reformation in the sixteenth century, which
derived much of its momentum from the development of print.
This new Reformation will bring ways of thinking as foreign to
religious thinkers today as did the Reformation then. Taylor ac-
quiesces to what he views as the inevitable: "We might as well
face the fact that more and more people who would otherwise
have belonged to our churches are going to be born again out of
television's experiential womb." Whether Taylor is right or not may
be proven only by the historical perspective to be gained by the
passage of time. It is possible that, as audience figures suggest,
this new Reformation may already have reached a plateau. In the
meantime, however, religious communicators must address the
problem as clearly and logically as possible, weighing the issues
involved even if they are forced, again in McLuhan's terms, to
use a logic gained from a rear-vision view.

Television's Control

The second objection to the religious use of mass media from
within the church arises out of concern for the implications of
the organization of the mass media themselves. Harvey Cox has
highlighted this problem:

> The problem with the mass media is not their content—though
> God knows that is bad enough. The trouble is their structure
> and the pattern of their control. They are massive one way
> signalling systems that allow for virtually no response. They are
> controlled by the rich and the powerful. . . . They are run for
> profit, for controlling people and selling them things.

This context, according to Cox, cuts right across the message of
the gospel, rendering it totally ineffective—"A gospel presented

in a context which contradicts the gospel is no longer the gospel at all." This is a problem particularly with those who receive the messages of American broadcasting outside the American system. Jesuit communicator Stefan Bamberger notes,

> Latin American Christians have very realistically brought to our attention the fact that the mass media in many countries are commercially and politically dominated. . . . How can one identify with a set-up which, in most parts of its program, flatly promotes the consumer society and often obeys political dictatorship?

This apparent conflict has never been a problem for the paid-time broadcasters, who consider it beyond the scope of Christian concern to effect social change except through the conversion of individuals, a process which can take place regardless of contexts and suggested identifications. Their task, as they see it, is not to change social structures but to use what tools are available for the purpose of spreading the gospel. This limited evangelical understanding of "spreading the gospel," understood largely as verbal content, lies at the base of much of the debate over religious uses of mass media. Other religious communicators feel that spreading the gospel also involves action on behalf of the poor, the oppressed, and those suffering because of powerlessness to resist exploitation.

Television Has Little Impact

Each year, about 2 million religious television and radio programs are beamed over some 7,000 stations. These programs have made little impact on non-Christians. More than 70 percent of Americans either have no religious affiliation or are Christian in name only. Religious television doesn't seem to significantly impact this group. In a survey we conducted of 40,000 church-related Christians, only .01 percent said they attend church as a result of mass evangelism, including religious radio and television. However, more than 85 percent said they came to Christ and the church primarily because of a friend, relative, or associate.

Win Arn, *Christianity Today,* October 16, 1987.

The alternatives suggested by the critics of current religious broadcasting reflect this broader concern to embody the gospel in action not only through television but also against television. Harvey Cox suggests that the proper function of the American religious communicator should not be a personally beneficial one but a surrogate one: "to be the voice of the powerless and poor of the world . . . to use the media to allow people to give expression to their fear, to let people cry out, and to make media accessible." Many mainline broadcasters assert that one of the major objects of their broadcasting is producing programs which raise issues of social concern and which give expression to minority groups and causes.

Theologian Robert McAfee Brown suggests that the most appropriate stance for the church to take in regard to the mass media is to use its facilities to counter the depersonalizing and privatizing effect of the media in society. In this case the church's mission to television may represent a massive clash of institutions, with the church becoming a paradigm of a counterculture or antienvironment organization in which human values are preserved and restored to their foremost position in society.

> If depersonalization turns out to be the greatest single threat in the future, it can be strongly argued that the church has the special role of warning about this and safeguarding the personal dimension against encroachment in the name of efficiency, progress, or technological necessity.

Various churches and church leaders have been following this approach. The media awareness program, *Television Awareness Training,* was developed by a group of churches to develop social awareness of the influence of television on social attitudes and values. The program is now being used internationally, with adaptations made for particular national contexts. The United Church of Christ has continually played an active part in media advocacy, devoting much of the time of their Office of Communication to media criticism, lobbying, and organizing community and legal-action groups against the television industry on behalf of disenfranchised groups.

Not Much Hope for Change

At the moment, however, it is unlikely that such action will become a universal strategy of the churches. Not only are there major theological differences between the groups which lead them to conceive the problem of media differently, but there is now major capital investment to be protected and justified, not only in television but in the large, related fields of religious music, publishing, entertainment, and alternate education. These gain their distinctiveness not from their rejection of the marketing approach in the name of religious faith but from their almost total integration of modern consumer marketing with religion, producing what Virginia Stem Owens identifies as a range of prepackaged, certified Christian life-styles to meet one's particular demands and aspirations, with appropriate seminars available to show a person how to fit into that life-style.

The answer, according to one group, is to be the mouthpiece for the poor and disenfranchised, to resist the imposition of the media, to be the counterculture in which human values are preserved. The answer, according to the other group, is for religious faith to ride the technological roller coaster wherever it goes, with a strong confidence in the capabilities of technology to contribute to the furthering of the Christian cause. The only potential limitation would be the money to enable the church to do it. "The church won't be able to do much if (the world) can keep it poor and underfinanced. The billion dollar category is what is needed to be truly effective," says paid-time religious broadcaster Pat Robertson.

It is apparent that the conflict within the church caused by the growth of evangelical broadcasting in recent years is more than just a case of "sour grapes" or "ego-defensiveness." It represents a marked difference in approaches to religious faith and practice arising out of theological, philosophical, social, and practical differences.

Manipulated by the TV Industry

These differences within the church have made it as a whole vulnerable to manipulation by the powerful television industry which in the past two decades has permitted and encouraged the growth of paid-time broadcasting because that approach is most in harmony with its own economic goals and methods. The paid-time religious broadcasters in general have not yet been able to perceive or acknowledge the use that has been made of them, or the power of the television industry to shape their message and their organizations. Nor have they acknowledged their vulnerability to possible future changes in broadcast policy according to the inclinations of the television industry. By undercutting the moral basis of representativeness in religious programming on television, the paid-time religious broadcasters have removed one of the major contributions that religious groups could have made in influencing television in America: that of acting as agents in challenging the television industry to act within its moral responsibility as a utility for genuine social communication.

Recognizing Statements
That Are Provable

From various sources of information we are constantly confronted with statements and generalizations about social and moral problems. In order to think clearly about these problems, it is useful if one can make a basic distinction between statements for which evidence can be found and other statements which cannot be verified or proved because evidence is not available, or the issue is so controversial that it cannot be definitely proved.

Readers should be aware that magazines, newspapers and other sources often contain statements of a controversial nature. The following activity is designed to allow experimentation with statements that are provable and those that are not.

The following statements are taken from the viewpoints in this chapter. Consider each statement carefully. *Mark P for any statement you believe is provable. Mark U for any statement you feel is unprovable because of the lack of evidence. Mark C for any statements you think are too controversial to be proved to everyone's satisfaction.*

If you are doing this activity as a member of a class or group, compare your answers with those of other class or group members. Be able to defend your answers. You may discover that others will come to different conclusions than you. Listening to the reasons others present for their answers may give you valuable insights in recognizing statements that are provable.

> P = *provable*
> U = *unprovable*
> C = *too controversial*

1. The mass media draw people away from reality and into fantasy.

2. Religious television reaches only a small percentage of the total viewing public.

3. Television evangelists are not the only clergy who mismanage church funds.

4. Television is by definition a tradition-smashing medium.

5. Modern communications technology has provided an important tool for the fulfillment of the Scriptures.

6. The *Charlotte Observer* has been investigating the finances of Jim Bakker's operation for ten years.

7. If St. Paul were alive today, he would use television.

8. Millions of American Christians contribute their time, money, and goods to ministries and charities around the world.

9. There are 1,108 religious radio stations and 65 religious television stations in the United States.

10. Religious television is simply entertainment.

11. The television evangelists have allowed television values to corrupt their message.

12. Politically oriented television evangelists speak to far larger audiences than Martin Luther King Jr. did when he was the leader of the civil rights movement.

13. The savage disputes among television evangelists result from the fact that they have no authority or certainty to which they can appeal.

14. Fundamentalists have a way of turning victories into defeats and vice versa.

15. Pat Robertson's "Operation Suffering" has provided medical examinations for the homeless, sent food and clothing to suffering Christians in Poland, and rehabilitated villages in South Lebanon.

16. Millions of sinners each week find Jesus through the ministry of the television evangelists.

17. Where there is no theology there is no religion.

18. Most television evangelists have no official affiliation with a larger religious body.

19. The television evangelists play a critical role in the continued growth of the New Christian Right.

Periodical Bibliography

The following articles have been selected to supplement the diverse views presented in this chapter.

Christianity Today	"The Great Transmission: Can Christianity Survive a 19-Inch (Diagonal-Measure) Gospel?" March 18, 1988.
William F. Fore	"The Church and Communication in the Technological Era," *The Christian Century*, September 24, 1986.
David R. Gergen	"On Christian Understanding," *U.S. News & World Report*, April 6, 1987.
Phillip E. Hammond	"For Many, PTL Stands for Truth, Beauty, Not Scandal," *Los Angeles Times*, June 4, 1987.
Barbara Grizzuti Harrison	"TV Evangelists: What a Heavenly Mess," *Mademoiselle*, November 1987.
McKendree R. Langley	"Televangelism's Crisis, Public Witness's Future," *Eternity*, June 1987.
Colman McCarthy	"Praise the Lord, and Pass the Loot," *Los Angeles Times*, March 29, 1987.
William B. Michaels	"Oh, to Be Rid of TV Evangelists," *The New York Times*, April 2, 1987.
Richard N. Ostling	"Enterprising Evangelism," *Time*, August 3, 1987.
Sanford Ragins	"When Stones Break: The Flaws in Clergymen Are Within Us All," *Los Angeles Times*, June 4, 1988.
Beth Spring	"A Study Finds Little Evidence that Religious TV Hurts Local Churches," *Christianity Today*, May 18, 1984.
Thomas H. Stahel	"War of the Evangelists: Unfunny Reflections," *America*, April 11, 1987.
Cal Thomas	"Repent, Ye Sinners in Thy Rich Pulpits!" *Los Angeles Times*, March 25, 1987.
Nicholas von Hoffman	"Jackleg Preachers," *The Nation*, March 5, 1988.
Kenneth L. Woodward	"What Profits a Preacher?" *Newsweek*, May 4, 1987.

What Is the Future of Religion in America?

Chapter Preface

Religion has not been exempt from the many changes sweeping American society in recent years. For example, many established Protestant denominations have experienced slow growth or decline in membership. At the same time, fundamentalist and pentecostal churches have increased rapidly.

Conservative Christians have gained prominence in business, education, and government as they continue to establish schools, universities, television stations, periodicals, and political organizations. Coinciding with this is the growing popularity of religions from outside the Judeo-Christian tradition, such as Buddhism and Islam. The New Age movement, another non-traditional religion, has become a recognized phenomenon in many parts of America.

What do these changes tell us about the state of religion in America? The authors in this chapter debate such issues as whether religion will continue to be important in the future, whether traditional Judeo-Christian religions will remain the most prevalent, and what impact the New Age movement will have in America's future.

"Religious faith in both the U.S. and the world as a whole will continue to decline indefinitely."

Religious Faith Will Decline

Burnham P. Beckwith

Burnham P. Beckwith is a futurist and the author of several books, including *The Decline of U.S. Religious Faith*, from which this viewpoint is excerpted. According to Beckwith, religious faith has been in decline for several centuries and will continue to decline as social progress and scientific advances make religion unnecessary.

As you read, consider the following questions:

1. What statistics does the author cite to prove that religious faith is declining?
2. According to Beckwith, how will increased education contribute to a decline in religion?
3. Are there any trends not listed by Beckwith that might contribute to the decline of religious belief? Are there any trends which might counterbalance this decline? What might Beckwith's argument be against such trends?

Burnham P. Beckwith, *The Decline of US Religious Faith: 1912-1984 and the Effects of Education and Intelligence on Such Faith.* Palo Alto, CA: B.P. Beckwith, 1985. Reprinted with permission of the author.

All scientific knowledge makes possible more or less reliable prediction of future events. A scientific hypothesis cannot be verified or disproven unless it implies a verifiable prediction. Therefore, if the conclusions based upon the data reviewed in this [viewpoint] are true, they must imply certain predictions about the future of U.S. religious faith.

In 1794 the Marquis de Condorcet (1743-94), the first and the greatest futurist, confidently predicted that the continued growth of knowledge and education would result in a long and continuous decline in religious faith. "The time will therefore come when the sun will shine only on free men who know no other master but their reason, when . . . priests . . . will exist only in works of history and on the stage. . . ."

Fortunately for his reputation as a futurist, he did not predict how soon this result would occur. In essence, he merely predicted a long-continued decline in religious faith. And this prediction has been fully verified to date. In 1794 the percent of the French who believed in life after death was probably over 95%. By 1975 it had fallen to 39%. And the religious editor of *Newsweek*, reported in 1977 that, "according to a recent public opinion poll, fully 30% of all French citizens between 15 and 30 profess no religious belief at all." D.B. Barrett estimates that the percent of the world population which is "non-religious and atheist rose from 0.2% in 1900 to 20.8% in 1980."

Religious Faith Will Decline

The most important general prediction which is supported by the data is that religious faith in both the U.S. and the world as a whole will continue to decline indefinitely, i.e., as far as we can see into the future. My chief general reason for making this prediction is that religious faith has long been declining, and that the same factors which caused the long past decline will continue to operate indefinitely in the future. I shall now list, and then discuss, the chief of these factors, roughly in the order of their importance. They are:

1. The growth of knowledge
2. The growth of formal education
3. The growth of informal education
4. The growth in the influence of very intelligent persons
5. The growth of freedom of expression
6. Economic progress
7. The improvement of health care
8. Progress in social reform
9. The rise of logical positivism or scientism

I shall now explain each of the causal factors.

1. The growth of knowledge has long tended to weaken religious faith. For instance, acceptance both of the idea that the earth is

Eric. Reprinted with permission from the *American Atheist*.

not the center of the universe and of the theory that human beings have evolved from lower animals caused many people to abandon some or all religious beliefs. Scientific knowledge is certain to continue to grow, and will enable men to explain and/or control ever more events without relying on supernatural beings or forces.

2. The continued growth and improvement of formal education will indefinitely increase the average person's understanding of both the old and the new scientific knowledge that enables people to solve their personal and social problems without believing in and relying upon supernatural spirits and help. In the absence of widespread education, knowledge has relatively little effect on the belief of the masses.

Even without any further growth of education, the past education of parents and future parents will continue to reduce the religious faith of their children, through home influence, for at least one more generation, and probably longer. Several studies revealed that college students whose parents had been to college were less religious than their fellow students. Future research will confirm this conclusion, and also will probably reveal that grandchildren are affected by the formal education of their grandparents.

3. Informal education is largely the result of reading books and periodicals, listening to the radio, and watching TV programs. There has been a vast and continuous growth of such education for many decades, and such education is likely to continue to grow and improve indefinitely. It probably has much the same effect as formal education.

Intelligence vs. Religion

4. The more intelligent people are, the less religious they are. It is highly unlikely that the average native intelligence of any large population will change significantly in the next 100 years. It may see, therefore, that the negative correlation between such intelligence and religious faith will not directly affect future trends in religious faith. However, there will probably be important indirect effects. All of our major institutions of education and information—schools, press, TV. etc.—are dominated by persons of superior intelligence, who have great influence on what is taught, published, and broadcast. Moreover, in every field of human behavior and thought there is a tendency for the less intelligent and successful to imitate the more intelligent and successful. Hence, it is likely that the less intelligent will increasingly accept the religious opinions of the more intelligent, i.e., will become less religious in faith. This trend should occur even among the most intelligent.

The continuing development of ever more efficient methods of selecting intelligent intellectual leaders in our universities, press, and other media, and the constant improvement of media technologies, will steadily increase the already strong influence of the most intelligent people over social and intellectual trends in all countries. Moreover, the continued growth of spontaneous selective eugenic breeding (when gifted students marry each other), especially in elite universities, will steadily increase the proportion of very highly intelligent persons in the U.S. population, which will increase the intellectual influence of such people, who are the least religious of all.

5. Freedom of expression for highly intelligent dissenters will continue to increase. Historically speaking, it is only a short time ago that outspoken religious liberals, dissenters, agnostics, and atheists—who were probably on average very superior in both education and intelligence—were arrested, imprisoned, tortured, and hanged or burned at the stake. Such measures were long effective in slowing the decline of religious faith. They are still used in some Catholic and Moslem countries.

There is still much room for further increase in freedom of expression. The National Opinion Research Center has conducted polls which have repeatedly and consistently revealed that most

Americans still believe that atheists should not be allowed to teach in U.S. schools, and that a very large minority of Americans believe atheists should not be allowed to speak in public.

A Better Life on Earth

6. Until recently the great majority of people in every country lived in poverty, serfdom, or slavery, and had little hope for any great improvement in their economic lot. The industrial revolution and the continued advance of technology has vastly improved the economic and political condition of the common man in all advanced countries, precisely those countries in which the decline of religious faith has gone the farthest. . . . If nuclear wars can be avoided or reasonably limited, such economic progress is almost certain to continue. It will enable more and more people to become educated, and will persuade them to rely ever more confidently on their own personal and social efforts to improve their lot. As a result, they will feel less and less need to believe in, and rely upon, supernatural aid and support. Hope for a better life on earth will continue to replace hope for a better life in heaven.

Religious Decline in California

Most progressive social trends have appeared earlier and/or gone further in California than in most other states. It is therefore significant that a 1983 opinion poll in the San Francisco Bay area (population 4.5 million) revealed that only 41% of the nearly 700 respondents classified themselves as Christians, that 19% called themselves nonreligious humanists, and that 12% called themselves atheists or agnostics. The only other large groups, "mystics and spiritualists" (22%), included many persons who believe only in some impersonal force or spirit. It will take many decades for the rest of the U.S. to achieve such secularization levels, but this result seems highly probable because it has already been achieved in this California area.

Burnham P. Beckwith, *The Decline of US Religious Faith*, 1985.

---

7. Religion arose and flourished in ages when wars, famines, and plagues repeatedly decimated the population, and doctors could do little or nothing to cure the sick or heal the wounded. In such conditions, men find it easy to believe that magic, sacrifice, prayer, worship, and religious faith can heal the sick. The vast recent improvement in scientific health care has greatly reduced illness and death rates, and thereby weakened the temptation to rely on prayer and religious healing. Further medical progress will continue to produce this effect indefinitely.

8. The past century has been an era of continuous political and

social reform in all advanced countries, and such reform will continue indefinitely. Every sound social reform, like the adoption of social insurance, makes life healthier, happier, and more economically secure for millions of people. All such progress reduces the imagined need to appeal to supernatural beings for aid and emotional support.

9. In recent decades English-speaking philosophers and students of scientific method have elaborated new theories of knowledge—analytic philosophy, logical or semantic analysis, operationalism, logical positivism, etc.—which have made it much easier to refute or discredit religious theories and dogmas. The continued improvement and spread of these positivist theories will continue indefinitely to weaken religious faith everywhere.

"The vision of a religionless future is but illusion."

Religious Faith Will Not Decline

Rodney Stark and William Sims Bainbridge

Rodney Stark is professor of sociology at the University of Washington. William Sims Bainbridge is professor of sociology at Harvard University. They are the authors of *The Future of Religion*, from which the following viewpoint is excerpted. According to these authors, religious belief has persisted. Stark and Bainbridge assert that particular religions such as Christianity, Buddhism, and Islam may decline, but that new religions will take their place because human beings will always believe in some power greater than themselves.

As you read, consider the following questions:

1. What statistics do the authors cite to prove that religious faith is not declining?
2. According to Stark and Bainbridge, how does secularization help, rather than hinder, religious belief?
3. Why have social scientists misread the future of religion, according to the authors?

Rodney Stark and William Sims Bainbridge, *The Future of Religion: Secularization, Revival and Cult Formation*. Berkeley: University of California Press, 1985. © 1985 The Regents of the University of California.

At least since the Enlightenment, most Western intellectuals have anticipated the death of religion as eagerly as ancient Israel awaited the messiah. Social scientists have particularly excelled in predicting the impending triumph of reason over "superstition." The most illustrious figures in sociology, anthropology, and psychology have unanimously expressed confidence that their children, or surely their grandchildren, would live to see the dawn of a new era in which, to paraphrase Freud, the infantile illusions of religion would be outgrown.

But, as one generation has followed another, religion has persisted. A third of Americans claim they are "born again" Christians, and 90 percent pray regularly. During the nationwide strikes in Poland, the workers did not raise the red flag, but the blue banner of Our Lady. The Soviet press angrily admits that 70 years of intensive education in atheism and severe repression of religion are a resounding failure. Nevertheless, most intellectuals remain confident that religion lives on borrowed time, and every sign of weakness in major religious organizations is diagnosed as terminal. All contrary indications, be they revivals of conventional religion or a lush growth of new religions, are dismissed as superficial. Fashionable opinion holds the trend toward secularism to be rapid and inevitable.

The argument developed in this [viewpoint] is very unfashionable. We think the vision of a religionless future is but illusion. We acknowledge that secularization is a major trend in modern times, but argue that this is not a modern development and does not presage the demise of religion. Rather, as we attempt to demonstrate, secularization is a process found in all religious economies; it is something that is always going on in all societies. While secularization progresses in some parts of a society, a countervailing intensification of religion goes on in other parts. Sometimes the pace of secularization speeds or slows, but the dominant religious organizations in any society are always becoming progressively more worldly, which is to say, more secularized. The result of this trend has never been the end of religion, but merely a shift in fortunes among religions as faiths that have become too worldly are supplanted by more vigorous and less worldly religions.

Revival and Religious Innovation

Secularization is only one of three fundamental and interrelated processes that constantly occur in all religious economies. The process of secularization is self-limiting and generates two countervailing processes. One of these is *revival*. Religious organizations that are eroded by secularization abandon a substantial market demand for less worldly religion, a demand that produces breakaway sect movements. Thus, out of secularization is born revival as protest groups form to restore vigorous otherworldliness to a conventional faith.

Secularization also stimulates *religious innovation*. Not only do worldly churches prompt new religious groups, which seek to revive faith, but secularization also prompts the formation of new religious traditions. New religions constantly appear in societies. Whether they make any headway depends on the vigor of conventional religious organizations. When new faiths that are better adapted to current market demand spring up, older faiths are eclipsed. Thus did Christianity, Islam, Buddhism, and the other great world faiths wrest dominant market positions from older faiths.

A Vital Role

Religion continues to play a vital role in American life. In the 1960's, there were signs of a declining influence of religion and an expectation that America would become a secular society. However, religion seems to be very much alive. Harvey Cox, who wrote *The Secular City* in the 1960's, revised his views in *Religion in the Secular City*, written in the 1980's. Whereas, according to the Gallup Poll, 75% of the American people thought in 1970 that religion was losing influence, only 46% were of that opinion in 1980.

Paul Bock, *USA Today*, July 1986.

In the beginning, all religions are obscure, tiny, deviant cult movements. Caught at the right moment, Jesus would have been found leading a handful of ragtag followers in a remote corner of the mighty Roman Empire. How laughable it would have seemed to Roman intellectuals that this obscure cult could pose a threat to the great pagan temples. In similar fashion, Western intellectuals scorn contemporary cults. Yet, if major new faiths are aborning, they will not be found by consulting the directory of the National Council of Churches. Rather, they will be found in lists of obscure cult movements. Thus, to assess the future of religion, one must always pay close attention to the fringes of religious economies.

Misreading the Future of Religion

Social scientists have misread the future of religion, not only because they so fervently desire religion to disappear, but also because they have failed to recognize the dynamic character of religious economies. To focus only on secularization is to fail to see how this process is part of a much larger and reciprocal structure. Having erroneously equated religion with a particular set of religious organizations, Western intellectuals have misread the secularization of these groups as the doom of religion in general. But it is foolish to look only at sunsets and never observe the dawn: The history of religion is not only a pattern of decline; it is equally a portrait of birth and growth. We argue that the sources of religion are shifting constantly in societies but that the amount of religion remains relatively constant. . . .

Rewards and Costs

We begin with a mundane axiom about human behavior: *Humans seek what they perceive to be rewards and try to avoid what they perceive to be costs.* In various forms, this is one of the oldest and still most central propositions about human behavior. It is the starting point for micro-economics, learning psychology, and sociological theories. However, when we inspect more closely this human tendency to seek rewards, we see two important points:

1. In all societies, many rewards are scarce and unequally distributed. Substantial proportions of any population have far less of some rewards than they would like to have and less of these rewards than some other people actually possess. Scarcity, both absolute and relative, is a social universal.

2. Some intensely desired rewards seem not to be available at all. For example, no one can demonstrate whether there is life after death, but everyone can see that immortality cannot be gained in the here and now, in the natural world available to our senses. But the simple unavailability of the reward of eternal life has not caused people to cease wanting it. To the contrary, it is probably the single most urgent human desire.

Compensators

Noting the strong desires for rewards that are available to many, as well as those that seem not to be directly available to anyone, we can recognize another characteristic human action: the creation and exchange of *compensators*. People may experience rewards, but they can only have faith in compensators. *A compensator is the belief that a reward will be obtained in the distant future or in some other context which cannot be immediately verified.*

We do not use the word *compensator* in any pejorative sense. By it we simply mean to recognize that, when highly desired rewards seem unavailable through direct means, persons tend to develop explanations about how they can gain this reward later or elsewhere. Compensators are a form of IOU. They promise that, in return for value surrendered now, the desired rewards will be obtained eventually. Often people must make regular payments to keep a compensator valid, which makes it possible to bind them to long-term involvement in an organization that serves as a source of compensators. Put another way, humans will often exchange rewards of considerable value over a long period of time in return for compensators in the hope that a reward of immense value will be forthcoming in return. . . .

When we examine human desires, we see that people often seek rewards of such magnitude and apparent unavailability that *only by assuming the existence of an active supernatural can credible compensators be created.* For example, since time immemorial, humans have desired to know the meaning of existence. Why are we here? What is the purpose of life? Where will it all end? Moreover, people have not just wanted answers to these questions; they have desired particular kinds of answers—that life have meaning. But for life to have a great design, for there to be intention behind history, one must posit the existence of a designer or intender of such power, duration, and scale as to be outside or beyond the natural world of our senses. Similarly, for humans to survive death, it is, at least thus far in history, necessary to posit supernatural agencies. Indeed, to accept that earthly suffering gains meaning as prelude to everlasting glory is to embrace the supernatural. Archeological evidence that our rude Neanderthal ancestors buried their dead with elaborate ceremony and with food and possessions to be used in the next world suggests that such concerns typify humans far back into prehistory.

Religion Will Grow

As people find no enduring grounds for meaning in their secularistic philosophies and no eschatology that provides any ultimate hope, they will turn to other sources. Many will look to the cults, and many more to Eastern religions, largely due to the influx of Asians in America. Outreach-minded Protestant denominations and parachurch agencies will experience solid growth as they meet the needs of a searching public.

American Catholicism will also grow for the same reason: it offers an alternative to an ultimately bankrupt secularism.

Kenneth S. Kantzer, *Christianity Today*, October 17, 1986.

Although in our more technical essays we are able to derive this line of reasoning from our theory, surely the point can stand on its own merit: Some common human desires are so beyond direct, this-worldly satisfaction that only the gods can provide them. This simple point has profound implications.

So long as humans intensely seek certain rewards of great magnitude that remain unavailable through direct actions, they will be able to obtain credible compensators only from sources predicated on the supernatural. In this market, no purely naturalistic ideologies can compete. Systems of thought that reject the supernatural lack all means to credibly promise such rewards as eternal life in any fashion. Similarly, naturalistic philosophies can argue that statements such as "What is the meaning of life?" or "What is the purpose of the universe?" are meaningless utterances. But they cannot provide answers to these questions in the terms in which they are asked. . . .

Movements lacking supernatural assumptions cannot successfully compete, over the long run, in generating mass commitment when confronted by movements that accept the supernatural. To be more specific: So long as humans persist in desires not directly satisfiable, the eventual fate of "demythologized" religious organizations is sealed. Or one can conclude that, although modern-day Communism is in conflict with religion, it is not itself a religion and remains permanently vulnerable to religious competitors, especially once Communist regimes come to power. To sum up, our analysis suggests that not only is the notion of a non-supernatural or naturalistic religion a logical contradiction, but in fact efforts to create such "religions" will fail for want of that vital resource that always has been the sine qua non of religions: the gods.

> *"Broader than reform, deeper than revolution,*
> *this benign conspiracy for a new human*
> *agenda has triggered the most rapid cultural*
> *realignment in history."*

The New Age Movement
Will Transform America

Marilyn Ferguson

In recent years the phrase "New Age" has been used to describe a variety of nontraditional beliefs, including reincarnation, channeling, astrology, and the practice of Eastern religions. The following viewpoint is taken from *The Aquarian Conspiracy*, which has been called the handbook of the New Age by *USA Today*. Author Marilyn Ferguson, publisher of *Brain/Mind Bulletin*, argues that traditional religions such as Christianity are being abandoned or transformed. She concludes the New Age movement will have a significant impact on America.

As you read, consider the following questions:

1. Why are Americans moving away from traditional religions, according to the author?
2. How does Ferguson differentiate the "Aquarian Conspiracy" from past movements for social change?

Marilyn Ferguson, *The Aquarian Conspiracy*. Copyright © 1980, Jeremy P. Tarcher, Inc., Los Angeles. Reprinted with permission.

A leaderless but powerful network is working to bring about radical change in the United States. Its members have broken with certain key elements of Western thought, and they may even have broken continuity with history.

This network is the Aquarian Conspiracy. It is a conspiracy without a political doctrine. Without a manifesto. With conspirators who seek power only to disperse it, and whose strategies are pragmatic, even scientific, but whose perspective sounds so mystical that they hesitate to discuss it. Activists asking different kinds of questions, challenging the establishment from within.

Broader than reform, deeper than revolution, this benign conspiracy for a new human agenda has triggered the most rapid cultural realignment in history. The great shuddering, irrevocable shift overtaking us is not a new political, religious, or philosophical system. It is a new mind—the ascendance of a startling worldview that gathers into its framework breakthrough science and insights from earliest recorded thought. . . .

A Turning Point

The crises of our time, it becomes increasingly clear, are the necessary impetus for the revolution now under way. And once we understand nature's transformative powers, we see that it is our powerful ally, not a force to be feared or subdued. *Our pathology is our opportunity.*

In every age, said scientist-philosopher Pierre Teilhard de Chardin, man has proclaimed himself at a turning point in history. "And to a certain extent, as he is advancing on a rising spiral, he has not been wrong. But there are moments when this impression of transformation becomes accentuated and is thus particularly justified."

Teilhard prophesied the phenomenon central to this [viewpoint]: a conspiracy of men and women whose new perspective would trigger a critical contagion of change. . . .

The future, Teilhard said, is in the hands of those who can give tomorrow's generations valid reasons to live and hope. The message of the Aquarian Conspiracy is that there is ripeness for a Yes. . . .

The New Age and Religion

The spiritual quest begins, for most people, as a search for meaning. At first this may be only a restless desire for something more. The prescient Alexis de Tocqueville remarked on the coexistence in America of a strong religious spirit and material ambition. But perhaps, he said, this was a precarious balance. "If ever the faculties of the great majority of mankind were exclusively bent upon the pursuit of material objects, it might be anticipated that an amazing reaction would take place in the souls of some. I should be surprised if mysticism did not soon make some advance among people solely engaged in promoting its own worldly welfare."

Indeed, our vigorous appetite for the material has led us to satiation. Zbigniew Brzezinski, chairman of the United States Security Council, spoke of an "increasing yearning for something spiritual" in advanced Western societies where materialism has proven unsatisfying. People are discovering, he said, that 5 percent per annum more goods is not the definition of happiness. *Traditional* religion, he conceded, does not provide a substitute:

> This is why there is a search for personal religion, for direct connection with the spiritual. . . . Ultimately, every human being, once he reaches the stage of self-consciousness, wants to feel that there is some inner and deeper meaning to his existence than just being and consuming, and once he begins to feel that way, he wants his social organization to correspond to that feeling. . . . This is happening on a world scale.

A Gallup poll released in February 1978 reported that ten million Americans were engaged in some aspect of Eastern religion, nine million in spiritual healing. Those involved in Eastern religions tended to be younger adults, college-educated, living on either of the two coasts, about equally men and women, Catholic and Protestant. "Although [they] are not as likely to be churchgoers. . . they are just as likely to say that their religious beliefs are 'very important' in their lives."

Creating One's Paths

I believe my intense search for self was motivated by the intuitive certainty that in myself lay the reflections of all there was. That all my curiosities regarding the outside world were in truth curiosities I had about myself. If I could know me, I could know the universe. . . .

When I began to see the world with karmic consciousness, the knowledge that we all create our own paths of our own free will made me recognize the cosmic justice in everything. I understood that there was a purposeful good in all occurrences if I allowed them to provide a path of experience and understanding.

Shirley MacLaine, *Dancing in the Light*, 1985.

Spiritual experience moved beyond the borders of the establishment so quietly that only the polltakers have measured the change. Addressing fellow scholars and historians in the field of religion, Jacob Needleman remarked ironically in 1977 that these ideas and practices are now—"without our prior permission, so to speak—entering the real lives of real people, causing trouble, having real effects on marriages, careers, politics, goals, friendships."

But the spiritual shift is not readily uncovered by sociological methods. It's an individual phenomenon, William McCready of National Opinion Research said. "If you try to gauge it by membership in groups, you won't see it. Because they aren't much for joining, the people involved in this inner search are hard to pin down statistically.". . .

Move Away from Traditional Religion

Needleman said Westerners were moving away from the form and trappings of Judaism and Christianity, "not because they had stopped searching for transcendental answers to the fundamental questions of human life but because that search has now intensified beyond measure." They were looking to Eastern traditions to see what they might offer "our threatened society and our tormented religions.". . .

Formal religion in the West has been shaken to its roots by defections, dissent, rebellions, loss of influence, diminishing financial support. Unlike the schools, churches are not mandated by law and their bureaucracies are not directly tax supported; they cannot pass bond issues or raise property taxes. If they cannot find new roles in a rapidly changing society, they may go the way of the railroads—without Amtrak. . . .

That most authoritarian of religious institutions, the Catholic church, has suffered what historian John Tracy Ellis called "a shattering of its fixity," a trauma apparent in the new variety of doctrine and discipline among American Catholics. "No one group has full authority nor the ability to impose it on other groups," Ellis said. The American church is "shaken and uncertain in an anxious, uncertain time." Laypeople are urging reforms, evangelizing and participating in pentecostal and charismatic movements; by 1979 one-half million Catholics were estimated to have become charismatics, speaking in tongues and engaging in healing practices. The number of nuns and priests declined dramatically during the seventies, theologians were dissenting from papal authority, parochial school populations were declining. Similar rebellions have been taking place in nearly every organized religious body in the country. . . .

Threat to Judeo-Christian Tradition

Cultural awakenings, as historian William McLoughlin noted, are preceded by a spiritual crisis, a change in the way human beings see themselves in relationship to each other and to the divine. During "great awakenings" there is a shift from a religion mediated by authorities to one of direct spiritual experience. Not unexpectedly, some religious groups see the emergent spiritual tradition as a fearful threat to the Judeo-Christian tradition. The fundamental Berkeley Christian Coalition, sponsor of the Spiritual Counterfeits Project [SCP], devoted its August 1978 journal to this threat:

> At this point in Western cultural history, it is an understate-
> ment to say that Eastern metaphysics and the New Con-
> sciousness have gained a significant following in our society. Just
> ten years ago the funky drug-based spirituality of the hippie and
> the mysticism of the Western yogi were restricted to the counter-
> culture. Today, both have found their way into the mainstream
> of our cultural mentality. Science, the health professions, and
> the arts, not to mention psychology and religion, are all engaged
> in a fundamental reconstruction of their basic premises.

The coalition blames the rise of New Age spirituality on the timid-
ity of the Christian church in America:

> Eastern metaphysics and the New Consciousness, on the other
> hand, derive their popularity in part from the fact that they
> directly challenge the oppressive assumptions of technocratic
> Western mentality. They have not been afraid to charge our ra-
> tionalist, materialist, mercantile culture with depleting the qual-
> ity of human life. . . . Leaders of these movements have stepped
> into the vacancy created by the church's prophetic silence.
> They call plastic plastic and poison poison in a society whose
> economy is built on convincing people that both are good for
> them. Moreover the followers . . . are hard at work developing
> workable alternatives to the death-dealing culture they condemn.

The idea of a God within was particularly disturbing: The
religious point of view embodied in the holistic health movement,
said the coalition, "is an integral part of the mystical worldview
that is making a coordinated thrust into every aspect of our
cultural consciousness. . . . It is not a fad, it will not go away, and
it is fundamentally hostile to Biblical Christianity."

A Significant Alternative

As techniques derived from the New Age movement become more
widely accepted, more Americans throughout the country are likely
to be affected, sometimes unknowingly, by transformational values.
The potential appeal of New Age philosophy cannot be
underestimated, for it speaks to genuine concerns about the nature
of God and man that many Americans apparently feel are inade-
quately addressed by more orthodox faiths. "The New Age movement has already become a significant alternative to the Judeo-
Christian tradition," says Carl Raschke of the Institute for the
Humanities.

Fergus M. Bordewich, *The New York Times Magazine*, May 1, 1988.

Ironically, every organized religion has been based on the claims
of direct experience of one or more persons, whose revelations
are then handed down as articles of faith. Those who want direct

knowledge, the mystics, have always been treated more or less as heretics, whether they were the medieval mystics within Christianity, the Sufis within the borders of Islam, or the Kabbalists within Judaism.

Now the heretics are gaining ground, doctrine is losing its authority, and knowing is superseding belief. . . .

Social Transformations

Historically, movements for social change have all operated in much the same way. A paternal leadership has convinced people of the need for change, then recruited them for specific tasks, telling them what to do and when to do it. The new social movements operate on a different assumption of human potential: the belief that individuals, once they are deeply convinced of a need for change, can generate solutions from their own commitment and creativity. The larger movement inspires them, it supports their efforts and gives them information, but its structure cannot direct or contain their efforts.

The power of individuals to generate broad social change is the basis for the Hunger Project, an international charitable organization launched by est founder Werner Erhard in 1977 and headquartered in San Francisco. The Hunger Project's goal is to speed up a solution to the world hunger problem by acting as a *catalyst*. It is an intense, sophisticated large-scale effort to hurry a paradigm shift—to "make an idea's time come," as the project's organizers put it. The successes of the project and the ways in which it has been misunderstood are instructive.

The Hunger Project

The Hunger Project assumes that solutions do not reside in new programs or more programs. According to the best-informed authorities and agencies, the expertise to end hunger within two decades *already exists*. Hunger persists because of the old-paradigm assumption that it is not possible to feed the world's population.

In less than two years, *seven hundred fifty thousand* individuals in dozens of countries have pledged their personal commitment to help end world hunger by 1997; enrollment in the Hunger Project is increasing at the rate of more than sixty thousand per month. Three million dollars has been raised explicitly to increase public awareness of the tragic proportions of the problem, the available solutions, and the ways in which individuals and groups can accelerate an end to hunger and starvation. . . .

To create a sense of urgency, the project draws on the power of the symbol and the metaphor, describing the toll of starvation as "a Hiroshima every three days." When a Hunger Project relay of more than one thousand runners carried a baton from Maine to the White House, they did not ask the government to solve the problem. Rather, their message spoke of their own commitment to help end hunger and starvation. . . .

So long as we thought we couldn't do anything about the world's starving millions, most of us tried not to think about them; yet that denial has had its price. The Hunger Project emphasizes a key principle of transformation—the need to confront painful knowledge:

> We have numbed ourselves so that we do not feel the pain. We have to be asleep in order to protect ourselves from the horror of knowing that twenty-eight people, most of them young children, are dying this very minute—twenty-eight people no different from you or me or our children, except that we have food and they do not.
>
> We have closed down our consciousness and aliveness to a level where it doesn't bother us. So if you wonder if it costs us anything to allow millions to starve, it does. *It costs us our aliveness. . . .*

A key point is made to those who sign up: A world in which hunger has ended will be not merely different or better but *transformed*. And those who take part will be transformed by their own participation—by telling friends, family, and co-workers of their own commitment, even if they feel self-concious, and by searching for answers.

A New Age

We stand on the brink of a new age, Lewis Mumford said, the age of an open world, a time of renewal when a fresh release of spiritual energy in the world culture may unleash new possibilities. "The sum of all our days is just our beginning."

Seen with new eyes, our lives can be transformed from accidents into adventures. We can transcend the old conditioning, the dirt-poor expectations. We have new ways to be born, humane and symbolic ways to die, different ways to be rich, communities to support us in our myriad journeys, new ways to be human and to discover what we are to each other. After our tragic wars, alienation, and the bruising of the planet, perhaps this is the answer Wallace Stevens meant—after the final No, the Yes on which the future of the world depends.

Marilyn Ferguson, *The Aquarian Conspiracy*, 1980.

The Aquarian Conspiracy is also working to ease hunger—for meaning, connection, completion. And each of us is "the whole project," the nucleus of a critical mass, a steward of the world's transformation.

In this century we have seen into the heart of the atom. We transformed it—and history—forever. But we have also seen into the heart of the heart. We know the necessary conditions for the changing of minds. Now that we see the deep pathology of our past, we can make new patterns, new paradigms. "The sum of all our days is just our beginning. . . ."

Transformation is no longer lightning but electricity. We have captured a force more powerful than the atom, a worthy keeper of all our other powers.

We find our individual freedom, by choosing not a destination but a direction. You do not choose the transformative journey because you know where it will take you but because it is the only journey that makes sense. . . .

In a wider state of consciousness one can sometimes vividly re-experience a past trauma and, in retrospect and with imagination, respond to it differently. By thus touching the source of old fears, we can exorcise them. We are not haunted so much by events as by our beliefs about them, the crippling self-image we take with us. We can transform the present and future by reawakening the powerful past, with its recurrent message of defeat. We can face the crossroad again. We can re-choose.

In a similar spirit, we can respond differently to the tragedies of modern history. Our past is not our potential. In any hour, with all the stubborn teachers and healers of history who called us to our best selves, we can liberate the future. One by one, we can re-choose—to awaken. To leave the prison of our conditioning, to love, to turn homeward. To conspire with and for each other.

"[New Agers] talk about bringing in a new era for the world, when war and hunger don't exist . . . but never make the transition from words to deeds."

The New Age Movement Will Not Transform America

Richard Blow

Richard Blow is a reporter for *The New Republic*. In the following viewpoint, he argues that the New Age movement is the new religion of the baby boom generation. Followers, he argues, seek spiritual satisfaction with little personal sacrifice. Blow states the movement will have little social impact because the focus of New Age adherents is self-fulfillment, not helping others.

As you read, consider the following questions:

1. What are the historical roots of the New Age movement, according to the author?
2. In what respects does Blow believe the New Age movement can be called a religion?
3. According to Blow, what is wrong with the Hunger Project? How does he argue that the project is typical of the New Age movement?

Richard Blow, "Moronic Convergence," *The New Republic*, January 23, 1988. Reprinted by permission of THE NEW REPUBLIC, © 1988, The New Republic, Inc.

Shirley MacLaine must be in seventh heaven. In 1983, when she published *Out on a Limb*, the book that detailed her faith in reincarnation, she worried that people would think she was crazy. Some did, but millions bought the book. MacLaine has since appeared in the television dramatization of *Out on a Limb*, written two more reminiscences, and has more in the works.

Since 1983 MacLaine has shepherded into the American mainstream a host of ideas and practices known as the New Age movement. Gallup Polls show that from 20 percent to 35 percent of the American public believe they have had a past-life experience. And according to a study by SRI International, a California-based social research center, some five percent to ten percent of the population have adopted other New Age beliefs. One is "channeling," a kind of psychic talk show in which human mediums call forth the voices of long-dead spirits. Another involves crystals, which are quartz rocks. Thousands of people believe that crystals have the power to cure diseases and transmit human thoughts. But perhaps the best-known New Age performance was summer [1987's] Harmonic Convergence, during which thousands gathered at "pressure points" around the world (Niagara Falls, Central Park), hugged, held hands, and chanted, united in the conviction that this would usher in a new era of world harmony.

Not Just a Fad

Many skeptics have written off the New Age as just another California fad. It's true that until recently the "movement" had no clear agenda, no well-known spokesperson, no momentum. That's changing. There's a leader now, in MacLaine. There will be a church of sorts: MacLaine is planning to build a spiritual center in Colorado with some of her New Age profits. There are New Age think tanks such as Palo Alto's Creative Initiative Foundation. Increasingly, too, New Agers are getting aggressive about conversion, renting out theaters and concert halls in cities across the country for mass meetings. And the people who attend these meetings aren't the kind who'd follow Jim Jones to Guyana. They're prosperous, well-educated, otherwise thoughtful individuals. New Age may have started on the fringes of society, but it's not just for hippies anymore.

The New Age movement (no one really knows when the term was first used) began in California in the 1960s with the spread of Eastern philosophy, particularly Buddhist and Hindu, among a small number of mostly white, mostly young Americans. Skeptical about modern medicine and technology, disillusioned by the Vietnam War, the New Age pioneers experimented with alternative lifestyles that emphasized spiritual well-being over material gain. They practiced techniques such as meditation, holistic healing, and acupuncture to help them escape the apparent hostility

Evan Wilson. Reprinted with permission.

of the outer world. Later their basket of Eastern mysticism would grow to include practices such as witchcraft, astrology, and rebirthing, a process in which one is "reborn" by regressing via hypnosis to the time of one's birth.

In the 1970s New Agers turned to ideas from America's history to reinforce their search for alternatives. Although not always spelled out, the individualist and transcendentalist theories of Walt Whitman and Ralph Waldo Emerson began to appear in the New Age universe. But the '70s were a time of disillusionment, and the practitioners of New Age capitalized on those feelings. To their utopianism they added a modern twist: the idea that devoting oneself to self-improvement was personally valuable *and* socially beneficial. They dubbed their cause the "human potential movement." Social pundits dubbed them the "Me Generation." Perhaps most indicative of the era was Werner Erhard's emotionally manipulative (and immensely profitable) est program, featuring weekend seminars at which you couldn't use the bathroom until you learned to love yourself.

In 1980 Marilyn Ferguson's *The Aquarian Conspiracy* was

published, and it rapidly became the New Age bible. Ferguson argued that the world was entering a new era of harmony and peace. Ordinary people could help bring this about simply through their awareness of its inevitability. The more people were aware of the trend, the faster it would become reality. Though the book didn't offer many specifics, it helped transform the movement into more than a motley collection of rituals. It became a way of thinking applicable to any aspect of modern life: psychology, medicine, business, music, you name it. Since bringing on the New Age involved thought rather than deeds, New Agers wouldn't teach you how to do anything; they would tell you how to think about it. Attitude had become more important than action.

The bedrock of New Age thought now is the fulfillment of individual potential, with the implicit consequence of bringing the New Age closer. How fulfillment is achieved—whether through meditation, pop psychology, physical fitness, est, whatever—and what form it takes (money, power, sex) doesn't matter. What counts is the awareness that one has such potential and can exploit it. Thus *Pathways*, a New Age newspaper in Washington D.C., defines itself with this credo: "The world public has become disenchanted with both the political and financial leadership. . . . All the individuals of humanity are looking for the answer to what the little individual can do that can't be done by great nations and great enterprises." *Pathways* then encourages the "'little individual' to join together in the dynamic process of personal and social transformation."

A New Religion

If all of this makes New Age sound like a religion, that's because for many adherents it is. Like most religions, it attempts to address believers' spiritual concerns with the promise of an afterlife (or rather, another life). And it demands that its believers have faith in things that cannot be scientifically proven—channeling, for instance. But there is no God in the New Age church. Rather, god is within everyone, a universal characteristic New Agers sometimes refer to as "god-force" or "pure consciousness." Reaching the god-force within you is easy if you know how to do it, like knowing the combination to a bank vault. And if you don't know how to do it, there are plenty of New Age teachers to show you how—for a price.

The belief certainly lends weight to the idea that the individual is capable of doing anything. By recognizing that "you are God," as MacLaine says, "you can create your own reality." Thus, during the Harmonic Convergence weekend, one convert explained to a *Newsweek* reporter, "Even if the whole thing was made up, just to have thousands or millions of people coming together and envisioning the same thing has power in itself. If it's real or not is something else." MacLaine is at least consistent: she argues that if your reality isn't so great—if you're poor or unemployed—you have only yourself to blame. You have victimized yourself by not living up to your potential. If a Republican said this, he'd be attacked as cruel and selfish, rationalizing his unwillingness to sacrifice for others. When New Agers say it, they congratulate each other on their openness to new ideas and faith in individual potential.

Appeal to Laziness

In Shirley MacLaine's universe, god and evil do not exist, nor does sin. This suits a lot of lazy people just fine. It allows them to do their own thing, confident that whatever they have chosen to do, it is their karma or destiny to do. Furthermore, with Evangelicals fighting internecine wars and Catholics and many mainstream Protestants painfully trying to come to grips with issues of sexuality and political activism and new technologies, the amount of faith, hope, and charity—to say nothing of discipline and patience—necessary to sustain religious belief and religious practices, and to remain loyal to religious institutions, appears to be phenomenal. Into what many are bound to see as muddle, Shirley MacLaine steps, tying everything up in one knot: "There is a reason for everything," she says. "A plan." And all you have to do is *know* there is a plan, you don't have to do a damn thing about it; you don't have to avoid sin, reflect on the world's suffering and sins—and do something about them.

Barbara Grizzuti Harrison, *Ms.*, July/August 1987.

The New Age way is not to deny differences between people, but to deny that they matter. It's an attempt to create an egalitarian society based not on equal distribution of wealth or property, but on spiritual equality—a sort of socialism of the mind. It's an illusion. But for New Agers, even an illusion can become real if you believe in it long enough.

Hippies and Yuppies

Why do so many people find this retreat into individualism so attractive? The truly counterculture New Agers—the hippies of 20 years ago—feel that it enables them to continue to harbor the discontent with middle-class values and the political status quo that they felt during the '60s. (Although the movement does nothing to challenge those realities.) For young people, born in the '60s and '70s, New Age is a concession to Ronald Reagan's success. They believe in progressive social change, but see its 20th-century vehicles—the Democratic Party, labor unions, college campuses—as moribund or apathetic. They don't like Reagan, but don't know how to beat him, so they adopt a philosophy that never mentions him.

New Age is more than anything else the religion of the baby boom, the people aged roughly 25 to 40 who dominate the New Age world. Turned off social activism by the assassination of their heroes, by Vietnam, Watergate, and Reagan, the boomers gave up and went to law school or Wall Street. New Age thought tells them there's nothing wrong with that. For a generation that has abandoned its collective sense of purpose, the idea that individuals can accomplish anything has obvious appeal. They don't have to march in the streets to change the world. They can do that from the comfort of their own couches.

Money without guilt—it's the one thing missing in the yuppie lifestyle. New Age gives it to them. Here again New Age language sounds suspiciously like Republican social policy. Economic growth leads to personal growth, and that is always worthwhile. Even better, the pursuit of profit will also take care of social concerns like poverty, hunger, and war. In the New Age lexicon, there is no mention of sacrifice, duty, or responsibility. Those concepts are regressive, unprofitable in any sense.

There is no tension in the New Age between reaping the rewards of capitalism and the desire to help others. Profit, after all, is simply the fulfillment of potential, the byproduct of spiritual harmony. "To be a spiritual person, you should have abundance," MacLaine said in one Seattle seminar, defending her $300-per-person fee.

Big Business

Not surprisingly, New Age condones big business because New Age *is* big business. In 1986 New Agers spent $100 million on crystals and $300 million on audio and videotapes that instructed them in ways of self-fulfillment. Then there are the hundreds of books and dozens of periodicals devoted to New Age, the seminars held by channelers and hypnotists and self-help groups like "Lifespring," and perhaps most lucrative of all, the music. . . .

But New Agers proclaim that they're not just traditonal capitalists. Rather, they've merged liberal political views with the ability to turn a profit. And it's true that New Agers are anti-war, pro-environment, anti-nuke, pro-feminist. What makes them different from other liberals is their approach to the resolution of these issues. Instead of seeing them as political concerns that the Democratic Party would support, New Agers completely depoliticize them. Under the guise of non-partisan change, New Agers address issues in ways guaranteed to offend no one. They never tackle issues; they hug them. They apply New Age optimism to problems like poverty and the environment, work to change people's attitudes and increase "awareness," and ultimately do nothing but give themselves a warm feeling inside.

One example is a group called Beyond War, founded by the Creative Initiative Foundation in 1982. . . .

Beyond War's mandate comes from a 1946 statement by Albert Einstein: "The unleashed power of the atom has changed everything save our modes of thinking and we thus drift toward unparalleled catastrophe." Changing our way of thinking is Beyond War's job. Through its literature, videotapes, seminars, a newsletter, and Beyond War "gatherings" at members' homes, it suggests a three-step process: "KNOWLEDGE, DECISION, ACTION."

To complete the first phase, one must "gain knowledge about our environment" and society's choice between "global life and global death." In part two, "we must then make a decision to choose the path which leads to global life." Easy enough. In the final stage of moving to a world beyond war, individual decisions will be transformed into societal change through "ACTION." What kind of action? Building "understanding that the world is beyond war through a process that does not impose the specific steps of the solution. . . ." And so the process comes full circle. It begins with gaining knowledge and ends with passing the knowledge along to others. Beyond War wants peace—but it's so intent on making friends, that it doesn't go so far as to say how peace can be achieved. . . .

Wishing Problems Away

On one level, the notion of Harmonic Convergence is a beautiful idea, the joining together of multitudes of people, all concentrating on the very noble desire for peace and harmony. On another level, it can be quite disturbing when you realize . . . these people have given up on the real world. They are turning their backs on scientific and technological progress to help find the solution to the problems facing the world. Instead, they are merely wishing these problems away by looking for some universal energy force or enlightened beings from outer space to make the world a better place to live.

Barry Karr, quoted in *The Skeptical Inquirer*, Winter 1987-88.

The New Age take on world hunger isn't much more reassuring. That problem is handled by something called the Hunger Project. The Hunger Project was founded in the late 1970s by est's Erhard. As it states in its newsletter, "A Shift in the Wind," the project's mission is to "generate a new context in which ending hunger could show up as a real possibility, to create an environment in which individuals could perceive, think, decide, plan, and act consistent with the end of hunger."

Like Beyond War, the people with the Hunger Project don't get too specific. They admit that "the Hunger Project never intended to tell people what to do, nor to offer a step-by-step blueprint [to end the problem of hunger]." That would be an imposition, a violation of believers' personal intellectual freedom. After all, why would their ideas for ending hunger be better than anyone else's? And if that's the case, why should they have *any* ideas for ending hunger?

Instead, the Hunger Project focuses on the previously little-discussed mental avenues for ending hunger. It tries to encourage individuals to "take a stand for the end of hunger" by realizing that the "end of hunger is an idea whose time has come." The group knows that because its research led it "to the inescapable conclusion that humanity could no longer make a case for the widespread existence of hunger." Somehow, once that mental bridge is crossed, the end of hunger will be a little bit closer.

The Hunger Project claims to have "enrolled" 5.2 million people. Since enrollment means little more than making "a personal declaration to create the end of the persistence of hunger as an idea whose time has come," the number may not mean much. Still, every one of those people represents someone who might be involved with the issue in a more serious way, but isn't because the Hunger Project says he doesn't need to be. Lester Brown of the WorldWatch Institute told *Mother Jones* magazine that the Hunger Project has "probably collected more money in the name of hunger and done the least about hunger than any group I can think of." Instead, the millions that the Hunger Project raises go mostly into spreading the word according to these New Age gods.

No Results

Groups like Beyond War and the Hunger Project embody all that is bad about the New Age. Draped in the sacraments of political correctness, they and other New Agers do nothing to solve the problems they claim to care about. They talk about bringing in a new era for the world, when war and hunger don't exist and people live in harmony, but never make the transition from words to deeds. Maybe one day there will be a New Age on earth—but not if these people can help it.

Understanding Words in Context

Readers occasionally come across words which they do not recognize. And frequently, because they do not know a word or words, they will not fully understand the passage being read. Obviously, the reader can look up an unfamiliar word in a dictionary. However, by carefully examining the word in the context in which it is used, the word's meaning can often be determined. A careful reader may find clues to the meaning of the word in surrounding words, ideas, and attitudes.

Below are sentences adapted from the viewpoints in this chapter. In each excerpt, one of the words is printed in italics. Try to determine the meaning of each word by reading the excerpt. Under each excerpt you will find four definitions for the italicized word. Choose the one that is closest to your understanding of the word.

Finally, use a dictionary to see how well you have understood the words in context. It will be helpful to discuss with others the clues which helped you decide on each word's meaning.

1. Religion arose and flourished in ages when wars, famines, and plagues repeatedly *DECIMATED* the population.

   DECIMATED means:
   a) helped c) destroyed
   b) increased d) maintained

2. Young people believe in progressive social change, but see its 20th-century vehicles—the Democratic Party, labor unions, college campuses—as *MORIBUND* or apathetic.

   MORIBUND means:
   a) vigorous c) dying
   b) sentimental d) expensive

222

3. We begin with a simple *MUNDANE* fact about human behavior: Humans seek what they perceive to be awards and try to avoid what they perceive to be costs.

MUNDANE means:
a) ordinary
b) silly
c) obscure
d) complicated

4. If one believes life has a great design, one must *POSIT* the existence of a designer.

POSIT means:
a) assume
b) study
c) doubt
d) argue

5. During "great awakenings," there is a shift from a religion *MEDIATED* by authorities to one of direct spiritual experience.

MEDIATED means:
a) opposed
b) interpreted
c) strengthened
d) clarified

6. In the New Age *LEXICON*, there is no mention of sacrifice, duty, or responsibility.

LEXICON means:
a) map
b) vocabulary
c) music
d) computer

7. The crises of our time are the necessary *IMPETUS* for the revolution now beginning.

IMPETUS means:
a) impediment
b) permission
c) disaster
d) driving force

Periodical Bibliography

The following articles have been selected to supplement the diverse views presented in this chapter.

Jonathan Adolph	"What Is New Age?" *New Age Journal's 1988 Guide to New Age Living,* Winter 1988.
Robert M. Bowman Jr.	"What's New in the New Religions?" *Moody Monthly,* November 1987.
Kenneth A. Briggs	"America's Return to Prayer," *The New York Times Magazine,* November 18, 1984.
Robert J.L. Burrows	"Americans Get Religion in the New Age," *Christianity Today,* May 16, 1986.
Charles Colson	"So Much for Our 'Great Awakening,'" *Christianity Today,* May 13, 1988.
Gary K. Griswold	"Religion: An Obstacle to a Better World?" *The Humanist,* March/April 1987.
William R. Hutchison	"Past Imperfect: History and Prospect for Liberalism—1," *The Christian Century,* January 1-8, 1986.
Kenneth Kantzer	"Time To Look Ahead," *Christianity Today,* October 17, 1986.
Andrew Kimbrell	"The Coming Era of Activism: New Left Meets New Age," *Utne Reader,* March/April 1988.
Barbara King	"The New Age War Against God," *The New American,* June 20, 1988.
Martin E. Marty	"What People Seek—and Find—in Belief," *U.S. News & World Report,* December 29, 1986/January 5, 1987.
Terry Muck	"Light in the New Dark Ages," *Christianity Today,* March 4, 1988.
Maxine Negri	"Age-Old Problems of the New Age Movement," *The Humanist,* March/April 1988.
Leon J. Putnam	"A New Age Looms," *The Churchman,* January 1987.
Raymond B. Williams	"Hinduism in America," *The Christian Century,* March 11, 1987.
Kenneth L. Woodward	"From 'Mainline' to Sideline," *Newsweek,* December 22, 1986.

Organizations To Contact

The editors have compiled the following list of organizations which are concerned with the issues debated in this book. All of them have publications available for interested readers. The descriptions are derived from materials provided by the organizations.

American Atheists
PO Box 2117
Austin, TX 78768-2117
(512) 458-1244

American Atheists is an educational organization dedicated to the complete and absolute separation of state and church. It opposes religious involvement in public schools. Its purpose is to stimulate freedom of thought and inquiry concerning religious beliefs and practices. It publishes *American Atheist* magazine, numerous books, and reprints of articles through American Atheist Press.

American Humanist Association
7 Harwood Drive
PO Box 146
Amherst, NY 14226-0146
(716) 839-5080

The Associations' members are devoted to humanism as a way of life. They do not acknowledge a supernatural power. The Association opposes school prayer and government aid to religion. It favors objective teaching about religion in public schools. The Association publishes numerous brochures, books, and journals, including the bimonthly *The Humanist.*

American Jewish Committee (AJC)
Institute of Human Relations
165 E. 56th St.
New York, NY 10022
(212) 751-4000

The AJC works to enlighten and clarify public opinion on problems of Jewish concern, fight bigotry, protect human rights, and promote Jewish culture and achievement in America. The Committee is the publisher of the monthly journal *Commentary* and numerous pamphlets on church/state issues, such as *AJC in the Courts.*

American Vision
PO Box 72515
Atlanta, GA 30328
(404) 988-0555

American Vision is a Christian educational and communications organization working to build a Christian civilization. American Vision believes the Bible ought to be applied to every area of life: family, church, education, law, medicine, science, music, art, business, and government. It publishes a monthly newsletter, *Biblical Worldview.*

Americans for Religious Liberty
PO Box 6656
Silver Spring, MD 20906
(301) 598-2447

Americans for Religious Liberty is an educational organization working to preserve religious, intellectual, and personal freedom in a secular democratic state. It opposes school prayer and any government involvement with religion. It publishes the newsletter *Voice of Reason* and numerous pamphlets on church/state issues, such as *Which Vision for America?*

The Association for Religion and Intellectual Life (ARIL)
College of New Rochelle
New Rochelle, NY 10805-2308
(914) 632-8852

ARIL is comprised of Jews and Christians involved in academic and intellectual pursuits. It strives to aid members in resolving conflicts that arise between religious beliefs and secular intellectual activity. It publishes the quarterly journal *Religion and Intellectual Life*.

Billy James Hargis's Christian Crusade
PO Box 977
Tulsa, OK 74102
(918) 836-2206

The Crusade is a Christian educational ministry whose stated purpose is to safeguard and preserve the conservative Christian ideals upon which America was founded. It is in favor of school prayer and Bible reading and against government policies that interfere with religion. It publishes the monthly *Christian Crusade Newspaper* and numerous books on religion in America.

Board of Church and Society of the United Methodist Church
100 Maryland Ave. NE
Washington, DC 20002
(202) 488-5600

The Board of Church and Society is a national agency of the United Methodist Church. It addresses social issues and represents the church's official positions. It publishes the monthly magazine *Christian Social Action* in addition to booklets and study materials.

Evangelical Council for Financial Accountability (ECFA)
PO Box 17456
Washington, DC 20041
(703) 435-8888

Founded in 1979, the ECFA is comprised of over 450 Evangelical Christian religious, charitable, and educational organizations. Its purpose is to enunciate and maintain a code of financial accountability. It assists its member organizations in making appropriate public disclosure of financial practices. ECFA publishes a pamphlet about charitable giving called *The Giver's Guide*, and a list of member organizations that subscribe to the council's principles.

The First Church of Christ, Scientist (Christian Science)
Committee on Publications
175 Huntington Ave.
Boston, MA 02115
(617) 450-2000

The First Church of Christ, Scientist is the Mother Church of the Christian Science denomination, which numbers 3000 branch churches in 57 countries. Christian Science teaches that by prayer that opens one's heart and mind to God, one can be healed spiritually and physically. Christian Scientists disseminate numerous publications, including the *Christian Science Journal* and *The Christian Science Monitor.*

Freedom from Religion Foundation (FFRF)
PO Box 750
Madison, WI 53701
(608) 256-8900

FFRF is a politically active organization of "free thinkers." Its purpose is to promote separation of chuch and state and combat fundamentalism. Its extensive publications include books, brochures, pamphlets, and the newspaper *Freethought Today.*

National Council of the Churches of Christ in the USA (NCCC)
Division of Education and Ministry
475 Riverside Drive
New York, NY 10115
(212) 870-2290

The NCCC is the agency of Protestant, Anglican, and Eastern Orthodox denominations comprising over 100,000 churches with over 40 million members. The agency provides educational materials and resources for missionary, social justice, and evangelization activities of the member churches. They publish the monthly *Ecu-Link* and the annual *Yearbook of American and Canadian Churches.*

National Council on Religion and Public Education
901 S. National Ave.
Springfield, MO 65804
(417) 836-5514

The Council is comprised of schools, organizations, and individuals who believe religion should be studied in public education in ways that do not promote the values or beliefs of one religion over another. It publishes *Religion and Public Education* magazine and resource materials such as "Teaching About the Bible" and *A Compact Guide to Bible Based Beliefs.*

National Religious Broadcasters (NRB)
PO Box 1926
Morristown, NJ 07960
(201) 428-5400

The NRB is an association of religious radio and television producers and station owners. It is dedicated to communicating the gospel and encouraging religious broadcasting. Among its publications are the monthly *Religious Broadcasting Magazine* and the *Sourcebook for Religious Broadcasting.*

The New Age Society
342 Western Ave.
Brighton, MA 02135
(617) 787-2005

The New Age Society is a resource center designed to explore the latest in New Age thought, philosophy, and values. It publishes the monthly magazine *New Age Journal,* and *New Age Society Newsletter.* The newsletter includes a comprehensive, updated list of New Age resources including books, retreats, and travel experiences.

The Rockford Institute Center on Religion & Society
152 Madison Ave., 24th Floor
New York, NY 10016
(212) 532-4320

The Center on Religion and Society is a research and educational organization that advocates a more public role for religion and religious values in American life. It publishes numerous articles on the relationship between religion and politics in the quarterly journal *This World* and the monthly newsletter *The Religion & Society Report*.

Spiritual Counterfeits Project
PO Box 4308
Berkeley, CA 94704
(415) 540-0300

The Spiritual Counterfeits Project is an evangelical Christian group that evaluates current spiritual trends and movements on the basis of the Bible. It opposes the New Age movement and such new religious institutions as the Unification Church. It publishes a quarterly newsletter and an annual journal in addition to books and booklets.

United States Catholic Conference (USCC)
Office of Public Affairs
1312 Massachusetts Ave. NW
Washington, DC 20005
(202) 659-6700

The USCC is the administrative agency of the American Catholic Bishops. It assists the bishops in formulating pastoral letters and official statements, and represents the bishops in Washington. The Conference's Office of Public Affairs publishes *Origins* magazine, which contains official statements from bishops' conferences and other Catholic documents of related interest.

Bibliography of Books

Robert N. Bellah and
Phillip E. Hammond

Varieties of Civil Religion. San Francisco: Harper &
Row, 1980.

Jim Castelli

10 Rules for Mixing Religion & Politics. Washington,
DC: People for the American Way, 1984. Pamphlet
available from People for the American Way, 1424
16th St. NW, Suite 601, Washington, DC 20036.

Furio Colombo

God in America. Translated by Kristin Jarratt. New
York: Columbia University Press, 1984.

Flo Conway and
Jim Siegelman

*Holy Terror: The Fundamentalist War on America's
Freedoms in Religion, Politics and Our Private Lives.*
Garden City, NY: Doubleday & Company, Inc., 1982.

Harvey Cox

Religion in the Secular City. New York: Simon &
Schuster, 1984.

John Deedy

American Catholicism: And Now Where? New York:
Plenum Press, 1987.

R. Bruce Douglass, ed.

*The Deeper Meaning of Economic Life: Critical Essays
on the US Catholic Bishops' Pastoral Letter on the
Economy.* Washington, DC: Georgetown University
Press, 1986.

James T. Draper and
Forrest E. Watson

If the Foundations Be Destroyed. Nashville, TN: Oliver
Nelson, 1984.

Wilbur Edel

*Defenders of the Faith: Religion and Politics from the
Pilgrim Fathers to Ronald Reagan.* New York: Praeger,
1987.

William F. Fore

*Television and Religion: The Shaping of Faith, Values,
and Culture.* Minneapolis, MN: Augsburg Publishing
House, 1987.

Razelle Frankl

Televangelism: The Marketing of Popular Religion. Car-
bondale, IL: Southern Illinois University Press, 1987.

Thomas M. Gannon, ed.

*The Catholic Challenge to the American Economy:
Reflections on the US Bishops' Pastoral Letter on
Catholic Social Teaching and the US Economy.* New
York: Macmillan Publishing Company, 1987.

Martin Gardner

The New Age: Notes of a Fringe-Watcher. Buffalo, NY:
Prometheus Books, 1987.

Douglas Groothuis

Unmasking the New Age. Downers Grove, IL: Inter-
varsity Press, 1986.

Eric O. Hanson

The Catholic Church in World Politics. Princeton, NJ:
Princeton University Press, 1987.

Carl F.H. Henry

The Christian Mindset in a Secular Society. Portland,
OR: Multnomah Press, 1984.

Carl Horn, ed.

Whose Values? Ann Arbor, MI: Servant Books, 1985.

James Davidson Hunter

Evangelicalism: The Coming Generation. Chicago:
University of Chicago Press, 1987.

Erling Jorstad

Being Religious in America. Minneapolis, MN:
Augsburg Publishing House, 1986.

Lay Commission on Catholic Social Teaching and the US Economy	*Liberty and Justice for All: Report on the Final Draft of the US Catholic Bishops' Pastoral Letter "Economic Justice for All."* Notre Dame, IN: The Brownson Institute, 1986.
Robin W. Lovin, ed.	*Religion and American Public Life.* New York: Paulist Press, 1986.
Charles P. Lutz, ed.	*God, Goods, and the Common Good: Eleven Perspectives on Economic Justice in Dialog with the Roman Catholic Bishops' Pastoral Letter.* Minneapolis, MN: Augsburg Publishing House, 1987.
Shirley MacLaine	*Dancing in the Light.* Toronto: Bantam Books, 1985.
David R. Mains	*The Rise of the Religion of Antichristism.* Grand Rapids, MI: Zondervan Books, 1985.
William Miller	*The First Liberty.* New York: Alfred A. Knopf, 1986.
Richard John Neuhaus	*The Naked Public Square.* Grand Rapids, MI: Eerdmans Publishing Company, 1984.
Mark A. Noll, Nathan O. Hatch and George M. Marsden	*The Search For Christian America.* Westchester, IL: Crossway Books, 1983.
Robert Peel	*Spiritual Healing in a Scientific Age.* San Francisco: Harper & Row, 1987.
James Randi	*The Faith-Healers.* Buffalo, NY: Prometheus Books, 1987.
Pat Robertson	*America's Dates with Destiny.* Nashville, TN: Thomas Nelson Publishers, 1986.
David Toolan	*Facing West from California's Shores: A Jesuit's Journey into New Age Consciousness.* New York: Crossroad, 1987.
United States Catholic Conference	*Political Responsibility, Choices for the Future: A Statement of the Administrative Board.* Washington, DC: United States Catholic Conference, 1987.
James E. Wood Jr., ed.	*Religion and the State.* Waco, TX: Baylor University Press, 1985.

Index

abortion, 101, 102-108, 109-114
Allen, Ethan, 82
Americanism
  defined, 44
  future of, 50-51
Aquarian Conspiracy, 207, 212
Argo, Edgar, 167
Armstrong, Ben, 172
Arn, Win, 186

Bainbridge, William Sims, 200
Bakker, Jim and Tammy, 151, 159,
  160, 162, 163, 177
Bamberger, Stefan, 186
Beckwith, Burnham P., 194, 198
Bellah, Robert, 49
Benestad, Brian, 100
Benjamin, Walter, 166-167
Bennett, William J., 52
Berkeley Christian Coalition, 209-210
Beyond War movement, 220-221
Black, Hugo, 128-129, 130
Blow, Richard, 214
Bock, Paul, 202
Bordewich, Fergus M., 210
Brown, Lester, 221
Brown, Robert McAffee, 187
Brzezinski, Zbigniew, 208
Buchanan, Patrick, 100
Burger, Warren, 123
Burnham, Walter Dean, 26

Canavan, Francis, 54
capitalism
  needs morality, 88-89
Caplan, Arthur, 133
Catholicism, 28
  and public policy
    bishops' letters concerning,
    86-101
    on abortion, 102-114
  and television evangelism, 176-181
  as declining, 209
  needs to set an example, 107-108
Chesterton, Gilbert K., 46, 76
Christian Broadcasting Network
  (CBN), 156-157
Christian Science Monitor, 141
Christian Scientists
  stance on medical treatment
    as positive, 139-145
    con, 133-138
Cobb, Sanford, 61
Condorcet, Marquis de, 195

Connecticut Mutual Life Insurance
  Company report, 29-32
Cormier, Jay, 176
Corry, John, 159
Cox, Harvey, 165, 177, 183, 185-186
Crouch, Paul, 180
Crowley, Pat, 160
Cuddihy, John Murray, 19, 21, 22
Cuomo, Mario, 102

Declaration of Independence, 40-41,
  46
Dierfield, R.B., 131
Douglas, Stephen, 113
Douglas, William O., 57, 71-72, 92,
  129
D'Souza, Dinesh, 94

Eastland, Terry, 33, 37, 75
Eckelkamp, Don, 35
Edwords, Frederick, 43
Ehrenreich, Barbara, 77
Eidsmoe, John, 39
Einstein, Albert, 220
Eliot, T.S., 74
Ellis, John Tracy, 209
Englehart, Bob, 184

Fairlie, Henry, 158
Falwell, Jerry, 41, 58, 79, 154, 174
Ferguson, Marilyn, 206, 212, 216-217
Fore, William F., 169, 178
Franklin, Benjamin, 45-46, 47, 49,
  53, 82
fundamentalism
  defined, 166
  see also television evangelism

Gaffney, James, 86
Gallup Poll, 20, 23, 30, 208, 215
Gannon, Thomas M., 89
Gaylor, Anne Nicol, 81
Gerbner, George, 153
Gergen, David R., 161
Gettysburg Address, 48
Goldberg, George, 120
Graham, Billy, 78, 123, 161, 173

Habermas, Jurgen, 168-169
Hadden, Jeffrey K., 171
Hansen, Marcus Lee, 21
Hargis, Billy James, 155
Harmonic Convergence, 215, 217,
  220

Harrington, Michael, 25
Harrison, Barbara Grizzuti, 218
Hayes, Nevin, 99
Heads Up literacy program, 156-157
Herberg, Will, 21, 27, 28
Hitchcock, James, 111
Horsfield, Peter G., 182
Hunger Project, 211-212, 220-221

Ingersoll, Robert, 44, 47, 48-49

Janeway, Eliot, 92
Jefferson, Thomas, 46, 49, 54, 58, 70,
    82, 83, 159
Judeo-Christian tradition
  as shaping national ideals, 41, 53,
    55, 57-58, 70, 73, 75, 79
  con, 43-51, 61, 77-85
  movement away from, 206-213

Kantzer, Kenneth S., 204
Karr, Barry, 220
Kennedy, D. James, 154, 155-156, 174
Kidwell, Kirk, 39
Kirk, Russell, 69
Kreitler, Peter G., 164

Ladd, Everett Carll, 19
Lay Commission on Catholic Social
  Teaching and the US Economy, 88
Lenski, Gerhard, 27-28
Lewis, C.S., 178
Lincoln, Abraham, 47-48, 49, 71, 83,
    84, 106, 113-114
Lindvall, Terry, 178
Lipset, Seymour Martin, 18, 21, 27,
    28
Locke, John, 55-56, 60
Luther, Martin, 36, 172

McClintock, John, 48
McCollister, Betty, 106
McCready, William, 209
MacLaine, Shirley, 208, 215, 217,
    218, 219
McLaughlin, Martin, 100
McLoughlin, William, 209
McLuhan, Marshall, 185
Maddox, Robert L., 21, 61, 127
Madison, James, 38, 54, 70, 82
Marlette, Doug, 79
Marty, Martin E., 17
media
  church should use, 176-181
    con, 182-188
  see also television evangelism

Meehan, Mary, 113

Michaels, William B., 162
Moral Majority, 42, 78, 80
Mormons, 50
Mouw, Richard, 161-162
Muggeridge, Malcolm, 184-185
Mumford, Lewis, 212
Murray, Jon G., 83, 124

National Opinion Research Center
  (NORC) studies, 19, 197-198, 209
Needleman, Jacob, 208, 209
Neuhaus, Richard John, 56
New Age movement
  as big business, 219
  as signficiant, 206-213
    con, 214-221
  growth of, 207, 208, 209, 215
  origins of, 215-217
New England Journal of Medicine, 143
New York Times, The, 49
Novak, Michael, 101, 103
nuclear weapons
  Catholic response to, 95, 97

O'Brien, George Dennis, 98
O'Donnell, Edward, 98
Owens, Virginia Stem, 183-184, 187

Paine, Thomas, 61
Pope John Paul II, 101, 108
Protestant Christianity
  decline of, 40
  virtues of, 33-42
public policy
  and religious values
    should guide, 69-76, 86-93,
      109-114
    con, 77-85, 94-101, 102-108

Raschke, Carl, 210
Reagan, Ronald, 81-82, 169, 218-219
Reese, Charley, 56
religion
  and government
    should intervene, 133-138
      con, 139-145
    strengthens, 52-58, 69-76
      con, 77-85
  and politicans
    should promote values, 109-114
      con, 102-108
  future of
    as declining, 194-199
      con, 200-205
    as New Age movement, 206-213
      con, 214-222
  in the US
    as cultural, 43-51

as protestantism, 33-42
role in society
  as important, 17-24, 27, 33-42
    con, 25-32, 43-51, 59-63
  should guide, 86-93
    con, 91-101
  traditonal
    as strong, 17-24
    as weak, 25-32
Reichley, A. James, 23, 71
Rifkin, Jeremy, 172-173
Roberts, Oral, 159, 161-162, 164, 177
Robertson, Pat, 79, 152, 154, 156-157,
  161, 166, 168, 174, 188
Robin, Eugene D., 144
Rosazza, Peter, 98-99

Schaff, Philip, 60
school prayer, 72, 169
  allowing
    as discrimination, 127-132
    as sponsoring, 131
  and Supreme Court, 123, 124,
    128-132
  as part of national heritage, 129-130
  banning of
    limits religious freedom, 120-126
  legislation, 123, 124, 125, 169
  statistics, 124-125, 131
Scopes Trial, 170, 175
Shaw, Anthony, 133
Shaw, Russell, 100, 101
slavery, 105-106, 113-114
Smith, Adam, 89-90
Solzhenitsyn, Aleksandr, 73-74
Stark, Rodney, 200
Stayskal, Wayne, 122
Stewart, Potter, 55, 129-130
Sullivan, Joseph, 107
Sunday, Billy, 39-40
Supreme Court
  and abortion, 101, 104, 114
  and prayer, 123, 124, 128-132
Swaggart, Jimmy, 177
Swan, Rita, 135, 137
Swomley, John M., 59, 63, 104

Talbot, Nathan, 139
Taylor, James, 185
Teilhard, Pierre de Chardin, 207
Television Awareness Training, 187
television evangelism
  abuses of, 153, 154, 155, 177
  as beneficial, 151-157, 176-181
    con, 158-164, 182-188
  as effective, 171-175
    con, 165-170
  as legitimate, 151-157

con, 158-164
as political, 172
legislation, 179-180

Tocqueville, Alexis de, 26, 27, 38, 53,
  58, 70-71, 207
Toles, Tom, 96, 129
Twitchell, Robin, 135-137

US
  Constitution of,
    and right to life, 135
    and school prayer, 124-125
    First Amendment to, 34, 56, 58,
      63, 70, 121, 128, 131, 141
    heritage of as religious, 43-51
  United States Catholic Conference
    (USCC), 99-101

van den Haag, Ernest, 73
Van Horn, James D., 143

Walker, Shauntay, 136, 137
Washington, George, 47, 71, 82, 84
Weber, Max, 27
Weyrich, Dawn, 151
Whalen, Joseph, 101
Wilson, Evan, 216
Wolfe, Christopher, 109
Wright, Steve, 151

Yoder, Edwin M. Jr., 131